Cities and Buildings

W9-CHE-597

Creating the North American Landscape

Gregory Conniff
Bonnie Loyd
Edward K. Muller
David Schuyler
Consulting Editors

Published in cooperation with
the Center for American Places,
Harrisonburg, Virginia

Cities and Buildings

Skyscrapers, Skid Rows, and Suburbs

LARRY R. FORD

The Johns Hopkins University Press
Baltimore and London

© 1994 The Johns Hopkins University Press
All rights reserved. Published 1994
Printed in the United States of America on acid-free paper

The Johns Hopkins University Press
2715 North Charles Street
Baltimore, Maryland 21218-4319
The Johns Hopkins Press Ltd., London

Library of Congress Cataloging-in-Publication Data will be found
at the end of this book.

A catalog record for this book is available from the British Library.

All photographs and figures are by the author. Some of the illustrations have been previously published, in *Geographical Review*.

Frontispiece: Skyline of Columbus, Ohio, in the 1980s.

Contents

Preface

Thinking about Cities; or,
My World and Welcome to It

The clocks that strike in my dreams are often the clocks of Columbus.
—James Thurber

I like to watch.
—Chaunce Gardiner, *Being There*

Looking back on it, I think that growing up in Columbus, Ohio, during the 1950s had a lot to do with my wanting to write this book. The many wonderful stories by James Thurber which were set in Columbus made it clear to me at an early age that observations of life in ordinary neighborhoods could be rich, vivid, and whimsical.[1] Thurber's aunt, for example, reportedly kept plugs in all of her "new-fangled" electrical sockets to prevent electricity from leaking all over the house if the switches were left on. Such stories made modernization and change in the American city come alive for me. But it was also the wide variety of streets, buildings, and other places that an adventurous child could explore at that time and in that place—the roof-tops, the alleys, the houses, the stores—that really made the city interesting. I have always wanted to convey somehow the excitement and importance of the nooks and crannies of my urban world to those who see cities in more abstract ways. This book is a small step in that direction.

Perhaps by briefly reviewing some of my early experiences with places in cities I can make my perspective a little clearer. To me, the rich variety of houses, stores, streets, and people in cities has never been adequately captured by census data dealing with such topics as "percentage substandard" or "average rent." Cities are made up of real buildings and the places between them. There is more to these places than socioeconomic categories suggest.

Growing up in a relatively poor neighborhood in the center of

Columbus during the 1950s meant coming into contact with all kinds of interesting people and places (it wasn't until much later, at the university, that I found out that I had been deprived). My mother and I shared a two-bedroom house with two other households—a "normal" nuclear family and a gypsy woman who sometimes burned incense and played "Sabre Dance" on her victrola into the wee hours of the night. On cold winter days, I would stay home from school, and the gypsy would read to me from the original *Frankenstein.*

Many of my friends lived in flats over grocery stores, cafes, and pharmacies, and we would endlessly compare the smells that wafted up from the commercial establishments below. Some of the kids I knew lived in tarpaper shacks with newsprint wallpaper and outdoor toilets. The streets where they lived, on the other side of the tracks, were not paved, in spite of their location close to downtown. It was rumored that wild beasts still lurked in the nearby woods, although I personally never saw any. There were, however, "bag ladies" in the alleys, and we would sometimes climb trees to "steal" fruit for them. There were also nicer streets with bigger houses, houses with fireplaces and formal dining rooms. Life in such houses was not always cozier or more interesting than it was on my street, although it did usually seem to be a bit quieter.

Cleveland Avenue, the commercial thoroughfare nearby, provided endless amusement. We (my gang and I) were "drugstore cowboys" at a place called the Sunshine Corner, a neighborhood hangout since 1919. Often we would sit outside Krauss Brothers Tavern and listen to the occasionally coherent stories of the men who cared to enlighten us with insights into the meaning of life. There was also a movie theater where kids could go to Saturday matinees by turning in a certain number of popsicle sticks or bubblegum wrappers in lieu of money. We knew the strip well. We played on the rooftops, decorated the windows for major holidays, and scavenged valuable materials from the storage areas and trash bins in order to build forts and other neighborhood "defenses." Even at the age of ten, I was fascinated by the great variety of residential and commercial structures to be found in my neighborhood alone. Today, decades later and living in another city, I still am.

By the time I was eleven, my ramblings were no longer confined to just one neighborhood. As a Boy Scout, I was able to usher at the Ohio State University football games. This gave me the opportunity to explore the cavernous (90,000-seat) Ohio Stadium as well as the mysterious buildings (labs? dorms?) to be found on the rest of the campus. Since we did not have a car, I usually walked the four or five miles to the university and so discovered and explored in some detail other types of neighborhoods. Urban gradations became apparent to me: from old to new, rich to poor, big to small, and so on. I often stopped at a diner or a White Castle restaurant—exotic building types not found in my neighborhood—for a treat on the way home.

I also went downtown a lot. Everyone went downtown a lot in the early 1950s, as there were no malls and major purchases required a trip, usually by bus, to a downtown department store. I, however, went downtown more than most people my age. One reason was that my mother worked downtown, and I often took a bus in order to meet her for shopping (and a soda) at the end of the day. I had started doing this at the age of six, but at that age the city went by too quickly to make any sense of its geography, and I was often confused. For example, since large numbers of blacks began to board the bus only as we passed the city's largest bakery, I was nearly seven before I realized that blacks did not necessarily smell like doughnuts. (I was very much in favor of integration.) By the age of eight or nine, patterns of land use and ethnicity were beginning to make more sense.

Even as a small child, I enjoyed the excitement and complexity of downtown Columbus. I liked the hustle and the bustle of the streets; I liked the statehouse; I liked the tall buildings; but most of all, I liked department stores. Lazarus, a Columbus department store seven stories high and covering three city blocks, was at that time the fifth largest in the nation. It was a city within a city, complete with pretty lights, ringing bells, seasonal decorations, and a bank of elevators just made for racing (once the operators were replaced by push button controls). Even without money, it was a great place to play.

There was also the Lincoln-Leveque Tower, the city's tallest skyscraper at 47 stories and the fifth tallest in the world when completed in 1927 (it seems that Columbus could never do better than fifth). Sometimes we would sneak onto the forty-seventh floor of the Lincoln-Leveque Tower (into the men's room, to be specific) with the idea of sailing promotional records (received from a local Saturday morning radio show) out across the rooftops. More often than not, we would simply look at the city from 550 feet up. I just loved doing that. I began to carry a mental "aerial photo" of the city in my head, complete with "spatial patterns" of land use and neighborhood character.

Sometimes we were discovered (having failed to pay the fee to go to the observation deck) and chased out of the building. Years later, I wrote my Ph.D. dissertation on American skyscrapers, with a special focus on those in Ohio. Luckily, no one in the building remembered me.

Given my utter fascination with the built environment of Columbus, Ohio, you can imagine my response to cities such as New York, Tokyo, and Cairo. I have walked and snooped and lurked for days on end in cities, making every effort to take it all in—to decipher the elusive essence of place. I like to watch. I like to look at the buildings and the changing ways in which people use them. To me, these microgeographies of real places provide essential insights leading toward an understanding of city structure and urban form.

For the most part, however, I did not find much emphasis on buildings as places in academia. Since I was already interested in cities by the time I got to the university, I took a variety of courses in a number of disciplines which dealt with urban issues—sociology, geography, economics, history, psychology, and so on. While I was introduced to a barrage of theories, methodologies, models, and data, all aimed at explaining the city, I felt that something was missing. Where were the real urban places that I found so interesting? We studied housing but not houses, retailing but not department stores, quaternary functions but not skyscrapers. We mapped low-income neighborhoods, but there was no mention of the Sunshine Corner. It wasn't mentioned in art or architectural history either.

I wanted cities to be explained through a thicker, more "real" discourse. Things got even fuzzier for me when abstract theories and concepts were used to explain spatial patterns which were really abstractions themselves—i.e., "a Marxist analysis of the inner city." Studies of real houses, stores, and towers, I felt, could help tie some of these ideas together. And so it came to be that, after twenty years of teaching and writing about urban geography, I finally sat down to write a book about cities and buildings—a book which I hope will tie together architectural and social history on the one hand, and some fundamental spatial patterns and processes on the other. This is really a sort of "spatial" (architecture in context) architectural history for urban geographers, social scientists, and other students of the American urban scene.

For a long time there wasn't enough published material to study systematically the built environment of American cities. That has changed dramatically in the past two decades. As I will suggest in the following chapter, there is now a voluminous literature on everything from shopping arcades and prisons to bungalows and diners. Indeed, there is far too much to compress into one book such as this one. I have simply selected a few of my favorite themes and topics in order to get the ball rolling. Still, I hope that this book will serve as a sort of reader for those interested in the relationship between architectural history and urban geography. The existing architectural literature, although plentiful, is scattered within separate books for each building type.

Similarly, work in urban geography seldom deals extensively with architecture and urban landscapes. I have tried to bring together some of this disparate literature by looking at a variety of building types in their spatial contexts.

I have attempted to write in a light style with a minimum of esoteric jargon. I have sought a conversational rather than a scholarly tone, and there is a minimum of footnotes, since nearly everything of importance that I have read has bubbled around in my head for years (if not decades). Although other works have been inspirational, the views expressed here are largely my own. Other views are partially or wholly assimilated into the way I look at cities; I won't attempt to pin them on anyone else.

In the spirit of postmodern pluralism, I hope that we can better integrate studies of architecture and landscape into our growing body of theory-informed and technologically sophisticated research. There is a lot to be learned by lurking, and you might be surprised by how much fun it can be.

Cities and Buildings

Abbreviations

CBD	central business district
DMZ	"dangerous movement zone"
FAR	floor area ratio
GDL	garage-dominant "L"
PLVI	peak land value intersection
SRO	single-room occupancy hotel
TDR	transferred development right

Introduction

Merging the Traditions of Space and Place

Call it architecture, call it history, call it landscape, or call it geography: regardless of what name it goes under, the built environment is becoming increasingly important in the popular literature. A visit to any bookstore will lead you to an array of books entitled *The Historic Architecture of . . .* or *The Beautiful Neighborhoods of . . .* as well as an ever-growing assortment of books on bridges, diners, pubs, fire stations, skyscrapers, bungalows, and apartment buildings. Kostof's *America by Design* (also a public television series), Girouard's *Cities and People*, Goldberger's *The Skyscraper*, Olsen's *The City as a Work of Art*, and King's *Buildings and Society* are but a few.[1] In other words, there is a growing interest in various types of urban architecture.

Readers are also becoming more interested in the social and economic character of cities. Books and articles that rate cities on a variety of factors from crime to pollution seem to appear almost daily. Many of these, such as Garreau's *Edge City*, focus on the evolution of new types of urban activity centers as well as the new forms of spatial organization that accompany such developments. Others, such as Wright's *Building the Dream* and Hayden's *The Grand Domestic Revolution*, demonstrate the relationship between architecture and social change.[2] While the need for increasing integration between the architectural and the social science approaches to understanding the city is gradually being recognized, there are still niches that beg to filled. The relationships between urban functions, spatial organization, and architecture need to be explored further.

The Architectural Approach to the City

Books on architecture and architectural history have traditionally focused upon individual buildings or types of buildings with little or no concern for their context. A few years back, I spoke at the national meeting of the American Institute of Architects and was privileged to go on several of the field trips. They were very different from the geography trips I was used to. Participants would generally read or talk until the bus arrived at a notable building, at which time everyone would rush off the bus to "photograph the hell out of it" and then return to the bus and their books and conversations. This emphasis on great and notable individual buildings pervades the literature. For architects, the seminal and unusual structures are what is important, for they epitomize individual creativity and chains of influence.

More recently, there has been more literature on general types of buildings. There are books on such things as terraced housing, apartment buildings, or factories, but there is still relatively little information on spatial context or urban form. Locations are rarely discussed. Factors such as the relationship of the building or type of building to transportation systems or changing social patterns are usually ignored. The focus is on the building, and that is that. There are a few exceptions. Recent works such as *Manhattan Manners* and *A History of Housing in New York City* do succeed in adding a spatial dimension to the architectural evolution of New York City.[3] Maps are used wisely, and the reader is introduced to the idea that where things happened is of some significance. Such efforts, however, are few and far between, and there have been no comprehensive works that aim to provide a "geography" of urban architecture.

The Social Science Approach to the City

Just as architects and architectural historians have tended to ignore spatial and social context in their descriptions of cities, social scientists have tended to ignore architecture. While many nineteenth-century students of the city did emphasize such things as topography, building materials, and the "look" of the place, the twentieth century brought new interests and concerns. Beginning in the 1920s, social scientists sought to "model" the universal city on the basis of its social, economic, and ethnic characteristics. Generalizations utilizing rings and sectors of "middle-class residences" or "industrial land uses" or "immigrant neighborhoods" were postulated. While some mention was made of general architectural types such as tenements, the look of the city ceased to be an important variable.

Social scientists came to rely heavily on census data at the tract level as they mapped and analyzed patterns of socioeconomic characteristics. While vast amounts of information were collected on income, education, and ethnicity, the census included no data on architectural style. Scholars could tell if housing was "substandard" or "overcrowded," but we could not tell if a building was a bungalow. Studies using aggregate data on housing cost and structural adequacy were common but told us little about cities as places.[4]

The development of computers and statistical techniques after World War II facilitated the manipulation of a large number of variables, and urban models became more sophisticated. The increasing interest in planning and zoning after the war also led to an emphasis on the two-dimensional city. As land uses were zoned (at least theoretically) into homogeneous areas, the resulting patterns were mapped and compared. The incredibly diverse, mixed-use tradional city, in which different social classes and economic activities occupied separate floors of the same building, gave way to an idealized urban area in which things were properly sorted into recognizable districts such as the central business district or skid row. Social scientists assumed that form would follow function as building types were erected for particular activities and social classes. Variations in architecture would simply reflect social patterns and so would be of little unique importance. The American preoccupation with sorting things out in space—zoning restrictions, single-purpose buildings, ethnic and economic ghettos—was mirrored in the social science literature.

Space must be "fleshed out" with architecture if we are to develop meaningful models of the real world. Buildings cannot be theorized out of their spatial context. In an architectural urban geography, both the buildings themselves and the imagery and ideology surrounding them create their own reality, a reality that is altered only with difficulty. While some social and spatial variables such as rent gradients and ethnic composition change continuously as the city grows, the built environment usually remains intact for some time, shaping and "reproducing" the character of place. Classic "spatial" geography suggests that things are continuously being sorted out according to current optimum locations. Architectural geography suggests greater stability, at least until mounting social or economic pressures lead to wholesale abandonment or massive intervention such as urban renewal.

Architectural imagery is also an increasingly important variable in urban spatial behavior. As the postmodern city has emerged, with its renovated warehouses, revitalized waterfronts, and chic restaurants in converted brothels, new aesthetic ideologies have had to be layered into conventional models of city structure. Cultural values other than "the most space per dollar" have come to the fore as rare, historic, or otherwise "placeful" architectural contexts attract attention.

While advocates of an architectural urban geography recognize whimsical and ideological dimensions of urban change to a greater degree than those using classical social science approaches, it does not

American cities vary significantly in their layout and their built environment. Do we monitor this adequately? Left, downtown Houston; right, downtown Pittsburgh.

follow that the traditional spatial and socioeconomic variables have become less important. Obviously, the best approach to understanding the city lies somewhere between the two poles—somewhere between a concern for the architecture of the built environment and a focus on the social characteristics of the population. The purpose of this book is to merge these two concerns by shedding some light on the relationship over time between the development of particular building types, on the one hand, and the spatial organization of the city on the other.

The unprecedented scale of twentieth-century development and the nature of the sprawling, multicentered metropolis make an understanding of the built environment increasingly important. Many generalizations which emphasize such things as decreasing land values from a central point lose significance in an age when single building projects can create their own centrality. The "staying power" of architecture is important as well. The fact that some central city neighborhoods remain desirable over long periods even in the face of surrounding disamenities while others succumb to massive deterioration cannot be attributed to relative location alone. Building style and architecture cannot be generalized out of the picture if location in space is to have any meaning.

Urban Architecture and Social Theory: Bringing Together Place and Process

A problem with much of the literature on cities is that often complex conceptual frameworks are used to "explain" other complex conceptual frameworks. Abstractions are used to explain abstractions, as in "the capitalist system has created an inner city underclass." Both the independent and dependent variables involve a great deal of interpretation and definition. Social theory, on the other hand, has become increasingly popular as it is recognized that social science without theory is sometimes little more than "slow journalism." The chal-

lenge, then, is to tie the various theoretical approaches more concrete-
ly to the development of real places, real cities.[5] We can start by
looking at the relationship between the development of particular
building types and the creation of various types of urban areas or
"zones" from the central business district to suburbia.

At the risk of overgeneralizing, social theory can be divided into
three levels of concern, which, for lack of better terms, I will dub
macro, meso, and micro. Macro-level theory deals with the overriding
political, economic, and cultural context. Examples might include
macroeconomics, Marxist critiques, or various brands of cultural de-
terminism. Theorists at this level invoke the "big picture" to explain
the city. Meso-level theory focuses on the roles of major individual
decision-makers (gatekeepers), such as political leaders and corporation presidents, in shaping urban form. Even given the economic
system and cultural values, there is nothing inevitable about the ways
cities evolve, since many urban landscapes are "authored" by powerful individual planners or developers. Understanding Paris and New
York means knowing something about Baron Haussmann and Robert
Moses. Finally, micro-level theory deals with how average people
perceive the city and make spatial decisions within it. Knowing about
the residential suburb means knowing a bit about the different ways
people trade off space, accessibility, amenity, and self-image in choosing a home. A major problem with the three levels of theory is that
they are often poorly linked. Marxists may explain the city in purely
economic terms while ignoring the roles of eccentric but powerful

individuals. Behavioralists may focus on the values and perceptions of individuals but ignore political and economic constraints on decision-making.

By focusing on the relationship between architecture and city structure, we can not only clarify some of the major theoretical approaches but also link them together. Since the focus is on real things such as skyscrapers and department stores rather than on abstractions such as the inner city or urban sprawl, it is easier to nail down various theoretical contributions. For example, by examining the construction of a major downtown office tower, we can focus in a very practical way on theory. Macro theory can be utilized to look at the roles of capital accumulation and flows, tax laws, occupational revolutions, and investment strategies that are related to the decision to put millions of dollars into a skyscraper rather than into other types of projects. We can also invoke meso-level theory to examine the roles of powerful individuals such as former New York governor Al Smith, who tirelessly pushed for the construction of the Empire State Building, in the midst of a depression, largely because he wanted to be the one to build the tallest building in the world. Finally, micro-level theory can be used to examine the location decisions over time of those who chose to occupy the tower. What did they feel were the trade-offs between accessibility, visibility, and prestige on the one hand and the cost and quality of space on the other. The interstitial areas between the various levels of theory may be tied together as the details of skyscraper construction are explored.

A Guide to the Following Chapters

The following seven chapters constitute a sort of architectural history for the social scientist. The emphasis is on vernacular building types rather than on magnificent and unusual seminal architecture. While a great deal is covered, much has been left out. There is very little mention of industrial or recreational buildings and no mention of institutional ones such as schools, prisons, hospitals, or military bases. I chose to emphasize common, pervasive building types such as offices, stores, and houses that average people know best and have the most contact with. I have also chosen to focus upon the older parts of the North American city from downtown to the outer belt and so have left out much discussion of new homes and suburban malls. Older buildings types and neighborhoods "have a history," and so it is possible to trace their evolution and staying power over time. Only in the last chapter do I speculate about what may be going on in the new suburban nodes that characterize the multicentered city.

The first three chapters deal with the evolution and spatial organization of the North American downtown. Chapter 1, the longest, is about skyscrapers. It deals with the evolution of the special-purpose office building and its role in shaping the North American downtown. In this chapter I include some discussion of the changing geographic characteristics of downtowns over time in order to better interpret the role of office buildings and set the stage for the discussions of skid row and shopping districts in the following chapters.

The office building was very likely invented in London, and it was there that the first segregated office districts evolved. The monumental office tower, however, was an American invention, and its adoption throughout the country played a very important role in creating the peak land value intersections (PLVIs) and rent gradients that geographers have since identified. The skyscraper office tower, perhaps more than any other type of architecture, has not only shaped the American downtown by pushing out all less intensive land uses, but has also provided an ideal focus for the study of such topics as capital accumulation, foreign investment strategies, individual decisions and aspirations of mighty entrepreneurs, and political conflict and confrontation over landscape tastes. Even the study of just one massive project such as the Rockefeller Center in New York City can tell us about how American downtowns came to be.

As elite and highly profitable activities increasingly located in a few major skyscrapers, the core of the central business district often shrank to just a few blocks. Many of the older buildings on the fringes of downtown were ignored and left to await future change. But change was often very slow in coming, and many structures remained in limbo for decades. Chapter 2 deals with the "zones in transition" that typically encircle the North American central business district. Mainly from an architectural point of view, this chapter describes the built environments of both "skid row" and the more upscale "zone of assimilation," and shows how they are related to the social characteristics of those places.

Chapter 3 deals with the kinds of places that have been designed to attract shoppers over the years. Shopping used to be the most important reason for having cities: that is, cities and markets were synonymous, and shopping dominated the central squares. Gradually, shopping activities moved into specialized quarters, including arcades, department stores, and most recently, "festival marketplaces." Architectural settings designed to attract shoppers can tell us much about our landscape tastes and preferences.

In Chapter 4 the focus shifts to the residential landscape. Here, I trace the evolution of the single-family "home" in England and North America as both a cultural ideal and a socioeconomic possibility. The impacts of changing building and transportation technologies are discussed, along with evolving images of the ideal family and society. From the row house to the ranch, the interweaving of ideologies and economics makes the story of the American house a fascinating one. It is in the home and garden that average people personalize their space and display their landscape tastes. In spite of a growing literature, there is much here that still needs to be explored.

Chapter 5 focuses upon various types of multiunit residential structures, including tenements and apartment buildings. Apartment buildings were common throughout central Europe by the mid-1800s, but they were very slow to catch on in the United States. They were introduced in New York City as the "French way of living" during the late 1800s, but were rare elsewhere in the United States until much later. The core areas of most American cities were initially "underbuilt" with single-family homes which often were converted to tenements as land values rose. Speculation and decay usually followed. Apartment buildings, on the other hand, were usually associated with luxury living until well into the twentieth century, although their role in recent decades has been mixed. The complex issues of density and design have had a variety of impacts on the American urban landscape.

The commercial thoroughfares, or "strips," that were extended outward from downtown to serve the growing population along mass transit lines are (fast) food for thought in Chapter 6. When Lowenthal, Blake, Venturi, and others wrote about American landscape tastes, it was the architecture of the commercial strips that garnered much of their attention. Compared to office buildings, department stores, and houses, the "decorated sheds" of the commercial strip have been modified continuously to provide everything from giant doughnuts to Assyrian temples for our motoring pleasure. In spite of being much maligned, the transitory architecture of the strip has worked and continues to work for a variety of economic and social reasons. It has helped to facilitate the invention and acceptance of many new functions (gas stations, motels, drive-in theaters) which were incubated on the American strip. We need to look behind the neon facades for a better understanding of this uniquely American phenomenon.

Finally, in Chapter 7 it is time to ponder some of the vast new, highly planned megadevelopments that are popping up in the multicentered American city. Many of these feature high-density, mixed-use buildings of the kind that we (as a culture) have just barely finished running away from in the central cities. Have our landscape tastes changed, or are we convinced we can do a better job of it this time?

Themes and Purposes

I hope that urban geographers and other students of the American city will gradually become more eager to examine the evolution and use of the ordinary American building types through the lens of a well-developed spatial framework. By thickening our two-dimensional spatial models with information on the built environment, we can understand more precisely the relationships between space and place. Our cultural ideologies, personal aspirations, economic constraints, and daily behaviors are all writ large in the structures we build and use. By fleshing out city structure with real landscapes, we can not only make better use of and add to the rich literature of urban and cultural geography but also those of architectural and social history, urban design, and social theory. I think it's worth a try.

1   Downtown Buildings

The Role of the Skyscraper in Shaping the American Central Business District

When one thinks of an American city, perhaps the first image that comes to mind is the skyline. While important cities have always had symbolic skylines made up of cathedrals, castles, palaces, and city halls, it was in the twentieth-century American city that the terms *city* and *skyline* became practically synonomous. No longer was the city a low-rise phenomenon with a few symbolic towers, but rather the functioning city *was* the skyline. The important activities of the city were housed within its symbolic structures. It is thus difficult, if not impossible, to understand the spatial organization of the city independent of the symbolic and aesthetic dimensions of the city. Space and place are inextricably intertwined.

The evolution of the American central business district (CBD) was shaped by, and in turn attempted to shape, the skyscraper office tower. It is a bit difficult to decide where to start a discussion of this phenomenon, since the tremendous concentration of activity in the American CBD is both the cause of and the result of the invention of the skyscraper. Since the initial development of CBDs long preceded the development of the special-purpose office skyscraper (but not the urge to build high), I will start there.

Definitions of Downtown: The Core versus the Frame

Most Americans use the term *downtown* rather than *central business district* when referring to the heart of the city. For our purposes, *downtown* refers to an area much larger than the CBD and one that is rather more difficult to delimit with any precision. *Downtown* refers to the center city in general, even if the land uses are quite mixed, including everything from parking lots and auto upholstery shops to hotels and warehouses. The CBD is the core of downtown and can be delimited precisely as that area which contains only CBD-type activities. In most American cities, this would mean the area that contains first-class office space (business and government) as well as some high-threshold retailing and associated hotel and entertainment facilities. The exact cut-off point for determining what belongs in the CBD may be open to some discussion, but in the typical American city, offices constitute by far the predominant use of space. For the purposes of this chapter, CBD will be used to refer to the district where the highest-level interactions and discussions occur. The CBD is the office core of the city. It is the place where movers and shakers meet to move and shake.

The downtown can thus be divided into two types of areas: the core and the frame. The core comprises the CBD while the frame contains a variety of support uses—parking, office suppliers, janitorial services, coffee shops, and some of the hotels, restaurants, and bars. In most American cities, the frame of the downtown is a bit ragged in appearance, often in contrast to the gleaming core. The frame, often referred to as the zone in transition or even skid row, will be discussed in the next chapter.

While all cities have something that can be called a downtown, not every city has a recognizable and distinctive CBD. Smaller cities, for example, may simply have too few central businesses to merit even one specialized office building. Some industrial or mining towns may have large populations but little in the way of a CBD. This chapter will therefore concentrate upon the larger, more dynamic cities, those which best illustrate the processes of CBD formation.

The emergence of the American CBD involves the interweaving of four separate dimensions—the functional, the cultural, the technological, and the political. The functional story traces the evolution of space for office functions as a separate, identifiable land use in the urban core. Early on, such activity did not take place in special locations but, rather, was carried on in the market square or at the docks. With the construction of special-purpose exchange halls which separated financial interaction from the stacks and barrels of the market, the office core was begun. The significance of this for the spatial organization of the central city is that because office activities requiring intensive interaction need only a very small amount of space, they therefore can outbid all other uses for a central location. While many other supporting activities may cohabit the CBD, it is office space which shapes and organizes it. As demand for a location in the center increases, land values rise as well, and eventually only very profitable activities can afford to locate there.[1]

The role of cultural values in shaping the American CBD is evidenced by the number of monumental skyscrapers. We may relate this to a long-standing European tradition of building tall, coupled with a dynamic and relatively unbridled economic system which encourages the display of success. Beginning in the late 1800s any company, city, or individual who could afford to do so built a tall and ornamental tower, and American cities soon bristled with competing "skyline" elements. Although it is difficult to provide, some definition of *skyscraper* is in order.

The most important dimension of the skyscraper for our purposes is that it is an extraordinarily tall building which contains useable space, as opposed to purely decorative towers such as the Washington Monument. There is no consensus as to just how tall or large a building must be before it is a skyscraper, since much depends on context; it must be tall enough to dominate the surrounding area. A dominant building in a small town would not be noticed in Manhattan. Also, what constitutes an unusually large concentration of useable space varies over time. For our purposes, a skyscraper will be defined as a building of at least 25 stories and/or 300 feet tall (often including a nonfunctional decorative tower). This definition clearly differentiates the skyscraper from the six- to ten-story structures found in many "traditional" cities. Skyscrapers were built to satisfy cultural demands for monumentality as well as to provide space for office functions. They could not be built, however, until the technology was available, which brings us back to the evolution of the CBD.

The story of technology is a major element in the shaping of the American CBD because a variety of architectural and transportation breakthroughs were necessary before it could evolve. Steel-frame construction; fast and efficient elevators; electricity for lighting, heating, and cooling systems; office machinery; and convenient mass transit systems were but a few of the inventions which were prerequisites for the emergence of the CBD.

Finally, political factors played an important role in the emergence of the CBD. Most American cities developed planning and zoning guidelines which allowed and even encouraged the construction of special-purpose office skyscrapers. While Paris continues to rigidly control the height of buildings, and most of London still abides by strict regulations enacted in the 1890s that keep all buildings below the 100-foot level, American cities show much less determination to control the skyline. Indeed, in many cities, from Buffalo to Los Angeles, the city government itself was the first to build a skyscraper.

A useful framework for understanding the most important processes in the creation of CBDs is provided by the six-stage model presented below:[2]

1. inception
2. exclusion
3. segregation
4. expansion
5. replication
6. redevelopment

During the inception stage, the CBD first begins to emerge as a special place, even though there are few if any special buildings associated with it. The homes and coffeehouses of the elite often serve to begin the process. During the exclusion stage, activities which are most obviously not appropriate for the CBD are forced away by a combination of high rents, social pressure, and architectural change. In other words, as a CBD develops, rents go up, new buildings are built, and some uses can no longer afford to be there.

Segregation occurs in the development of a CBD when uses begin to sort themselves out on the basis of both rent and type of required interaction. Typically, the larger the CBD, the more segregation. In the largest, there may be special districts within the CBD for legal services, financial services, government services, and so on. All of this requires expansion, and CBDs have usually needed to grow in area, vertically, or both. In some cases, areal expansion is contiguous, while in others, growth must "leapfrog" unsuitable or undesirable locations. Similarly, vertical growth may be unbridled, or it may be controlled by building ordinances regulating the height of structures. The replication stage may be reached when expansion becomes difficult and a replica of the CBD must be located elsewhere in the city or even in a suburban area. Finally, successful CBDs are rebuilt continuously so as to compete for the highest-level activities and most prestigious buildings. This is known as the redevelopment stage.

The Central Business District: Renaissance Precedents

The traditional European preindustrial city did not have a CBD but, rather, contained a variety of mixed residential-economic zones in which people lived and worked, often in the same building, according to their respective crafts. The typical building was a "burgher house" of perhaps four or five stories including a cellar. Goods could be stored in the cellar, retailed or wholesaled at street level, and manufactured in the attic, all by people who lived on the second and third floors. Since the best place to do business was in the center of town, the best place to live was also there. Thus, while buildings may have varied in size and quality, with the best being in the center of the city, they did not vary much in type, at least during medieval times (roughly 1000 to 1400 A.D.). The major exception to this homogeneity occurred in late-medieval northern Italy, where "family towers" of up to 250 feet were constructed in cities such as Siena and Florence. These towers were essentially fortified extended-family compounds which served to protect the wares of competing trading organizations. Significantly, however, they also served to create monumental skylines—perhaps the first secular skylines in the world.

In the larger cities, activities of a certain type tended to concentrate together; the only real economic segregation involved noxious activities such as tanning or dyeing, which were usually pushed to the edge of the city or at least downstream. Most of the manufacturing and storage in a city took place in houses, while most of the business of the city took place on the street.

With the arrival of the Renaissance (roughly 1400 to 1600 A.D.), the medieval city began to open up. Piazzas, plazas, and squares were built, sometimes on a monumental scale. Such plazas provided a sense of nodality or "centerness" to the city and thus a place where a new civic culture could be displayed and acted out. Indeed, the ideal Spanish-American city as codified by the "Laws of the Indies" in 1573 required the most important activities of the city to be concentrated on and around the central plaza.

With the sense of openness and centrality that arrived with the Renaissance came an increased awareness of the aesthetic and symbolic importance of individual buildings.[3] While monumental cathedrals had been evolving at least since the eleventh century, they tended to be embedded in the cityscape, with various and sundry buildings around and in front of them—a situation which still typifies many important mosques in Islamic cities such as Fez (Morocco) that were largely untouched by the Renaissance. Increasingly, it became important not only to have but to *see* the important buildings of the city. Buildings such as cathedrals, palaces, and city halls were set apart on open plazas where they could be visually as well as socially dominant. The center of the city became a symbolic and monumental place. The city came to be identified with its skyline.

With the possible exception of the cathedral, the most important building in many cities was the town hall. Usually located on the main square, the town hall was a multipurpose structure which sometimes included large meeting rooms over a covered market. With buying and selling going on below, important citizens could meet in the halls in order to debate more subtle political and economic questions. Like cathedrals, town halls were often monumental in scale and grandeur. In some of the most successful cities, a group of important buildings was constructed around one or more plazas. In Bruges by the year

The belfry in Bruges, Belgium, is an early (fourteenth-century) "skyscraper" and urban symbol.

1500, for example, one square was surrounded by the town hall and two major churches, while a second square was dominated by a market hall with a 350-foot belfry. Separating the two squares was the wool hall. Bruges had a splendid ceremonial center which in many ways was a forerunner of the CBD, since the important "business" of the city took place in a centralized set of monumental halls and squares.

In order to have a CBD, of course, there must be business. With the increasing importance of trade and banking during the fifteenth and sixteenth centuries, special-purpose buildings and squares evolved to provide space for high-level interaction. As cities such as Antwerp, Amsterdam, and London came to dominate what was rapidly becoming world trade, they also led the way in developing early versions of the CBD. By 1469, Antwerp had constructed a building that came to be known as the "Old Bourse" (after the Buerseplaats, or main square, in Bruges) and in 1531 opened a new, larger exchange hall where merchants could meet on a regular basis. Both halls were built in the form of a cloister, with shops around the court and meeting halls above. Over the next century, the idea of a large central exchange hall was copied throughout Europe. One was constructed in London in 1566–70 and one in Amsterdam in 1608–13. The cloister, or enclosed court, which had served for centuries as a religious and civic ideal in monasteries and central plazas, also worked well for business activities. Merchants could mingle in the halls, along the covered walkways, or in the middle of the paved courtyard, depending upon the nature of their activities.

Most of these early buildings and spaces were places for people rather than stuff. That is, there was little in the way of fixed and permanant furniture and records (city charters were often kept locked away in belfry towers) and nothing in the way of business machines. By the early 1600s special-purpose banks and warehouses were springing up around the exchange halls. They were characterized by a greater degree of specialized space, but only in a very limited way. For the most part, business activities still took place in a variety of settings, including coffeehouses, private homes, along the wharves, and in the street. While monumental town halls and exchange halls were becoming common in many important urban places, the vast majority of buildings were still relatively multipurpose and undifferentiated.

As long as cities were small, the number of people involved in business few, and business environments relatively unspecialized, the town hall/exchange hall model worked well. Most important cities had fewer than 100,000 people up to the 1500s, and no one was very far from the main square. By the late 1500s, however, there were some new trends on the horizon.

Baroque ideas of urban design, which grew out of the Renaissance, were bringing a new scale to the European city by the early 1600s. On the Continent, broad boulevards and gardens were making their appearance as city walls were either breached or demolished. Medieval compactness was becoming a thing of the past. Cities such as Paris and London were approaching metropolitan populations of nearly 500,000 by the mid-1600s, and one central exchange hall to handle the business of the city was no longer enough.

The Specialized Business District Evolves in London

Perhaps the first city in the world to develop something akin to a modern CBD was London. Some have argued that a CBD was emerging there as early as 1600 as certain economic activities gathered together on Cheapside between the Exchange and St. Paul's Cathedral. The size of the city (between 150,000 and 200,000) plus its importance as a political and commercial center provided the necessary activity threshold to overcome the inertia of inherited medieval urban form.

For perhaps the first time in history, large numbers of buildings were built specifically to house businesses with the idea that the merchants would live elsewhere and commute to the business district. Specialized "sheds" were constructed of up to five stories for the sellers of luxury goods and later for wholesaling and storage. Thus, London illustrates very nicely the stages of inception and exclusion in the making of a CBD.[4] A prestigious location on high ground (away from but with good access to the busy waterfront) between the Royal Exchange and St. Paul's Cathedral led important people to congregate there (in places like Lloyd's Coffee House) to discuss business. Exclusion occurred as buildings were built, rents were charged commensurate with the business role of the district, and residences were forced out.

If the specialized business district in London was just emerging by 1600, it was certainly well developed by 1700. The plague and fire of 1665–66 had caused most of the old walled city to be depopulated and leveled. The elite, and anyone else who could afford to, had taken up residence to the west toward the palace at Westminster and had no desire to return to "the City." The tremendous costs associated with reconstruction together with post-fire building codes (no wooden structures, no "medieval" overhanging lofts, recessed window frames, etc.) meant that only substantial, profitable buildings could be built in the center of the city. The height of buildings was determined by the width of streets, which were widened only with great difficulty due to the power of property owners even after the fire. Thus, a combination of planning and building codes coupled with the emergence of a steep rent gradient began to mold an urban core largely given over to the needs of business (the exclusion stage).

The linear character of central London, focusing upon a series of major east-west streets paralleling the waterfront activities along the Thames (fishmarkets, etc.), coupled with the need for total reorganization after the fire facilitated the emergence of the CBD. In addition to traditional mercantile activities, London began to specialize in such areas as insurance and banking associated with the development of oceanic commerce (the Bank of London was established in 1694). Soon, large trading organizations such as the British East India Company evolved as well. After the fire, some of the major streets were widened and paved to facilitate the increasing use of carriages (which also allowed for increased commuting distances) and to encourage the construction of bigger buildings (usually four stories). While Greater London contained 575,000 people in 1700, only about 200,000 lived in the City. The urban core never regained its pre-fire population.

While the core of Georgian (roughly eighteenth-century) London was extremely mixed in land usage and unspecialized architecturally by the standards of today, it was recognizable as something new—a commercial core developing in conjunction with residential suburbs. That is to say that some places were developed specifically for business, while others were designed to be homogeneously residential. This was a rather new idea when accomplished on a large scale. The refinement of this new type of spatial organization advanced only very gradually over the next 150 years. Until the advent of new building technologies and transportation innovations in the mid-1800s, the CBD could not become truly specialized.

Once the idea of a CBD was established, it could diffuse to places with lower population and business threshold levels, especially if those places were new and did not need to overcome the inertia of medieval urban form and building types. Such was the case in the New World.

The Emergence of the Central Business District in the United States

While Boston had a commercial exchange in 1740, the first specialized business district to emerge was in New York City. By around 1810, Wall Street was becoming the financial center of the region, if not the nation, even though the city had a population of only 80,000. Even though New York had been established in the 1600s as a walled city, its medieval traditions were weakly rooted, and by 1810 an expanding grid pattern was drawing exclusive residential districts away from the burgeoning port and emerging financial core. Philadelphia and other major American cities soon followed suit in developing what in New York came to be known as "downtown" due to the location of the financial district at the southern tip of Manhattan. As the American frontier moved westward, the threshold population necessary for a CBD decreased, so that many newer western cities established after the mid-1800s were laid out with specialized "business blocks" at the time of initial settlement. The stage of inception was no longer gradual but was planned from the beginning.

Even though a CBD was a prerequisite for urban stature by the early 1800s, few architectural innovations had evolved to facilitate its development since the time of the town halls and commercial exchanges of Renaissance Europe. Old photographs of cities such as New York and Boston show that buildings in the central district looked very much like buildings in other parts of the city. Wall Street was still dominated visually by the spires of nearby churches. While warehouses and port facilities were rapidly becoming specialized, business buildings were not. Indeed, the use of the term *house* provides insight into the situation. Until the development of specialized architecture in the mid-1800s, nearly every building was referred to as just another type of house, be it a warehouse, storehouse, schoolhouse, banking house, or whorehouse. A house was a house from New York to Boston regardless of the uses contained therein. While facades and window treatments varied, the possibilities for developing the central district were limited.

The two major exceptions to the above generalization, at least by the 1820s in New York City, were the Merchants' Exchange (1825) and "Classical-style" banks. These were special-purpose buildings suitable only for financial activities. The Merchants' Exchange, unlike

Lower Manhattan: Classical Greek Revival banks dominated the early commercial city.

its earlier predecessors, was much larger than the buildings around it and had considerable interior space.[5] It was not just a small hall built over a market. In addition, it had a monumental dome which towered over Wall Street as if to proclaim that a financial district of some importance had arrived. The second exception was the "Classical" bank building—that is, a bank in the form of a Greek Revival temple. Although small with only a one- or two-story open interior hall, these banks were symbolically different from the rest of the buildings on the street.

American cities faced two problems in the development of a CBD—how to build it and where to put it. Initially, there were very few examples of monumental bourses or exchanges, as was the tradition in Europe, and so even the most important corner in an American city could look like a residential street. Second, lacking any sense of permanent center as around a cathedral or a central plaza, the business district of an American city was free to wander anywhere, and often did. In Philadelphia, for example, the business district moved some fourteen blocks during the nineteenth century, from near the waterfront to City Hall. Obviously, the dual problems of how and where to build the CBD were related, in that it was difficult to increase the density of the business district while building nothing but "houses." Consequently, an expanding district often meant a moving one. Thus, the stages discussed above need not necessarily be sequential; expansion can sometimes occur instead of exclusion as the newly forming CBD searches for a place to land.

Technological and Aesthetic Innovations, 1850–1890

By the mid-1800s, the emergence of a combination of architectural and transportation innovations had drastically altered the structural and visual character of the American city. The most important of these innovations were the special-purpose office building (especially the proto-skyscraper) and the commuter railroad (both above- and below-ground).

Before the Civil War, most major American cities had a European profile with blocks of homogeneously low buildings and an occasional monumental structure. In cities such as Boston, New York, Philadelphia, and Washington, the architecture then in vogue was termed *Federal* and was really a relative of the English Georgian (patriots found it difficult to name a style after King George). The emphasis on symmetry and uniformity in these styles contributed to a sense of tasteful blending even when Classical or Italianate embellishments were added. The look of such cities can still be seen today in such neighborhoods as Beacon Hill in Boston or Georgetown in Washington. Shortly after the Civil War, however, the look of the city began to change.

The late 1800s have been referred to as the Victorian era, and it was in the context of Victorian architecture that the American skyscraper office tower was born. The urge to build tall, imposing structures as opposed to uniformly low ones was a Victorian characteristic. As the egalitarian, democratic uniformity of the classical Georgian city gave way to the competitive exuberance of the Victorian era, ornamental towers of considerable height began to appear on factories, offices, and houses. Competition for height, once limited to cathedrals and town halls, now became a game many could play. The reason was partly technological. The increasing use of machine tools and ready-made components meant that embellishments could be added easily to almost anything. The reason was also partly sociocultural in that people in some places, especially Britain and the United States, thought Victorian architectural excesses were wonderful. In other places, such as Paris, people were more cautious and modified the new style to fit existing traditions. Obviously, places participating in the new industrial economy of the nineteenth century were most likely to be playing the game.

Once interest in taller buildings was established in America, a variety of technological innovations were utilized to facilitate the reach for the sky. Among the most important were the elevator, steel-frame construction, and electricity.

In 1853, Elisha Graves Otis came to New York City hoping to interest somebody in a safety brake he had invented for freight hoists. Three years later, the first passenger elevator was installed in a five-story building belonging to a dinnerware company. The idea caught on, but it was not until 1873 that the first tall building was planned with the elevator in mind—the ten-story Western Union Building in New York City, equipped with four Otis elevators. Three were run by steam, and the fourth was a water-balance design. Improvements in the elevator and increased building heights progressed together. In 1887 the first electric elevator was installed, and in 1904 the first electric gearless traction elevators made buildings over 500 feet tall feasible.

Ironically, there was so little demand for office space during the early years of experimentation with the passenger elevator that its impact was predicted to be primarily on residential buildings. An article appearing in 1872 stated: "We have all heard about the European method of living in flats. . . . It is possible for us to greatly improve upon the European method since by establishing steam communications between each floor and the street, we may carry buildings as high as we please and render the top floor the choicest of them all."[6]

Another technological innovation necessary for the development of the utilitarian tall building was steel-frame construction. Decorative towers of great height were nothing new, and many of them, including the Cologne Cathedral and the Washington Monument, exceeded 500 feet. When such structures are built of masonry, however, they need such massive amounts of stone at the lower levels (and sometimes flying buttresses as well) that there is little usable interior space, at least in relation to the size of the lot required. Even nineteenth-century commercial buildings of limited height necessitated massive foundations and walls at the lower levels. This problem was solved with the invention of steel-frame construction—that is, the erection of a steel skeleton upon which non-load-bearing walls of a variety of materials could be hung.

Steel-frame construction was invented in Chicago. The Chicago fire of 1871 leveled much of the emerging CBD, and architects and engineers from around the nation gathered to participate in its reconstruction. Various ideas were tried in order to improve upon traditional building methods, including the use of interior cast iron columns to brace the walls. Legend has it that the steel skeleton owes its origin to the fact that William Le Baron Jenny came home early one afternoon and noticed that a small wire birdcage was easily supporting the heavy book that his wife had laid upon it. The steel skeleton was first used in the First Home Insurance Building in Chicago in 1883, a ten-story structure that was visually unremarkable. Nevertheless, the Home Insurance Building is often referred to as the earliest example of a skyscraper because it was the first to utilize "skyscraper construction."

Because Chicago had to rebuild quickly, it was far less conservative than New York in trying new building types, and it soon led the way in the use of steel-frame construction. The invention of the Bessemer process in the 1870s and the presence of the steel industry in Chicago may have spurred acceptance, since steel was becoming readily available and was relatively inexpensive. While Chicago had a number of buildings in the 15- to 18-story range by the 1890s, a true "skyscraper aesthetic" had not yet emerged. Most tall buildings were simply traditional ones made taller through the addition of a few more stories or a "tacked on" decorative tower. Rarely was height an integral part of the design. Train stations, for example, as symbols of civic pride and progress, sometimes had immense towers modeled on the monuments of Europe. Grand Central Station in Chicago (1890), had a 247-foot tower complete with an 11,000-pound bell to warn travelers of the time. As a by-product, Chicago was getting a skyline.

Throughout Europe and North America, the tower tradition, which had lain largely dormant for several centuries, was revived in the name of civic pride. New town halls (city halls) of towering heights were constructed in cities such as Leeds, Manchester, Munich, and Philadelphia. Towers adorned train stations in London as well as Chicago. Department stores and universities from Glasgow to Berkeley added towers, and in London the Tower Bridge became an instant historical landmark. Proper cities needed proper skylines. American cities, lacking Gothic cathedrals, medieval towers, and castles, were especially susceptible to tower-mania, as were many of the "new" industrial cities in northern Europe. Nevertheless, the champion in the new "tower as civic emblem and sign of progress" competition was Paris. The Eiffel Tower, at over 900 feet in height, was by far the tallest structure in the world. It was a naked skeleton or, as some have termed it, a bridge set on its end.

Surprisingly, New York City was slow to join in the race to reach new heights. In the 1880s, the tallest structures in New York were the support towers for the Brooklyn Bridge. The steel skeleton was not used in New York until 1888, when a finger-thin (25-foot-wide) 11-story structure was built on Broadway. The building was considered to be a joke, and the skeleton was used only because the narrow lot precluded any other type of construction. It was called the Tower Building.

The Emergence of the Office Tower as a Building Type

Until the mid-1800s, office activities required very little specialized space. Both commercial banks and merchants' exchanges tended to have one main hall or banking room with only a few "offices" tucked away around the edges. By the 1820s and 1830s, however, some new financial activities were emerging. Savings banks were spinning off from commercial banks and becoming independent entities. Trust companies, a medieval invention, but one that was not introduced into America until the 1820s, evolved to facilitate the emergence of corporations, nonprofit institutions, and family estates. Insurance companies grew in number and size as their activities expanded beyond the shipping industry. Life insurance, for example, considered to be an unnecessary luxury in the early 1800s, became fully established by the 1830s. By 1834, New York City alone had more than thirty insurance companies, more than were in the entire United States in 1800.[7]

The opening of the Erie Canal in 1825 helped to focus economic activity in New York, and on Wall Street in particular. A chamber of commerce was formed and a new custom house constructed. Clearing houses evolved to facilitate the banking industry, and offices began to evolve as a special kind of architectural space. By 1860, Wall Street had become the financial center of the United States as New York City captured the majority of foreign trade. Still, the office landscape of the city was subdued. Most office buildings were still Classical in design, Greek Revival temples in a sea of Georgian houses. After the hiatus imposed by the Civil War, this landscape began to change rapidly and drastically.

By the 1880s, it was both possible and popular to build impressive towers in the central districts of large American cities, as well as in cities in many other parts of the world. It was not always clear, however, just what they should be used for. The true office building was only just being invented in the mid- to late nineteenth century. In the early 1800s, most firms simply leased space wherever it was available or else did business in a coffeehouse, such as Lloyd's Coffee House in London. It is not clear when the very first office building was built, but the Sun Insurance Office in London was certainly one of the first.

The Sun Insurance Office was built in 1849 specifically to house the activities of an insurance company. Previously the company, like most companies of the day, simply made do with whatever space was available, preferably near the Royal Exchange. The company was growing rapidly (26 employees in 1806, 56 in 1866), and appropriate work spaces and storage areas were becoming necessary. Still, no one knew exactly what an office building was. The building was designed to look like an Italian palazzo from the outside, a symbol of corporate solidity, while the inside was designed very much along the lines of a fashionable house. It was sort of an "office house" with a sequence of great and comfortable rooms similar to what one might have found in the best residential squares of the city. The cozy and decorative fireplaces, the tables and chairs, the bureaus and bookcases for storage—all were similar to a residential interior.

London, the first city in the world to have large numbers of office workers, pioneered the effort to develop an appropriate office environment. The Inns of Court, designed to house lawyers and associated clerical staff, followed the model of the English university, with Georgian houses facing cloistered yards. One could go from Oxford to London with little change of atmosphere. As long as office space in London occupied buildings similar in scale to those around them (low and small), areal expansion was necessary, since increased densities could not be achieved on site. At the same time, the processes of exclusion and segregation were somewhat stymied by the lack of architectural differentiation.

Gradually, new types of office arrangements emerged. The Oriel Chambers, a four-story office building completed in 1864 in Liverpool, broke away from the "domestic-cum-college" style of earlier British offices. It contained a series of small three- and four-person units or cubicles arranged along an interior hallway. Since the vast majority of office firms were tiny, this arrangement allowed for a large number of small companies to coexist and to expand and contract as times changed. It was a true office building. Its simple repetitive spaces were unlike those found in a house. As the office building diffused to America, it increased in size and monumentality. In 1873, the Tribune Building in New York City was built to nine stories and decorated with an ornamental tower. It was perhaps the first office tower to dwarf its five-story neighbors. It would not be the last.

From about the 1870s on, the number of both office workers and office buildings grew rapidly. In 1800 only a tiny fraction of the work force could be called office workers by any stretch of the imagination, and over the next few decades growth in such employment was gradual. Between 1870 and 1920, however, the demand for office space in America increased tenfold—and the boom was only just beginning. Since the 1920s, the skyscraper office building, corporate capitalism, and a transactional civilization have all developed together.

The office tower as a building type matured during the late 1800s as the demand for special types of office space developed. While most buildings continued to be designed as a series of cubicles à la the Oriel Chambers building, other versions were perfected as a result of the emergence of giant corporations, increased use of office machinery (typewriter use increased from 146 in 1879 to 65,000 in 1890), and even "time and motion" studies aimed at perfecting the efficient office environment. Electric lighting made it possible to build larger interior spaces, and heating (and cooling) technologies made such things as the fireplace obsolete. By the 1890s, 20-story, "modern" office buildings were taking over the CBDs in New York and Chicago and beginning to appear in Pittsburgh and Buffalo. The 21-story, 305-foot Masonic Temple in Chicago was the tallest office building in the world in 1893 as the Columbian Exposition brought "City Beautiful" designs to the American city.

Deciding that the low skylines of Boston and London (and Paris) provided a more appropriate aesthetic model than a ragged skyline, Chicago opted for a 130-foot height limit by the late 1890s, and New York City took the lead in the development of skyscraper office buildings. London, Paris, and most other European cities also expressed concern about the aesthetic impact of tall buildings and passed some type of height control ordinance. Consequently, the CBDs in these cities continued to expand horizontally.

Transportation Technologies and the American Central Business District

The relationship between transportation innovations and the dynamics of CBD evolution has not always been an easy thing to understand. In London, for example, an excellent transportation system enabled the business district to sprawl from the Tower of London to Knightsbridge, while in Chicago it served to perpetuate a compact downtown core. These differences are at least partly a matter of timing.

While carriages, stagecoaches, omnibuses, and other types of wheeled vehicles had allowed people who could afford it to move about cities for some time, the first real improvements in intra-urban land transportation since the chariot occurred only in the mid-nineteenth century. The horsecar, a large wagon pulled by horses along fixed rails, appeared in the 1850s and greatly increased the speed of travel, since rails largely eliminated the need to deal with mud, cobblestones, and dust. Indeed, many were frightened by the incredible speeds of 10 to 15 miles per hour these new monstrosities could reach. Commuter rail lines, cable cars, and electric streetcars soon followed; and by the end of the century subways and elevated railways also contributed to intra-urban mobility.

By the time these innovations arrived, cities such as London and Paris were already quite large, and space was too valuable (and sacred) to give over very much of it to transportation uses. Railroad stations, for example, were located at the edge of the existing cities, so that there tended to be several peripheral stations rather than one "grand central." Also, by the time new transportation technologies arrived, the CBDs of London and Paris had already expanded, house by house, from the Royal Exchange to Westminster and along the Champs Elysées, respectively. Horsecars and streetcars helped to tie the periphery together and to connect one railroad station to the next. Indeed, the subway (underground railway) was invented in London in 1863 for the purpose of connecting peripheral rail stations (known today as the Circle Line). Only later was it pushed into the heart of the city.

In most American cities, transportation innovations, rapid urban growth, and office building developments came onto the scene together. Nowhere was this truer than in Chicago. The city of Chicago grew up around the railroad, and massive new stations were built along with the new central business district after the fire of 1871. The stations reinforced the idea of downtown. Similarly, streetcars (and for a while cable cars) focused on the new center, all coming together at a site that was more or less still under construction. The Loop, a small district encircled by an elevated rail line, became the undisputed heart of the city, and it soon filled up with large office buildings as well as other new, large building types such as the department store. The compact downtown skyline that emerged served as a model for what the American city should be like.

The focusing of transportation lines at a particular corner of the CBD gave rise to what has been referred to as the "peak land value intersection," or PLVI. The PLVI is, theoretically, the point of maximum accessibility and maximum potential interaction. It is "where it's at." Land values at the PLVI rose quickly in comparison with land only a few blocks away as everyone wanted to locate at or near the center of things. Because of the invention of the tall office building, many businesses indeed could locate at the PLVI, and this is what made American cities different. In most European cities, the "center" consisted largely of sacred or ceremonial space or of buildings that by the late 1800s were already considered to be historic. The largest cities, such as Paris and London, already had several centers based upon centuries of religious and civic monument layering.

The older American cities of the East Coast were hybrids. While not nearly so large and old as those of Europe, they were nevertheless very much in existence before the arrival of the railroad and the office tower. This is one of the major differentiating features of American cities even today. While Boston's CBD merges gradually with residential areas around it, having been inserted into a preexisting city, the downtowns of cities such as Los Angeles and Houston seem far removed from any neighborhoods, since business blocks and transportation lines were almost from the start built to be apart and different from residential areas.

New York City represents not only the biggest but also the most complex case in the development of the American downtown. Wall Street had become the business center of the city by the early 1800s, and the CBD gradually expanded to cover the lower tip of Manhattan by the late 1800s. As the area filled, many activities once associated with the core, such as retailing, began to migrate northward. The business district no doubt would have moved as well had not the skyscraper office building come upon the scene. By the 1890s, lower Manhattan was bristling with 20-story towers—a memorable scene for newly arriving immigrants approaching the city from the sea.

Transportation and technological innovations contributed to both the continuing success and the relative decline of New York's financial district. During the late nineteenth century, tall office buildings that included elevators could be built only in lower Manhattan. The first district to be electrified was in lower Manhattan (1880s), and for a considerable time after that, direct current was available only in the traditional financial district. Since elevator manufacturers had not yet developed a satisfactory method of speed control with any but direct current motors, a highly concentrated downtown emerged. Perhaps the tightly packed skyline that came to symbolize New York, and eventually the American city in general, was an accident resulting from technological constraints. Whatever the origin, the compact CBD turned out to be good for business.

Other developments worked against the continuation of Wall Street as the undisputed center of the business world. While lower Manhattan was the traditional center of the city, it became, during the railroad era, increasingly off-center from the point of maximum accessibility. The New York Central Railroad helped to create a second downtown. Attempts to bring the railroad to the financial district had met with considerable opposition. After being annoyed by the smoky, noisy, and sometimes dangerous railroad engines, Bowery mobs even tore up the tracks in lower Manhattan. In 1859, the southern limit for the Central was 26th Street, but it was soon after moved back to 42nd, thus determining the location of the old Grand Central Station, which opened in 1871.

In 1875, a train wreck in the inadequate tunnel serving the station led to a demand by the city that a new right-of-way be opened. In order to pay for a new, partially underground, way into the station, someone hit upon the novel idea to sell the air rights over the tracks. By 1903, when the new Grand Central Station opened, the airspace over the tracks along Park Avenue was lined with large buildings. At first hotels and apartment buildings were attracted to the area, but the availability of newly carved large lots coupled with excellent transportation connections gradually made midtown Manhattan the New York City PLVI. Consequently, by the 1920s, most major skyscrapers were being constructed there. New York City, therefore, provides the first example of the CBD replication stage, as downtown and midtown became competing foci. This eventually led to another round of segregation as the two nodes increasingly specialized in different types of office space.

Types of Office Employment, 1870–1914

The advantages of intensive face-to-face contact were addressed in a speech to the annual meeting of the U.S. Chamber of Commerce in 1927: "The reason that America today is leading the world is because her businessmen have had the sense and the foresight to carry on their affairs in limited, concentrated areas where they can get at each other."[8] This raises an intriguing question: What role has the morphology of the American CBD played in the development of the American economy? Just as there are arguments today that the economic flexibility of places such as Hong Kong would not be possible without immediate access to a wide variety of participants—so that, for example, orders can be taken before suppliers are found—the wide variety of contacts possible in the early decades of the skyscraper office tower may have shaped as well as been shaped by the nature of the financial community. In the more traditional CBDs of European cities, important locations tended to be less defined, and access to information tended to be through more formal channels.

Before the rise of corporate capitalism and the huge firm during the early years of the twentieth century, most office buildings contained a variety of small tenants. Close spatial proximity was vital for the successful interaction of many small firms with one another and with the newly emerging large firms. Until the First World War, the typical large office building contained a fine-grained mosaic of occupants. Although the new office towers usually carried the names of major corporations, those corporations initially occupied only a fraction of the available space. In Toronto in 1914, for example, a typical 10- to 20-story, 100,000- to 200,000-square-foot office building contained a range of 30 to 100 tenants.[9] The 15-story Canadian Pacific Railway Building accommodated 53 establishments, while the 10-story Old Dominion Bank Building had 37 separate firms.

During the early years of the twentieth century, a typical downtown office building might contain a variety of small business service and professional workers such as accountants, auditors, lawyers, stockbrokers, insurance agents, and advertising professionals whose offices existed in close association with large corporations. There were also a number of engineering firms, transportation companies, and governmental operations more directly involved with running the city. In addition, there were companies involved with mining, lumbering, and other activities whose direct linkage with the financial core was more problematic but nevertheless possible when one considers that face-to-face contact for the purposes of organizing, financing, and insuring a wide variety of activities was probably very necessary in the precomputer, and especially in the pretelephone, era.

One of the most important reasons for the creation of unprecedented amounts of office space during the early twentieth century was to make room for clerical workers. In the early 1800s, clerks were well paid, highly skilled, male, and few in number. By the early 1900s they were becoming poorly paid, semiskilled, female, and numerous. The managers, accountants, and lawyers of the new corporate economy needed vast numbers of typists, filers, switchboard operators, and secretaries. Big rooms full of desks replaced cubicles in some newer office buildings, but this was still the exception rather than the norm, as very few firms had as many as 200 employees. The development of the really large office building was still a few years away as well, both in terms of height and volume. In 1900, very few buildings contained as much as 100,000 square feet of space.

The Emergence of the Skyscraper as a Corporate Symbol

In the early years of the twentieth century, the uniquely American factors which gave rise to the monumental skyscraper were beginning to come together. While most office-space users continued to be small firms, giant national corporations were emerging in the United States and Canada. These corporations needed both large amounts of office space under one roof and memorable corporate symbols to help to spread the company name (in association with a nationally distributed product) across the land. Large office buildings became necessary, and tall office buildings were most desired.

At roughly the same time, a variety of technological improvements were being made. Chief among these was the development of a high-speed, gearless electrical elevator (1904) which would make possible buildings considerably higher than the "normal" maximum of about 20 stories. With Chicago and several other cities hamstrung by height limits, New York City was very much alone in the new, unprecedented race for the sky. As an added impetus, by 1903, office rents in New York were four times those of Chicago.

In 1908, the Singer Building doubled the height of the tallest point on the lower Manhattan skyline, a skyline that had been merely creeping up over the previous five decades. The Singer Building consisted of a base structure 14 stories high containing 330,000 square feet of gross floor space, topped by a 27-story tower which added only another 130,000 square feet of space. With its 4-story, decorative lantern top, the tower peaked at 612 feet, second only to the Eiffel Tower in the world's-tallest contest. This was the first really successful effort at merging the tradition of the tower as civic monument (as exemplified by everything from the Bruges Belfry to the Philadelphia City Hall) with the office building as corporate necessity.

The Singer Building was clearly a hybrid in that the company could have created the same amount of office space by constructing a 20-story building covering the full lot rather than a 14-story base and a slim tower. The tower was only 70 feet square and contained four elevators as well as stairways, hallways, and service rooms. It was clearly not the most efficient way to create functional office space. Nevertheless, it served as a role model for those who would create a prestigious skyscraper office tower. Unlike the towers which gave cities identity and importance elsewhere in the world, such as Victoria Tower (Big Ben), the Singer Building was completely private: any company with enough money could build one. It also illustrated that a tall building could be an important advertising symbol for companies that wished to do business nationally. If you could build a tower like the Singer Building, you must be able to make good sewing machines.

Between 1908 and 1915, there was a tremendous nationwide boom in office building construction which facilitated the acceptance of the skyscraper. The tallest buildings, however, continued to be built in lower Manhattan. The Metropolitan Life Building (1909) was the first to surpass 700 feet. Modeled after the campanile in St. Mark's Square in Venice, it confirmed the idea of the office skyscraper as a civic as well as corporate monument. The most impressive skyscraper of the era, however, was Cass Gilbert's Woolworth Tower, which, at 792 feet, remained the tallest building in the world until the 1930s, when it was surpassed by the Chrysler and Empire State buildings. It remained the fourth tallest in the world until the office building boom of the mid-1970s. Referred to as a "Cathedral of Commerce," this lacy Gothic monument is still widely considered to be one of the most beautiful buildings ever built.

Attempts to Control the Skyline

Not everyone was pleased by the new architectural wonder. In Boston, concern over the impact of skyscrapers on the congested, late-medieval city center led to the imposition of a 12-story height limit, leaving the city with only the 450-foot Custom House Tower on its skyline. Philadelphia decreed that no skyscraper should exceed the height of the 500-foot-tall City Hall so that its statue of William Penn could look down on the city in perpetuity (or, as it turns out, until the 1980s). Washington, D.C., banned tall buildings so that its national monuments could continue to dominate the skyline. Los Angeles limited the height of office buildings because of fear of what would happen to them during an earthquake. Chicago could not make up its collective mind. Between 1893 and 1902 it had a 10-story limit, partly due to lobbying by the owners of existing tall buildings who wanted to have a monopoly, but the limit was raised to 260 feet in 1902 (and then lowered to 200 feet after a building boom created a glut of space). All across the nation, cities wrestled with the sticky problem of determining just how tall downtown office buildings should be.

Some cities established height limits for the entire city (with some of these limits as low as 35 feet), while others established height districts, thus adding political direction to the growth and expansion of the CBD. Others determined that the height of buildings should be related to the width of the street (an idea that had been practiced in European cities for centuries) so that light and air could reach the sidewalks. As usual, New York City led the way.

Construction of the Equitable Building (1915) in lower Manhattan broke the tradition of low bases with slender towers. The Equitable Building, although "only" 39 stories tall, covered an entire city block and contained 1.2 million square feet of office space. It was thus of concern for two reasons. First, its mass blocked the light and air of the buildings around it and the street below at a time when natural lighting and cooling were still of some importance. Second, the creation of such a massive amount of office space at one time led to increasing concerns about congestion and the overloading of the infrastructure should very many builders follow suit. Clearly, the mass of the central business district had to somehow be monitored and controlled. The result was the nation's first zoning law aimed at controlling the height

Lower Manhattan: here we see a collage of skyscraper styles, from the Equitable Building (lower left), which led to the first zoning regulations for height and bulk in 1916, to the slim towers of the 1920s, to the glass box of the post–World War II era.

and bulk of buildings. Some forms of land use controls had been in existence previously, but comprehensive zoning ordinances were an innovation.

New York's law initially established height districts such that building height was related to the width of the street. For example, a "two" district would allow buildings twice the width of the street, thus encouraging those who would build tall buildings to find wider streets (as in midtown). But the type of zoning that eventually emerged related building height to floor area ratio, or FAR. That is, if a FAR of 10 was in effect in a certain district, then a 10-story building could be built covering the entire lot or a 20-story building could be built covering half the lot or any combination of the above. This created a "zoning envelope" within which only so much space could be created on a certain size lot. The architectural style that resulted was the "setback" or "wedding cake" style which featured buildings flush with the street at street level with a series of setbacks eventually culminating in a slim tower. Most cities eventually adopted some form of FAR zoning. The days of complete laissez faire building were over.

The controversy that emerged as a result of the new downtown buildings made the term *skyscraper* a household word. At first there was a great deal of confusion about just what these things should be called—cloud scrapers, cloud piercers, etc. The word *skyscraper* as an adjective describing tall buildings first appeared in 1884, and its use as a noun occurred first around 1889. Indeed, as late as 1933, the *Oxford English Dictionary* provided six different definitions of the word *skyscraper*, including a high-standing horse and a very tall man. Generally speaking, however, almost everyone knew what a real skyscraper was by the advent of World War I.

By 1915, New York City had nine buildings over 400 feet tall, and five of those were over 500 feet tall. New York was developing a skyline—a term first coined in the mid-1800s as something synonymous with "horizon" but which, by the 1890s, was increasingly associated with groups of buildings. While skylines could include groupings of church steeples and traditional palaces, by World War I having a skyline was beginning to mean having tall buildings. This also meant that civic pride and concern for congestion often worked at cross-purposes.

The Impact of Skyscraper Office Buildings on the Central Business District

The emergence of huge and very expensive office skyscrapers epitomizes the stages of exclusion and segregation in the evolution of the American CBD. Land costs soared to reflect the potential value of the land if built upon to the maximum allowable extent, regardless of what was currently on the site. Thus, many businesses were forced out, unable to pay the rents charged even in older, marginal space. Zoning made the differences between the core of the CBD and surrounding areas even more pronounced. If a district was zoned for tall office buildings, its value was *de jure* very great.

As early as the 1920s and early 1930s, books and articles discussing the rapidly reorganizing central city began to appear. Scholars in a variety of disciplines attempted to identify the trends and forces which were sorting out activities in and around the CBD. For example, Charles Colby identified a variety of centrifugal and centripetal forces which were leading to increasing differentiation of the city into functionally identifiable inner and outer zones.[10] He argued that while high land values, high taxes, congestion, and inability to find or build appropriate space were driving many activities out of the central area, the functional convenience and prestige associated with the central district was attracting other activities to it. The mixed-use central city was on its way out. Special-purpose tall office buildings came to symbolize the forces of exclusion and segregation.

Geographers have described the evolution of the specialized CBD in terms of a series of rent gradients with distance from the PLVI. Rents are highest at the PLVI and become lower with increasing distance from it, but the gradients, or slopes, are not the same for all uses. For example, office space typically locates at the PLVI for a variety of reasons. First, office uses can generate the most profit per square foot since these users deal with information rather than actual goods. It takes less space to decide to manufacture something than to actually manufacture it. Second, office space can occupy space intensively because the skyscraper is an appropriate building type for it. People with information can travel easily by elevator. Third, office users feel that they benefit greatly by an identifiable, prestigious location. "We are located in the Chrysler Building" is better than "we are located at 609 Elm Street." This means that the rent gradient for office space is very steep—users will pay a lot for a location at the PLVI but will not bid at all for a location just five blocks away. Thus, the steepness of the office "bid-rent curve" determines the extent of the central business core. Other activities must locate farther out.

Hotels and department stores cannot bid quite as much to be at the PLVI, since they do not generate enough profit per square foot and since the skyscraper is not quite as appropriate a structure (although some recent hotel developments have pushed the limit dramatically upward). Department stores, for example, must have large amounts of goods delivered and so need more space around them. In addition, there is a limit to how high people will go to obtain goods or services. "It is on the 63rd floor, sir" may well dissuade someone in search of a necktie. However, department stores need to be accessible, and so a location close to the PLVI is important. They will bid for space at the center but will, in most cases, be relegated to a space just beyond. And so it goes. Traditionally, at least some manufacturers were located close to the center of the city for convenient distribution of goods and because many employees commuted to work by public transit. Today, most industry has decentralized in search of horizontal space on cheaper land. Typically, housing is located farthest out, since it generates no profit per square foot (except as commuting time is valued) and since many Americans have a cultural bias against living in high-density environments.

While the bid-rent curve largely determines the location of major activities (those which occupy large amounts of space), small-space users such as cafes, specialty shops, and bars are included or excluded from the CBD depending upon whether spaces are provided for them somewhere within office buildings. For example, early skyscrapers tended to have bases flush with the sidewalk and relatively traditional frontages lined with shops. Later, as the tall building became the established downtown norm and as setbacks for plazas became common to conform to FAR lot coverage regulations, street-level doors disappeared. Today, the presence or absence of small shops is often a result of political decisions because governmental design guidelines can influence whether there will be a plethora of plazas or an abundance of arcades. These issues came to the forefront of urban design planning in the 1970s.

The Perfection and Diffusion of the Skyscraper, 1880–1930

During the early decades of the nineteenth century, the idea of a specialized business district and the idea of the special-purpose office building diffused simultaneously. Towns and cities of all sizes adopted the new spatial form. For example, Classical-style bank buildings, or "the strongbox on Main Street," appeared in both large cities and small towns all across America as this architectural form came to symbolize solidity and permanence. The construction of such buildings required neither large amounts of capital nor a great demand for office space

Similarly, in the middle years of the nineteenth century, the two- to four-story "office block," usually Italianate in style, diffused widely to cities of a variety of sizes. While such blocks came to symbolize the specialized business center of the town, or "Main Street," they did not serve to differentiate cities according to size. The same type of buildings were built in downtown Cleveland and downtown Zanesville, in both Philadelphia and Wilmington, and in Chicago and Peoria.

By the late 1800s and early 1900s, some differentiation began to occur, as not every city could afford to build "elevator buildings." The typical major office structure of this period was the 5- to 12-story masonry or perhaps steel-frame, cubicle-filled office "tower." Such buildings appeared in any city large enough to have a CBD, from Lima, Ohio, to San Diego, California, around the turn of the century. These buildings created a jagged skyline, as most of the central district remained low-rise. They also served to stake out the PLVI and set in motion the stage of exclusion, since the new building type was almost always built exclusively for office space. In some smaller cities, where civic pride demanded a tall building but where there was insufficient demand for office space, a tall hotel was often constructed at the PLVI. It was in the hotel, then, that the real business of the city was carried out. Nevertheless, geographic studies aimed at "delimiting the CBD" could be carried out in a wide variety of places because the core of the typical American city came to have certain accepted architectural characteristics.[11]

The truly monumental skyscraper was much slower to diffuse because it required not only a large investment but also significant architectural and engineering expertise. Firms specializing in skyscraper construction emerged in a few major cities, and their cost and availability helped to determine diffusion routes and possibilities.

Before World War I, very few buildings over 20 stories existed beyond New York City. There were a few notable exceptions. By 1914, for example, both Cincinnati and Seattle had an office tower exceeding 500 feet. The Cincinnati Tower was constructed by the Union Central Insurance Company, while the L. C. Smith Tower in Seattle was constructed by a typewriter manufacturer. The Smith Building remained the tallest building on the West Coast for over 50 years. Tall buildings were also built in Chicago, Pittsburgh, Buffalo, and other cities, although a combination of building regulations and lack of local leadership in need of a "civic-corporate symbol" coupled with the advent of World War I, meant that skyscrapers were still relatively rare outside New York in 1920.

It was during the late 1920s that the skyscraper as a symbol of the American city really took hold. World War I was followed by a recession and considerable economic reorganizing as corporate capitalism and a national consumer economy developed and matured. Few major office buildings were constructed until after 1925. Between 1925 and 1931, however, the skyscraper became the symbol of the "roaring twenties" in both New York City and elsewhere. In New York, dozens of buildings were built in the 500- to 1,000-foot category, with two—the Chrysler Building and the Empire State Building—exceeding 1,000 feet. The Empire State Building remained the tallest in the world, at 1,250 feet, until the Sears Tower in Chicago surpassed it by 200 feet in the mid-1970s.

By the late 1920s, there were plans afoot to build "mile-high" skyscrapers covering several city blocks when the Great Depression intervened. Since FAR regulations were now in full force, "wedding cake" setbacks became the architectural norm. In order to build unusually tall towers, full city blocks were often required, as in the case of the Empire State Building. Since large corporations were becoming increasingly common, at least in New York City, a large amount of open, horizontal office space was desired in order to facilitate intra-office communication. The skyscraper thus encouraged lot assembly, and the morphology of the city changed greatly as many small lots and uses gave way to a few large ones. Exclusion and segregation were in full swing. In New York during the 1920s, most of the new skyscrapers were built in midtown Manhattan, as large lots were more readily available there. In addition, the midtown core was focused by political as well as economic considerations. Since 1916, Manhattan had been zoned for commercial and residential uses; since office towers could not be built in areas preserved for residential uses, the northward expansion of office buildings was halted at the edge of the posh Upper East Side (and Central Park). The demand for vertical space increased.

Most Americans were convinced that skyscrapers were good for business. Advocates pointed out that, except for peak rush hours, traffic was lighter in skyscraper zones than elsewhere, since people were traveling by elevator rather than by taxi. Others compared Boston and Chicago in order to show that while the two cities attracted roughly the same daytime populations into their central districts, Boston (with its 125-foot height limit) appeared to be more crowded because its business took place over a larger area and people had to move about on the streets. Kingston and Clark referred to London in 1930: "In the city of London, which is probably a 4-story average over the city and in which there are no skyscrapers, if you attempt to make three business appointments a day you will do very well, because they will be scattered over every portion of the city and you will only add to the congestion of the street."[12] Also, by concentrating office space in vertical buildings, some maintained, you could make room for such things as a theater or restaurant district.

It was also during the 1920s that a "skyscraper aesthetic" was developed and architectural styles appropriate for tall buildings emerged. The earliest tall buildings were simply short buildings made taller with additional stories. The towers of the early 1900s largely emulated Gothic and Renaissance forms. With the Chrysler Building and the Empire State Building, however, American tower design achieved maturity. Strong vertical lines and sleek towers helped to accentuate the sense of height.

During the 1920s, the spatial separation of different corporate functions accelerated. As the rent gradient steepened and as space-extensive activities were pushed out of the business districts, top management had to decide whether to follow the factory to a more remote location or to stay downtown close to the heart of the financial world. For many, staying meant building because finding adequate space under one roof was often difficult even if citywide vacancy rates were high. Thus, most of the new towers carried corporate names. It also became evident during the 1920s that office buildings were a good place to invest capital, although this idea went through a rough maturation process during the Depression. Banks and insurance companies, in particular, by definition had huge amounts of money to invest, and land and buildings (especially famous and prestigious buildings) were seen as attractive. Because of massive investments, much downtown redevelopment over the years has been "defensive" in that too much has been invested to allow it to be thrown away. Political pressure to use government funds to enhance the environments of important headquarters buildings has become intense at various times.

While the skyscraper as corporate headquarters and as a new architectural form was being perfected in New York City, it was also being diffused more widely than earlier towers had been. Although there were still lower limits to the size of cities which could create a skyline, these limits could be pushed downward by an enterprising entrepreneur.

The Skyscraper: Cultural Values and Urban Morphology

By 1930, the American CBD as a special kind of place was fully developed. Not all of the development, however, can be seen as the natural expression of economic forces at work. In some cases, a strong will allied with economically "irrational" cultural values shaped the emerging CBD. Because of its enormous size and its prestige value, a skyscraper could have tremendous impact on the spatial organization of the emerging CBD. Cleveland is a case in point.

During the early 1900s, the Cleveland CBD was experiencing the stage of expansion/extension as newer office buildings were pulling the heart of the CBD eastward along Euclid Avenue. The old heart of the city, at Public Square, had become peripheral and was no longer the PLVI. In 1906, the Van Swerigan brothers obtained suburban property ideally suited for a prestige residential development (Shaker Heights) and wanted to serve that development with a commuter railroad. They purchased a rail line which entered the city just downslope from Public Square and decided that if the commute, and thus the residential development, were to succeed, Public Square had to be shaped into a major employment attraction—that is, it had to contain an immense and well-known office tower. In order to defray the costs of rehabilitating the railroad and building a tower, the brothers asked the city to relocate its main railroad station in the proposed development. The city repeatedly refused, but finally the Van Swerigans promised to build a 52-story skyscraper modeled after the Giralda Tower in Seville, Spain, with 2.2 million square feet of space (450,000 in the tower). Enthusiastic about the possibility of having such a landmark—at 708 feet it was to be the tallest building outside of New York—the city reconsidered and the station was moved.

The building was completed in 1928 and was known as the Terminal Tower, since it was built over the railroad station. Its location also made it an attractive place for railroad companies, and so much of the space was taken by corporations such as the Baltimore and Ohio and Chesapeake and Ohio railroads. The construction of the tower complex reshaped downtown Cleveland. Public Square became the center once again, for the Terminal Tower Complex contained as much first-class office space as the rest of the CBD put together, in addition to a department store, a hotel, a shopping arcade, three smaller (18-story) office towers, and the railroad station. Covering over 35 acres, the

Terminal Tower became nearly synonymous with the Cleveland CBD as it absorbed office activities formerly scattered throughout the CBD. In comparison, the rest of the downtown became marginal, peripheral space as the CBD retreated into one immense complex.

While CBD expansion occurred horizontally in towerless cities, it occurred vertically in at least some American cities, thus encouraging the emergence of an economically marginal "transition zone" of semi-abandoned smaller buildings only a few blocks from the PLVI. Such properties often suffered from disinvestment as owners waited expectantly for a skyscraper builder to express interest in their property. Shultz and Simmons, in their book *Offices in the Sky*, maintain that

> every year the erection of office buildings in every city has been increasing the value of land in the central districts, not only of the lots on which the new buildings were built, but also of the land under adjoining old buildings. Unfortunately, except for the very best locations, not one [of the older buildings] in ten was ever able to cash in on this unearned increment. High taxes on old properties made it impossible for owners who could not afford to rebuild or keep buildings in repair (especially since the new skyscrapers attracted the top tenants). As a result, these were the start of blighted areas.[13]

In other words, the skyscraper served to compact the core of the CBD while enlarging the frame. The zone in transition was drawn inward as once-central buildings became peripheral to the skyscraping center.

Not every city could afford a project as big as the Terminal Tower. Some cities did follow suit, however. Cincinnati built the Carew Tower Complex, a 568-foot office tower which also included a shopping mall and hotel. In Los Angeles, the city itself broke the rules (in this case a 150-foot height limit) to build a 450-foot civic monument—the Los Angeles City Hall. In Columbus, Ohio, the retiring president of the American Insurance Union wanted to build a tower as sort of a memorial to his reign but found it difficult to do so in light of the rather limited demand for office space in the city at that time. Eventually, an agreement was reached so that space in the new 556-foot, 47-story AIU Citadel would be shared by a hotel, a palatial movie theater, and the home offices of the insurance company, with the remainder used as speculative office space. Eighteen stories of the 20-story base were occupied by the hotel and the other 2 stories of the base by the AIU; the slim tower was used by a variety of small concerns such as law and accounting firms. While the Citadel, as it was called, had less impact on the Columbus CBD than did the mas-

The Cleveland Terminal Tower (1928) was the tallest building outside of New York City for nearly 40 years. The building provided a new focus for downtown Cleveland.

sive Terminal Tower Complex on Cleveland's central district, it did serve to anchor the CBD both visually and functionally to its traditional center at Broad and High.

In medium-sized cities such as Columbus, it was clear that the skyscraper was not simply another, merely taller office building. The AIU Citadel became the symbolic and visual center of the city, in competition only with the nearby state capitol building. When the tower opened, a plane flew over, showering the edifice with "myriads of flower petals" while secretaries marched down the street singing an "ode to the citadel." The American city had found its symbol. The American CBD had also been reorganized. As William Starrett wrote in *Skyscrapers and the Men Who Build Them*,

> One singular and significant fact of skyscraper construction here stands out, and that is its power to move the centers of cities. Under the old order, the cross-roads, vast traffic streams, and dense population knew no law but itself, and intensive building submissively remained where density ordained it should stay. But now it is different. Great structures can actually beckon the trends of population and traffic and, in a measure, can compel the shifting of economic centers of gravity.[14]

With the arrival of the Great Depression in the 1930s, many of the forces shaping the American CBD were put on hold.

The Impact of the Great Depression

By the year 1930, there were literally thousands of 10- to 20-story office buildings in cities and towns of all sizes across the nation. The American downtown had become a predictable place. The skyscraper, however, had not yet become quite ubiquitous, although the extent of its diffusion obviously depends upon its precise definition (i.e., some small cities built "skyscrapers" of only 15 stories, but these were far taller than anything else in the CBD). Using a stricter definition of skyscraper, we can map more precisely the diffusion of the tall building as of 1930, when the Depression brought a 30-year hiatus to skyscraper construction. Only New York City and Cleveland had buildings over 600 feet tall, but cities from Boston to Los Angeles had at least one building in the 400-foot category. The particular diffusion routes were often determined by intercity competition. For example, Cleveland, Cincinnati, and Columbus all had dominating towers, and each was well aware of the notoriety skyscrapers were receiving in the other cities. San Francisco and Los Angeles, Houston and Dallas, Memphis and Nashville—all had similar civic competitions.

The Depression had a major negative impact on construction of all kinds, but its impact on the CBD was especially pronounced because it brought financial ruin to many skyscraper owners and builders who had become overextended during the building boom of the late 1920s. The value of the towers often plummeted and remained depressed for decades. It was not until the early 1960s, for example, that the Terminal Tower in Cleveland could be sold for what it had cost to build it. It took a long time to convince corporations that downtown buildings were a good investment, and the second wave of skyscraper construction did not begin until the mid-1960s. In most American cities, the tallest building in 1929 was also the tallest building in 1959.

Throughout the 1930s to the 1950s, most CBDs remained overbuilt. In the economic euphoria of the 1920s, corporations and speculators had built massive office complexes in the expectation that office needs would continue to expand indefinitely and that future needs should be considered now while the building boom was on. When the market crashed, many companies went under and the space went begging, especially in less prestigious buildings. Even the Empire State Building had problems. Not completed until after the Depression began, it took a full decade to fill. Some have jokingly suggested that the only large tenant during this period was King Kong. The American Insurance Union in Columbus went bankrupt in 1933, at least partially because of the vast sums spent building the AIU Citadel. The building, which had cost $8 million to construct in 1927, was in effect sold for $3.5 million in 1933. The Van Swerigan brothers went bust in 1935, taking two local banks down with them.

Most of the new skyscrapers were not empty during the Depression. Some had more people working in them then than at any time before because of the doubling up that often occurred during the 1930s and 1940s. Although there were 88 vacancies in the Terminal

Tower in 1932, it was not uncommon for other offices to have lawyers, accountants, real estate agents, and a small company of some sort all sharing a few desks. Instead of renting extra space for expected growth as they did in the 1920s, most firms crammed into small offices in the expectation of further decline. A large number of vacancies meant a revenue shortfall for the building owners, but it did not necessarily mean an empty building.

In some cases, declining rents and limited demand meant that prestige buildings could be occupied by tenants not normally associated with such space. Directories from the period include references to such occupants as Christian Science reading rooms, the *Dairyman Monthly Review*, and the Lantern Slide Bureau in the Union Central Tower in Cincinnati. In other cases, large-space occupants, such as the 38 railroad companies that had offices in the Terminal Tower in 1932, could expand indefinitely and use generous amounts of space. In nearly every city examined, the Chamber of Commerce occupied space in one of the tallest buildings.[15]

The glut of space and the declining economy affected marginal buildings the most. In Columbus, two formerly prestigious buildings in the northern part of the CBD lost many of their tenants to the AIU Citadel during the late 1920s and never really recovered. In nearly every major city, large amounts of marginal space coupled with increasing numbers of homeless drifters served to make the edges of downtown into a sort of skid row. Municipalities, themselves hard-pressed for funds, were reluctant to lower taxes on downtown land and buildings, if not totally resistant to the idea, adding to the difficulties of property owners.

Urban Renewal and Civic Monumentality in the 1930s

While private construction ground to a halt during the 1930s, CBDs throughout the nation experienced some growth and change during the decade. Cities took advantage of lower land costs to create and expand monumental civic centers. New city halls, public libraries, auditoriums, museums, and concert halls were built, sometimes together in one extensive complex. The architectural style was nearly always classical, a bit of Athenian grandeur to brighten the bleak economic landscape.

Civic centers were usually built close to the core of the CBD, and their relatively low structures served to provide "breathing room" as well as greater visibility to the tall office buildings of the previous decade. In some ways, the era was analogous to the peeling away of medieval accretions to Gothic cathedrals during the Renaissance. Spacious plazas and malls appeared for the first time in many American cities, and fountains and statues often embellished them. In addition, new bridges and river embankment projects added to the beauty of American downtowns and gave them a more finished look. In some cases, as in Cleveland, the mall tended to tie together the major skyscraper with the rest of the CBD. In other cases, as in Columbus, the new expenditures beautified the area just around the new tower.

Most of the civic structures built during the 1930s were low and space-extensive. They served to perpetuate the trend toward lot assembly, with the consequent disappearance of street-level nooks and crannies and a fine-grained diversity of activity. Malls also perpetuated the trend toward the marginalization of peripheral space, that is, those buildings remote from both the new skyscrapers and the civic center.

Perhaps the most important downtown project to be built during the 1930s was Rockefeller Center in New York City. Although it was intended to be a mixed commercial-civic project focused on a new home for the Metropolitan Opera, the Depression led to a change in plans. Of all the original backers of the project, only Rockefeller remained after the crash of 1929. He was left holding a 24-year lease on 12 acres of prime land (owned by Columbia University) in the midst of an economic crisis and a glut of office space. The only way to get tenants was to create a project of such high quality that it could not be ignored.[16]

Since the public expected that the parcel would house an opera theater sited on an open plaza, Rockefeller felt obliged to keep some civic dimension in the new center. Pedestrian walkways, a 6,000-seat theater, the now-famous skating rink, and a considerable number of artistic embellishments were the result. The original center was the largest planned office project in New York, with 14 buildings containing nearly 6 million square feet of office space focused on the 70-story, 850-foot-tall RCA Building. The center was simply too big to be ignored, and it featured a large number of innovations, including underground parking, subterranean walkways, air conditioning, and pedestrian plazas which were unusual even in New York. Still, it was not until 1941 that it was a financial success.

The size, quality, and fame of Rockefeller Center has served to fix the core of the midtown office district at 5th Avenue and 50th Street for the past 60 years. Although office construction has crept northward during the past two decades, the rapid movement that characterized pre–Rockefeller Center New York has stopped. Rockefeller Center served to turn office construction westward to 6th Avenue and beyond.

The Skyscraper Comes of Age: Downtown Revival and the Office Boom

In spite of the increasing importance of office transactions in the American economy, private investors remained skeptical of the need for major new projects in the CBD until well into the 1960s. While office employment increased from 4 percent of total employment in 1900 to 18 percent in 1960, the office tower was still out of favor. The race for the sky had led to so many bankruptcies during the 1930s that major investments were still seen as risky. Four major trends were beginning to affect the American CBD during the 1950s: (1) the sub-urbanization of many activities, especially retailing and manufacturing but some kinds of office space as well; (2) the use of federally funded urban renewal projects to revitalize the downtown; (3) the architectural trend toward modern, minimal, understated, and modestly sized glass boxes largely devoid of the ostentation that characterized the 1920s; and (4) the emergence of a very affluent economy dominated by tertiary and quaternary office employment.[17]

Suburbanization

In 1950, many activities were still located in the CBD because there were few options. Nothing much had been constructed anywhere in the city since the 1920s, and since space was readily available downtown, many activities continued to locate there even when the space was considered to be increasingly suboptimal. As construction revived during the late 1940s and early 1950s, and as shopping centers and industrial parks siphoned off activities once located in the downtown, many began to predict the demise of the central city.

As other activities moved out, office space could be created quickly and inexpensively by converting structures once used for retailing or storage. Between 1945 and 1966, more office space was created in the Chicago Loop through conversion than by new construction. Because of the vertical expansion of office space during the early years of the twentieth century, very few office buildings had been torn down. As late as 1967, over two-thirds of the office space built during the 1890s in Chicago was still in use. While much of this space was aesthetically and functionally marginal, in the cautious days of the early 1950s, when memories of the Depression were still fresh, it was seen as the option of least risk by those seeking to stay in the urban core. In many cases, the core expanded as the frame or transition zone was pushed outward with the refurbishing of older buildings.

As the suburbanization trend accelerated in the mid-1950s, certain types of offices, especially those not requiring intensive face-to-face contact with clients or customers, began to head for either scattered locations or locations in urban subcenters such as along the "Miracle Mile" in Los Angeles. Many cities—including Chicago, Detroit, St. Louis, and Toronto—developed major office nodes only a few miles from the traditional CBD (the Manhattan syndrome).

One of the first major types of office-space users to decentralize was the life insurance company. According to Gad and Holdsworth,

> The growth in business led to the development of life insurance policies as standardized mass products. In turn, the old linkage system of the downtown district fell apart, primarily due to the removal of directors and even top managers from the day-to-day conduct of business. . . . At the same time, standardization of the product and rationalization of the production process allowed the adoption of low-wage labor. Large departments on single floors are one expression of this new form of production.[18]

Manufacturer's Life, for example, moved to a newer, lower building with landscaped grounds in Toronto's midtown area.

Technological changes also encouraged some firms to move from the older towers in the CBD. In the mid-1950s, Union Central Life Insurance in Cincinnati, which then occupied about 150,000 square feet of space in the tower (1913) that bore its name, began looking for a place to put its new electronic computer department. Leapfrogging in search of more space was getting too complicated, and neither scattered space in a number of buildings nor a location in a tall, thin tower would do. In 1958, the company decided to abandon its own building and head for the suburbs. The president explained: "We don't have to be in a place where there is maximum land value . . . we have little dealings with the public at the home office." New computer rooms required not only horizontal space but modern, air-conditioned space as well. Decentralization was considered to be the progressive thing to do in the 1950s.

Urban Renewal

The second major trend affecting the CBD during the 1950s was federally sponsored urban renewal. Many older cities had experienced considerable deferred maintenance between 1930 and 1950 and needed something more than ad hoc, here-and-there new buildings to revitalize the image and reality of the central city. In addition, many cities needed complete spatial reorganization on a scale not seen since the nineteenth century, when monumental plazas and boulevards were created in the capitals of Europe. Skyscraper towers located on streets little wider than alleyways coupled with increasing reliance on automobiles and buses meant that infrastructures had to be re-designed. Cities had to be opened up in order for them to function. In some cases, the laissez faire attitudes of the 1920s had enabled too much to be built in too small a space.

The first city to have its central area reshaped by urban renewal was perhaps the city that needed it the most, Pittsburgh. The Golden Triangle, consisting of gleaming skyscrapers set around a grassy park, replaced a jumble of industrial warehouses, railroad tracks, and bridges in the mid-1950s. Pittsburgh became the first city in the country to attempt to change its image from that of a grimy and dangerously smoky industrial town to that of a bright and classy headquarters city. As its image changed, so too did investment strate-gies. By the late 1960s, monumental new skyscrapers such as the 841-foot U.S. Steel Building proclaimed that downtown Pittsburgh was here to stay.

Baltimore, Hartford, Cleveland, and St. Louis also experienced massive renewal projects during the late 1950s and early 1960s. In the early 1950s, Baltimore possessed one of the dreariest, most congested and obsolete downtowns in the country, and many of its buildings were abandoned. Urban renewal cleared the way for One Charles Center: "The shock of seeing the Charles Center going up, something no one ever believed would happen, has given the whole town a new lease on life."[19] In most cases, early urban renewal projects concen-trated on facilitating the building of office towers as the only likely saviors of an apparently dwindling downtown. Skyscrapers could also change the image of a city: a gleaming new skyline was proof that something was going on.

Other massive federally funded projects, such as freeways and "slum clearance" (often for stadiums and cultural centers), also helped to reorganize the central city and to revitalize the CBD. Eventually, federal "seed money" became widely used in all kinds of cities in order to rouse private investors into action.

Minimalist Architecture

The third major trend impacting the CBD during the 1950s and 1960s was the complete infatuation with Modern, minimal architec-ture. While most of the towers built during the 1920s were blatantly decorative, there were some clues by about 1930 that the simple glass box then being championed by Europe's Bauhaus school of architec-ture would soon arrive on this side of the Atlantic. The 39-story Philadelphia Saving Fund Society Building, completed in Philadelphia in 1931, was clearly a harbinger of the streamlined look. Only the Depression blocked further acceptance. The glass box made its debut to rave reviews with the relatively small 21-story Lever House in New York City, which served as a model for downtown construction soon after its completion in 1951. While the Lever House was well-designed and used quality materials, developers soon learned that they could put up simple 20-story unadorned glass boxes relatively cheaply. Before long, there were lots of them in New York City, but they made little visual impact. Shultz and Simmons reported in 1959 that, "with all the vigor of New York's new boom, there has been no attempt to revive the old race for height by going higher than the Empire State Building. No new building has exceeded 60 stories and only 20 of the 109 buildings erected in Manhattan since 1947 are 30 or more stories tall and of these only 5 exceed 40 stories."[20]

At least New York City had an office building boom during the 1950s. Most cities did not start rebuilding their CBDs until much later. Even Chicago did not begin to build again on a grand scale until after 1956, when the 41-story Prudential Tower began to rise, utilizing the air rights over the lakefront railroad tracks. In San Francisco between 1945 and 1954, the downtown gained only 746,000 square feet of office space, in spite of a massive and highly concentrated office market. San Francisco did not begin to build downtown until 1959, when 1,437,000 square feet of space were added, and it was not until 1965, when the 33-story Hartford Building was completed, that a new tower exceeded the height of the 1928 Russ Building. Between 1963 and 1977, however, approximately 23 million square feet of office space went up in the San Francisco CBD. Nearly all of this space was in conservative glass boxes. By the late 1960s, this conservatism was beginning to wane with regard to both design and size. In 1969, the 52-story Bank of America Building added 1,771,000 square feet of space to the CBD, and in 1972 the Transamerica Pyramid stuck its pointed top 853 feet into the sky. People began to be worried about the impact of tall buildings for the first time since the 1920s.

The Office Economy

The final major trend affecting the CBD in the postwar years was the development of a mature office (some would say "transactional") economy, one based on the exchange of information rather than on the production of material goods. The percentage of the work force involved in manufacturing plummeted in most metropolitan areas, and an office job became the norm in many. As discussed above, however, office jobs do not necessarily have to be downtown, and many of them are not. Nevertheless, much of the very highest-level interaction remained in the CBD, and this gave rise to a demand for new kinds of space, especially prestige space.

In addition to the general increase in space required by the growth of office activity—including clerical work, administrative activities, computer complexes, and professional offices—there was also a large increase in per capita floor space as business machines got larger and affluent firms shunned the cramped quarters associated with earlier eras. In part, the large increase in per capita floor space reflected the increasing percentage of professional and technical office workers in a given building. In 1947, there were an average of 53 professional workers to every 100 clerical workers, while by 1965 the ratio was 80 to 100. Space became a nonwage "perk" aimed at enhancing executive self-image. According to a report in *Fortune*, "It's a whole new ballgame with space. You need it if you are going to attract people to work for you."[21] In 1963, the average per capita floor space in a "normal" New York office building was 165 square feet, while in "executive-heavy" buildings, it was 337 square feet. By the 1960s, top employees were coming to expect a full range of amenities as well as lots of space, and this often meant new buildings even when there were plenty of vacancies in older buildings.

The Geography of Tall Buildings

Obviously, the evolution of the skyscraper office building and the CBD has affected some American cities much more than others. A major difficulty facing the writer who would monitor trends in downtown development is the lack of centralized information. The *World Almanac* began to list tall buildings by city in 1954, providing the height and number of stories for tall buildings throughout the nation. While it is not always possible to determine the use of the building (office, hotel, apartment) or its location (in the CBD or elsewhere) from this listing, in most cases, the vast majority of skyscrapers are downtown. Another problem is that the almanac does not provide the size of the buildings in square feet of space, and especially for the earlier buildings, tall does not necessarily mean big. For example, the L. C. Smith Building (1913) in Seattle was 500 feet tall but included only 170,000 square feet of space. For postwar buildings, however, there is usually a very close relationship between height and rentable square feet.

Until the late 1960s, most large office towers were concentrated in New York City. In 1954, for example, New York City had 36 towers of more than 500 feet and 8 over 700 feet. In all of the rest of North America (United States and Canada), there were 20 buildings over 500 feet and only one over 700 feet. All of these buildings dated from

Evidence of the office building boom: top, *midtown Manhattan, ca. 1960;* bottom, *midtown Manhattan, ca. 1980*

the pre-Depression building boom or earlier. As another example, there were approximately 141 buildings exceeding 300 feet outside of New York in 1954 and about 100 in New York.[22]

Perhaps more significantly for the shaping of the CBD, in 1954 New York City was the only city to have a number of buildings with vast amounts of office space under one roof. For example, the 50-story Metropolitan Life Building (1909) was the first office building complex to have over 1 million square feet of space (1.3 million). The Woolworth Tower (1913) added 990,000 square feet. By the early 1930s, New York had 15 office buildings with more than 1 million square feet of space, led by the Empire State Building with 2.8 million. Outside of New York, such buildings were rare indeed. In addition to the Terminal Tower complex in Cleveland, only the low-rise Chicago Mechandise Mart (not really a downtown office building) had more than a million square feet of space. Famous towers such as Chicago's Wrigley Tower (220,000 square feet) and Tribune Tower (640,000 square feet) were small by comparison. Major towers outside of New York and Chicago rarely exceeded 500,000 square feet and were more likely to have around 250,000.

By 1990, nearly every large North American city could boast of an impressive skyline. In 1993, there were 72 buildings over 700 feet tall outside of New York City, in addition to the 29 in Manhattan. In addition, there were about 214 buildings between 500 and 700 feet tall outside of New York, with 42 cities having at least one such building. New York City had 103. In other words, 500-foot towers increased in number from 57 in 1954 to 418 in 1993. The almanac listed 583 buildings of between 300 and 500 feet tall outside of New York (none below 500 feet and 460 feet, respectively, are listed for New York and Chicago), and the list is very incomplete. There are at least 1,000 buildings over 300 feet in North America, and the number is increasing rapidly.

Most of these buildings are not only tall but also large. In 1962, Houston became the first city except for New York, Chicago, and Cleveland to build an office tower of more than 1 million square feet. In 1968 Atlanta, Boston, and Philadelphia followed suit, as did San Francisco and Dallas in 1969. By 1983, million-plus buildings were becoming quite common in more than a dozen North American cities from Toronto to Los Angeles. In some cities, really super "megastructures" began to single-handedly reshape the CBD. In Detroit, the Renaissance Center created 2.5 million square feet of office space along with a 72-story hotel and shopping mall, while in Chicago, the Sears Tower (the tallest office building in the world) added 3.4 million square feet of space to the Chicago CBD. In New York, the World Trade Center twin tower complex added an incredible 11 million square feet of space to lower Manhattan, more than the total amount of space in most American downtowns. The CBD was shrinking in area and expanding vertically. The rent gradient was becoming even steeper.

Not every city experienced this building boom. Tremendous amounts of office space were created in some cities along with ex-

Table 1. Office tower construction, 1970–1983

City	New office space (millions of sq. ft.)	Office towers of 25 + stories
New York City	73.0	239
Chicago	36.0	71
Houston	30.0	27
San Francisco	23.0	36
Denver	17.0	20
Dallas	14.0	24
Los Angeles	13.0	15
Atlanta	11.5	16
Pittsburgh	9.0	15
Minneapolis	7.0	5
Detroit	5.5	15
Cleveland	4.0	6
Baltimore	4.0	7
San Diego	3.0	2
Miami	2.5	2

tremely impressive skylines while other cities were largely inactive. Between 1970 and 1983, for example, some CBDs changed more than others, as can been seen in Table 1.

Many other fairly sizable cities experienced almost no increase in CBD office space. Cities such as Akron and Fresno, for example, appear to be below the threshold for major downtown development. In general, downtown skylines provide excellent clues to the importance of downtowns, especially in cities that serve as the major "control points" of the economic system; thus, New York, Chicago, and San Francisco have the most impressive skylines. There are other important factors, however.

In order to compare various cities on the basis of skyline significance while adjusting for differences in metropolitan population, I have devised a measure called a "skyline score." Using the formula $S = (B/P) \times H$, where S is the skyline score, B is the number of buildings over 300 feet tall, P is the standard metropolitan statistical area (SMSA) population in millions, and H is the combined height of the three tallest buildings in thousands of feet, we can come up with a skyline score for each metropolitan area that can serve as a rough guide to skyline importance. By using both B (number of buildings) and H (height of tallest buildings), we can recognize the importance of having either a large number of moderate towers or a few very tall ones. For example, the score for New York City would be 52.5; that is, 52.5

Table 2. Skyline scores for selected cities

City	Skyline score	CBD office space (millions of sq. ft.)
New York	52.5	350.0
Chicago	32.8	99.0
Houston	25.1	75.5
San Francisco	15.0	50.5
Atlanta	14.7	28.5
Boston	9.7	50.1
Detroit	4.9	28.5
St. Louis	1.8	12.5

$= (239/18) \times 3.95$, where 239 is the number of buildings over 300 feet tall, 18 is the New York metropolitan population in millions, and 3.95 is the combined height of the World Trade Center (two towers) and the Empire State Building in thousands of feet. Skyline scores are a handy way to predict certain metropolitan characteristics. Selected skyline scores using 1983 data (a year for which a detailed study of CBD office space exists)[23] are presented in Table 2.

Cities with impressive skyline scores tend to have several characteristics in common, in addition to being corporate headquarters with large office space requirements. For example, high-scoring cities with limited space, especially for the CBD, such as Boston, San Francisco, and Pittsburgh, tend to have taller buildings than those that are free to expand. Also, cities with high skyline scores tend to be regional capitals or central places dominating a large hinterland. Such cities try to convey the message that they represent "the city" for miles around, and so a skyline is important. Cities such as Atlanta, Denver, and Dallas epitomize this image, while low-skyline cities such as Milwaukee and San Jose labor in the shadow of more impressive nearby cities. This is especially true for newer regional capitals with no older, mid-rise stock of office buildings. These cities tend to have a few very tall buildings dominating many very small ones. There is little in between. Miami epitomizes this type of skyline.

Cities which have industries with lots of money to invest suddenly (such as energy-related industries during boom periods) and those which display technology (such as steel or glass industries) through skyscraper construction tend to have many tall buildings. Houston, Denver, and Pittsburgh illustrate this tendency. Obviously, banks and insurance companies invest huge sums by definition, and so cities with a strong financial component would have impressive skylines.

Since most skyscrapers are located in the CBD, cities with strong centralized downtowns tend to have more impressive skylines than those in which office activity has scattered to a variety of suburban locations. Cities like Chicago have impressive skyline scores since the CBD has never been replicated, while the Los Angeles CBD has had several successful and attempted replications.

Urban design policies also shape the skyline. Washington, D.C., has kept strict height limits throughout its history in order to perpetuate the visual dominance of the traditional monuments. Washington has therefore created vast amounts of office space in "European-style" mid-rise buildings. Until recently, Philadelphia required that its 548-foot City Hall remain the tallest structure in the city, and its skyline score is only now beginning to creep upward. New York, on the other hand, has always allowed, if not encouraged, skyscrapers, while San Francisco has recently adopted a much more restrictive stance which will mean that the Transamerica Pyramid will remain the tallest in the city for the foreseeable future.

There are also some less rational explanations for the geographic variation in skyline scores. In addition to the competition that has often occurred among entrepreneurs within a city, there is often inter-city competition. There can be no doubt that rival cities such as Dallas and Houston, Oklahoma City and Tulsa, Los Angeles and San Francisco, and many others were well aware of increasing skyline monumentality in the competing city. It was true for cathedral cities in medieval times, and it is true today. Such competition helps to explain why Cleveland, Columbus, and Cincinnati all had 500-foot towers by 1928 even though such towers were far from ubiquitous at that time.

Perhaps the major independent variable in the development of high-rise CBDs is city size. Metropolitan areas below a certain threshold size simply cannot afford the type of investment in public infrastructure required to support an impressive skyline. Neither do they usually have sufficient demand for office space of the type that requires face-to-face contact in prestige towers. No metropolitan area with fewer than 500,000 people has much of a skyline, and a million people seems to be a more important cut-off point. We are thus experiencing an era similar to the baroque. During the height of the baroque, larger, more important cities were drastically redesigned with a built environment of a totally different scale than that which prevailed during the Middle Ages. Palaces, opera houses, boulevards, and cathedrals added monumentality to the baroque city. Smaller, less important places remained medieval in scale and organization. Paris and Carcasonne became more and more different. Similarly, Boston and Erie are becoming very different types of places today.

Skyscrapers and Urban Design: Problems and Prospects

The monumental office skyscraper has had such a major impact on the American CBD that it is no wonder it has also become very controversial. Many authors have argued that skyscrapers are ruining the city—blocking the sun from both the street and the newly constructed plazas, creating wind tunnels, and fostering an impersonal, dehumanizing scale—while others argue that they have saved the city through economic revitalization. There are an almost endless number of emotional debates that could be outlined in a section entitled "The Skyscraper and Urban Design," but I wish to concentrate on three: (1) the skyscraper and the overconcentrated CBD, (2) the skyscraper and diminished downtown diversity, and (3) the skyscraper and the skyline wall.

Skyscraper Concentration: Environmental Problems and Core-Frame Contrasts

The office tower has served to concentrate and focus the American CBD at least as much as the more commonly recognized PLVI or point of maximum accessibility, although the two factors often work together. The development of a concentrated focus has generally been a very positive contribution to the American city, since, with no central plaza or cathedral to anchor it, the American CBD has often moved about and scattered with little reason to be one place or another. Cities such as Phoenix, which have built few major downtown office towers, often have no focus, no consensus node of activity. Cities which did build towers that came to be the functional and visual focus of the city have most often seen that nodality reinforced by subsequent construction. The AIU Citadel (later the Lincoln-Leveque Tower) in Columbus, Ohio, helped to anchor the CBD at Broad and High; and four new office towers, two of them with over 1 million square feet of space, have recently been built around it. There is no doubt about where the CBD core is located.

While famous towers have served to anchor the North American CBD both functionally and visually at least since the 1920s, there is some danger that they have also overconcentrated it. In many American cities, the CBD has decreased in area to only a few blocks with perhaps a dozen or so massive buildings huddled together. There is no place to walk, since a stroll of only a few blocks may lead you to a sea of parking lots and abandoned structures. Truly massive complexes, such as the Renaissance Center in Detroit, can sap the life from even major office towers, as everyone wants to be where the action is. Clustered skyscrapers make sense from the standpoint of business

Downtown Toronto: at the compact, vertical central business district the mass transit system links with underground pedestrian zones.

togetherness but not from the standpoint of urban design. Many famous buildings can no longer be seen because taller buildings have gone in all around them. At least the Empire State Building, which guessed wrong in the search for the midtown core, is still plainly visible—all alone on 34th Street. Offices on the fiftieth floor of many buildings have only a view of the fiftieth floor on the opposite side of the street. Perhaps this keeps busy workers from daydreaming or lingering over spectacular sunsets.

Clusters of massive skyscrapers have also been the cause of some rather interesting environmental problems, especially in northern cities where wind velocities can be quite high. In some cases, tall buildings have clustered so as to form wind tunnels which can, at times, make the street a dangerous place for people under a certain weight threshold. Very often, decorative fountains have to be shut down, since the spray can carry for several blocks. In a few cases, winds have caused considerable damage by blowing out windows. Microclimates that result from reflective glass and steam from heating and cooling systems are also being studied with increasing interest. The potential health hazards associated with indoor, air-conditioned workplaces provide an additional area of concern. In order to minimize some of these problems, a recent San Francisco skyscraper featured a "new" architectural innovation widely seen as something that can cut air conditioning costs and hazards—windows that open!

Skyscraper concentration has taken several forms, from a tightly packed cluster to a "strip" of tall buildings along a prestige-address street. Whatever the form, the vertical city can make for underutilized streets. This has become especially true in recent years as underground tunnels and second-level walkways connecting office towers to parking garages and to each other have further served to remove pedestrians from the street.

While skyscraper concentration has been very hard on the downtown frame in terms of decreased investment, it has more or less ensured the perpetuation of the downtown core. The vast amounts of money spent on CBD office space and related amenities means that these projects cannot be allowed to fail. The only politically possible panacea for downtown problems in cities with skyscrapers is more skyscrapers because such defensive development is thought to ensure the continued existence of the downtown as a very important place and so protect past investments. Fifty-story buildings cost too much to throw away. In the long run, "if you build them, they will come."

The Large Office Building and Downtown Diversity

The second major design problem inherent in the skyscraper CBD is the problem of diminished downtown diversity. Since large buildings require large lots, the close-grained diversity made possible by large numbers of small structures has largely disappeared. Early skyscrapers generally featured street-level facades that conformed to the traditional idea of what an urban street should be, in that the ground level often contained shops and cafes. Beginning in the late 1920s and especially by the 1950s, when "modern" glass boxes appeared, this variety began to diminish. Planners concerned about "urban congestion" and designers who wanted greater visibility for their buildings decided that plazas in front of towers were good ideas. Instead of meeting FAR requirements for less than full lot coverage through setbacks higher up, minimal lot coverage could be achieved by placing the box in the middle of an open plaza. Trees and fountains could then be added. In order to acquire a sufficiently large lot, many smaller structures had to be cleared, and towers ended up taking far more space than they actually occupied. While the city was opened up to some extent, just as it was during the baroque, much of the life of the CBD was lost.

Most of the postwar towers consisted of buildings with just one street-level door for the public, usually leading to a large hall with elevator doors and an information/security desk. The cafes were gone. In many cases, blocks which had contained dozens of small buildings during the early 1900s had room for only one or two large

The importance of street-level doors: mixing the old and the new in San Francisco

ones by the 1970s, and this meant one or two street-level doors. The amount and diversity of street-level activity was thus permently precluded by the size and architecture of the office towers. A study of the 16-block core of downtown San Diego using street directories to determine changes in the number and variety of street-level activities over time showed that while there were over 1,500 street-level doors in the CBD in 1927, there were fewer than 500 by 1980, and many of these led to parking structures.[24] Blank walls and repetitive plazas were replacing the small shops and cafes of earlier decades.

The diminishing architectural diversity of the CBD has also been very hard on those who preserve historic structures. John Costonis points out in *Space Adrift* that much of the destruction of older downtown buildings has been unnecessary.[25] Older buildings which are in excellent condition and provide handsome profits for owners are often destroyed so that a tower can be built at the other end of the block. Since huge lots must be assembled in order to build tall towers, the space must be acquired even if it is only to be cleared for an empty plaza. He points out that in the early 1970s, Chicago zoning permitted a 140-story tower if a full city block could be acquired. The preservation of smaller, historic structures is very difficult when such temptations exist.

Costonis recommends the utilization of development rights, or "air rights," over older buildings in order to preserve them. For example,

Will transferred development rights (TDRs) help protect historic landmarks in New York City?

if a developer wanted to put up a 60-story building in a district where the FAR, or floor area ratio, was 20, he would need a lot three times larger than the base of the building (presuming the building had no setbacks above the base). Instead of clearing the buildings nearby, he could buy the air rights above them and so use up their "zoning envelopes." The owners of the older buildings would obtain cash in exchange for their right to redevelop at a higher density in the future. The total volume of the block would not be increased beyond the zoning limit (the reason for zoning in the first place is to guard against overloading the infrastructure) but simply shifted to one lot. The older buildings could then be rehabilitated for ancillary uses serving the new tower, such as fancy restaurants and shops. This would help to maintain architectural and historical variety in the CBD.

Transferred development rights (TDRs) have been used to a limited degree in large cities like New York and San Francisco, usually for adjacent buildings. It has been suggested that such transfers could be used to a much greater degree through the creation of a "development rights bank" which could buy and sell the right to add space to the CBD. If the entire CBD was a special development rights transfer district, the owner of a small but historic building in part of the CBD could sell the rights to develop over that building to the bank (or donate it and take a tax write-off). Perhaps years later a would-be tower builder could buy the right to add extra space to a planned skyscraper while the maximum CBD volume as allowed by zoning would not increase. So far, this has not happened.

In order to encourage a greater sense of diversity and activity at street level while still facilitating the construction of office towers, many cities have resorted to "zoning bonuses." A zoning bonus is the right to build additional space which is given at the discretion of the city as a reward for desired urban design characteristics. For example, a 1980 report from the city of San Francisco suggests that an additional

Protecting the theater district through zoning bonuses in New York City

FAR of 2 be given for "excellence in architectural design and enrichment of the pedestrian environment."[26] It suggests that the same bonus be given as an incentive to provide features which "prove to be bona-fide public amenities, i.e., arcades, pedestrian ways, open space." It also allows for a FAR increase of up to 4 for the provision of "urban parks, community facilities, and public works of art." In other words, if a building developer constructs a public arcade with lots of shops and cafes, a garden, and an art gallery, he may be able to build the equivalent of four extra stories covering the entire lot (or a great many more in a thin tower). Zoning bonuses are also sometimes given to buildings that include direct access to subways. It should be noted that in recent years San Francisco has backed away from such guidelines and has argued that all buildings should have such amenities as a matter of course. Not all cities can be so demanding.

One problem with zoning bonuses is that whatever is desired often soon becomes excessively abundant. Bonuses were once given for open plazas in midtown Manhattan, and soon there were four or five unused plazas per block. An additional problem with interior arcades is that, while they may seem lively, they are actually owned and policed by the building owners. They are open only at certain hours and, in reality, only to certain kinds of people. Still, on expensive land in the heart of major central business districts, perhaps the only way to get small-scale street life is to include cafes and theaters in tall office towers.

Urban Aesthetics and the Skyline Wall

A third major urban design problem associated with attempts to control and manage skyscraper development is the downtown "wall syndrome." In any major city, at any given time, there is a tendency to build office buildings of roughly the same number of stories. The office market will normally absorb only so much new space each year, in increments of say 300,000 square feet in a city of 1 million or

Smaller, postmodern towers in the San Francisco skyline: a cap on office space and new design guidelines are having an impact.

800,000 square feet in a city twice as large. If someone builds a very large structure as a corporate monument, the costs of the lag time in rentals must be absorbed by that one building. If several moderately sized buildings come onto the market at once, the costs are spread around. Consequently, for example, San Diego has over a dozen new buildings all between 22 and 27 stories, while office towers in Denver tend to be 10 stories taller. The additional costs in elevators, heating systems, bracing, and the like make for certain major cost threshold points in any given market. Except for corporate symbols, most buildings are built below that point.

Building regulations also tend to homogenize the skyline. A certain CBD-wide FAR limit, for example, would tend to make most of the buildings end up being the same height. In some cases, absolute height limits set the maximum allowable height. In its attempt to control the increasing bulk of the city and to preserve the ambiance of rolling hills and bay views, San Francisco established height and bulk districts with an absolute maximum of 700 feet in a very small core surrounded by a much larger area with a 600-foot maximum. By the mid-1980s, San Francisco had 21 towers between 450 and 600 feet tall, most of them located along Market Street so as to connect directly with the Bay Area Rapid Transit system (BART). From both street level and a distance, the Market Street skyline looms as a 500-foot wall with no peaks or valleys and no turrets or towers. From Corona Peak it looks like a half-mile long glass box. So much for height control.

The Market Street wall is not only unpleasant from an aesthetic standpoint but is also dysfunctional in that it accentuates a long-standing San Francisco problem. Since the blocks are extra long on Market Street (compared to the small blocks in the CBD core to the north), access to anything south of Market Street is psychologically if not physically difficult. There are few routes to "south of Market." The wall of massive buildings does not help. Recently, the city has encouraged skyscraper construction in this area through the use of FARs that are quite generous in comparison to those in the already overdeveloped northern CBD.

In order to minimize the wall syndrome, urban designers in San Francisco are rethinking the glass box. The "postmodern" movement in architecture, with its emphasis on historical forms and playful embellishments, makes such rethinking more palatable for builders. The basic idea is to lower the center of gravity for new towers and bring back the slim, decorative tower. New buildings, for example, must have the bulk of usable space in the lower one-half of the building. The Transamerica Pyramid, once considered to be controversial, now serves as an aesthetic role model. Setbacks, pyramids, and decorative towers should make the skyline more pleasing and memorable as well as provide gaps for light and air.

If all goes well, the skyscraper can contribute both new, close-grained diversity to the city at street level and a culturally valued, highly imageable skyline.

The New CBD and the Structure of the City

Since World War II, the American economy has experienced what has become known as "restructuring," as the number of manufacturing jobs has decreased and the number of jobs in services such as finance, insurance, and real estate has increased. This has especially been the case in large cities. New York City has led the way: in 1980, the number of jobs in services and finance in New York City surpassed those in manufacturing, and the gap has widened since then.[27] As recently as 1977, there were 540,000 manufacturing jobs in the city, compared to 420,000 in services and finance. By 1984, there were nearly 580,000 jobs in services and finance, and only 430,000 in manufacturing—a massive reversal. In 1982, 30 percent of employed New Yorkers held a professional, technical, or managerial job, compared to 14 percent working in semiskilled or unskilled blue-collar jobs. New York City was in the midst of an office employment boom that slowed only during the recession of the late 1980s.

Unlike manufacturing jobs, office employment, as we have seen, tends to be extremely concentrated. Downtown and midtown Manhattan have absorbed most of the new jobs. Although new office construction has boomed, housing construction has not. While it is estimated that the city grew by 78,000 people between 1981 and 1984, there was an increase of only 11,000 in housing units and an actual decrease of 33,000 in rental units. Commuters from outside the city are playing an ever-increasing role in the New York City economy. There is a mismatch of jobs and housing. The continued success of the CBD may well depend on the provision of more close-in housing that is affordable to the new work force. Manhattan rents have climbed to ridiculous levels.

A study of the Boston office boom points up a related problem. In general, the new office towers need employees with skill and education levels not found in the inner city. While jobs in the CBD go begging, unemployment rates in nearby neighborhoods are often very high, as manufacturing and warehousing employment diminishes. The CBD must look elsewhere for employees.

San Francisco is also experiencing an office boom. Indeed, some in the city have worried about increasing "Manhattanization," by which they mean a city of office towers filled each day by hordes of suburban commuters. In order to mitigate this problem, the city has linked new office construction to new housing construction through the use of a citywide housing production formula. When proposals for new office projects are put forward, the city estimates the impact of the developments on housing demand. Those office projects that include adequate amounts of new or rehabilitated low- and moderate-income housing as part of the package receive highest priority and quickest approval. In addition, the city has rezoned parts of the CBD fringe residential and offers a 20 percent FAR bonus for residential uses within the CBD. In the future, the tallest buildings could be condos, as they are in much of the rest of the world.

Conclusions: The Sky's the Limit

It appears that both the skyscraper office tower and the CBD are here to stay despite many predictions to the contrary. Like the death of Mark Twain, the death of the American downtown has been greatly exaggerated. While much office employment has moved to the suburbs, it is increasingly moving to specific suburban development nodes, such as the Costa Mesa–Irvine area in Orange County, California, which are beginning to look very much like central business districts. This may be CBD replication (the midtown Manhattan syndrome) rather than an entirely new phenomenon. Already such places are developing impressive skylines. Large metropolitan areas may simply need more than one CBD.

The prediction that skyscrapers would become passé was also premature. During the 1950s, many thought that the Empire State Building would remain the tallest in the world forever, with new buildings hovering around modest heights of 20 or 30 stories. This has not proven to be the case, but there are signs that the race for sheer height has cooled, at least temporarily. The Sears Tower, the tallest in the world, was completed in 1974, and the World Trade Center in New York was topped off at about the same time. The Transamerica Pyramid, completed in 1972, remains the tallest skyscraper in San Francisco. Only New York, Chicago, Houston, Atlanta, and Los Angeles have buildings over 1,000 feet tall, although several other cities are pushing closer.

Still, the dream of building a supertower remains. Frank Lloyd Wright talked of a mile-high skyscraper for Chicago, and recently a team of architects "designed" (with no intention to build) a 500-story tower to be located on nine city blocks in downtown Houston. Nevertheless, concern about earthquakes, wind, soil, housing, urban design/aesthetics, and a variety of other issues have combined to limit interest in quantum leaps in building height.

Some have suggested that the future "tallest building in the world" will be located in East Asia rather than North America. Some of the tallest office towers outside of North America as well as the tallest hotel in the world are currently located in Singapore. Tokyo and Seoul have towers in the 700-foot category, while Hong Kong now leads the pack with a 1,200-foot skyscraper. With real estate prices in the Tokyo CBD the highest in the world, it would seem to be only a matter of time before the Japanese, in spite of concerns about typhoons and earthquakes, build the world's first 2,000-foot building.

2 The Downtown Frame

Buildings in Transition

The development of a skyscraper-filled CBD has been very hard on the fringes of the typical American downtown. This area, known as the downtown "frame," often appears to be ragged and underutilized as a result of the vertical concentration of high-level functions in a relatively small number of office towers. The frame is sometimes referred to as the "transition zone" for several reasons. First, the frame is a mixed-use zone which is transitional between the office core and the residential neighborhoods beyond. Second, the frame itself is in transition because many of the functions associated with it (such as light industry, warehousing, auto repair, and single-room-occupancy hotels [hereafter referred to as SROs]) appear to be no longer appropriate for expensive downtown land and are clearly on their way out. Finally, the buildings themselves within this zone are in transition, since most are not up to code and the owners are speculating on the land while deferring maintenance on the structures.

The North American transition zone is far more pronounced than similar areas in other developed countries or even those in Third World cities. There are a variety of social and economic explanations for this, but our concentration is on the spatial organization of the built environment.

The Moving Peak Land Value Intersection

Without a major plaza or cathedral square to anchor it, the peak land value intersection (PLVI), or office core, often migrated considerable distances in the North American city. The frame around the core can thus be divided into two distinctive areas—the zone of discard and the zone of assimilation. The zone of discard is the area from which the PLVI is moving, while the zone of assimilation is the area the PLVI is moving toward. Typically, the PLVI moved over time from the semi-industrial chaos of the waterfront, with its possible flood hazards and congestion, to an area on higher ground which was once a zone of better residences. Both areas became zones in transition, since the former, being discarded, had to accept a variety of new, often transitional uses in order to pay the bills, while the latter often experienced piecemeal redevelopment as houses were gradually replaced by bigger buildings. Both still appear to be somewhat disheveled and sometimes even sleazy and contribute substantially to the negative image of the North American downtown.

The particular character of these two zones is related to the character of the office core. In cities where major office complexes absorbed high-level activities and stabilized downtown at an early point in time, the zone of discard may nearly surround the core, since the CBD diminished in size and retreated inward and upward. Cleveland provides a fair example. Cities in which the office core is anchored by a major symbolic feature such as State House Square in Columbus, Ohio, may not experience much PLVI shifting. In such places, transition zones develop as the edges of the CBD fluctuate and threaten surrounding areas even in the absence of PLVI migration. In cities without major office towers or other anchors, the CBD sometimes "wandered" for decades, creating classically different zones of discard and assimilation. San Diego, at least until recently, epitomized this type of city, with the PLVI migrating seven blocks northward over a 60-year period. Most North American cities have at least some frame landscapes associated with both types of zones. Let us examine each type in more depth, beginning with the zone of discard.

The Zone of Discard: Code Enforcement and the Making of Skid Row

The zone of discard can be divided into two types of areas—uninhabited and inhabited. The uninhabited area is characterized by warehouses, storage yards, recycling centers, parking lots, and the like. This zone tends to be on the extreme fringes of downtown and once constituted the support district for the original CBD. The inhabited part of the zone of discard tends to be the area closer to the original CBD, the area where the early office buildings, hotels, restaurants, and theaters were located. Many of the old hotels have become residential hotels, and many of the theaters now show pornographic films. This is the area that is often referred to as "skid row."

The term *skid row* was coined in Seattle to describe the zone of cheap hotels and eateries that lined Yesler Way, the road logs were "skidded down" from the wooded hills above to the waterfront below. The term caught on as a vivid description of a waterfront zone of discard, and eventually of all zones of discard, where "rough and ready" men congregated in cheap hotels and seedy bars. All major world cities have, to some degree, the clientele for a skid row, and most have cheap lodgings and cafes of some kind, but few have entire downtown districts given over primarily to this kind of landscape. The North American–style skid row does not exist in Paris, Tokyo, or Buenos Aires.

In 1963, Donald Bogue published a study in which he mapped skid rows for 45 large American cities.[1] Although these areas varied greatly in size, shape, and intensity, every city had at least one. Some cities, such as Baltimore, had one large, concentrated skid row between the CBD core and the waterfront. Others, such as Cleveland, had several small skid row nodes all around the CBD core, with some skid row characteristics pervasive throughout the downtown. Cities like Portland, Oregon, were neatly bifurcated, with half the downtown being skid row and the other free of skid row characteristics, while in St. Louis, there was no skid row core, but the entire downtown was semi–skid row.

Skid row originated from leftover space. As the CBD moved and as newer, better, bigger buildings absorbed the demand for space, the zone of discard was created. There was little demand for the older (in some cases only a few decades older) buildings. Rapid architectural change meant rapid obsolescence. Buildings without elevators, modern plumbing, air conditioning, and prestige lost value as more space was created than could be filled, especially during an economic recession.

Very often, city codes and regulations contributed to the creation of skid row conditions in the zone of discard. During the nineteenth century, disastrous fires were a common reality and a constant threat in the thrown-together, largely wood and brick American city. While most large European cities had banned wooden construction centuries before, American cities remained highly flammable into the twentieth century. When zoning and building codes were developed in the early 1900s, a common goal was to encourage the rebuilding and redevelopment of the downtown area with "up-to-code" steel and stone structures. The preservation and rehabilitation of older buildings was discouraged. While such regulations had worked well in sixteenth-century Paris (since compact, walled cities had little choice but to rebuild on site), in American cities it was easier to simply move on. A key point here is that building codes aimed at encouraging the replacement of older buildings were introduced at the same time that the skyscraper (or at least proto-skyscraper) began to concentrate activity in a few large buildings. As a result, very few of the older buildings were actually replaced.

Not only did fire codes become increasingly restrictive (especially in high-density downtown areas—sometimes referred to as Fire District One and subject to especially strict regulations) but seismic codes, health codes, and safety codes added to the difficulties of the zone of discard, especially in the context of a declining demand for space in the older buildings due to skyscraper mania. Codes requiring fire escapes, structural bracing, fire-resistant materials, and other reasonably obvious safety features were joined by codes requiring stairs to be a certain width, banisters a certain height, and windows a certain dimension.

Codes tended to have several impacts on the American skid row. Since the PLVI was moving and new towers were going up elsewhere, rents declined in the older buildings and redevelopment was not feasible in a zone of rapidly declining prestige. Nevertheless, most of the buildings were in solid, if not good, condition and would have been used for a variety of mixed residential and commercial activities had they been in Europe. In American cities, zoning sometimes ruled out residential uses in commercial and industrial areas and so some flexibility was lost. Even when residential uses were permitted, converting a commercial building to housing required a change of use permit, which often required that the building be brought up to code—that is, be renovated to meet all current fire, seismic, and safety regulations. Such total rehabilitation was clearly uneconomic, but this did not bother city officials because they wanted the "old and dangerous" buildings replaced, not rehabilitated. And so nothing happened. Commercial buildings retained marginal commercial uses (everything from plumbing parts to porno movies) rather than developing new, possibly more profitable uses that would have required massive expenditures to meet building codes.

Many cities discouraged gradual maintenance by requiring total code enforcement if more than a certain amount of money (usually a certain percentage of the assessed value of the building) was spent on rehabilitation in a given year. Sometimes this figure was so low, especially during inflationary periods, that a building could not be re-roofed or replumbed without bringing it up to all codes. And so, in a hypothetical skid row building, the roof continued to leak, the upper floors were no longer used, and the occupants became more economically marginal. As older buildings emptied out, owners deferred all maintenance and simply waited in the hope that someday someone would want to build a skyscraper on the lot. Sometimes buildings were condemned and were replaced by parking lots. Often they mysteriously burned or fell down.

In addition to building and fire codes, other city policies also contributed to the marginal character of the zone of discard. Typically, the infrastructure of the area was allowed to deteriorate because city plans often called for eventual large-scale urban renewal and reorganization. Since, for example, plans often called for the elimination or relocation of streets, there was no point in repaving them. Potholes the size of Volkswagons appeared on skid row streets. Weeds the size of small trees grew up through cracks in the sidewalks, and streetlights were seldom repaired. Defaced and crooked stop signs hovered over mounds of blowing trash because cities could see no point in spending money on an area that was scheduled for clearance and politically powerless.

The combination of old buildings that did not meet codes and a decrepit infrastructure that was ignored in the expectation of eventual massive renewal made it impossible for skid row property owners to obtain any type of financing for any type of project. In Seattle, for example, it was not until the early 1970s, after nearly a decade of owner-financed rehabilitation efforts, that financial institutions would make loans in Pioneer Square, the original skid row.[2] Sometimes banks and savings institutions avoided making loans even on buildings which did meet codes and were not located in a potential renewal area simply because the mixture of land uses was considered to be inappropriate (mixed residential/industrial or hotels and junkyards). This was especially true along traditional waterfronts.

Financial institutions were not the only organizations to "redline" skid row. Insurance companies were reluctant to insure buildings which were considered by the city to be fire and safety hazards. Without insurance, "respectable" businesses, at least those with an inventory of reasonably valuable goods, would not locate in the area. Skid row became the place for shoestring and fly-by-night operations. Examples of catch-22 situations were everywhere.

Nonconforming Buildings and Nonconforming People: Hotel Living on Skid Row

Hotels constituted one of the major land uses in the zone of discard. Some of these were once the finest the city could offer but, like the older office buildings, could not compete with the newer, larger hotels. Others were built initially as residential hotels, probably an American invention. The large hotel first appeared in Boston in the 1820s.

For at least a century, hotel living was considered an acceptable and respectable housing alternative for (male) bachelors, retirees, and others who were not interested in the task of running a home. While the rich might take a suite at the Plaza, office workers might stay in less ostentatious hotels until they were ready and able to "settle down." In the 1870s, boosters reported that San Francisco was the greatest hotel city in the world. One visitor stated that "furnished lodgings, so difficult to obtain in the majority of towns, abounded in San Francisco."[3]

In some cases, residential hotels were built to house workers recruited for a particular project. In San Diego, for example, a large residential hotel was built to provide housing for workers building the streetcar lines. A major reason for the importance of residential hotels in the North American city was the relative absence, in most cities, of the apartment building. Outside of New York, Chicago, San Francisco, and a few other cities, the primary options for those who could not afford a house in the early 1900s were hotel living or boarding in someone else's house.

Architecturally, the earliest residential hotels were probably little different from office buildings. In fact, there were lot of conversions back and forth (before zoning and building codes). Rooms above a store could be let as housing, offices, storage, or even space for light industry as supply and demand changed. Lacking the magnificent lobbies and ballrooms of expensive hotels, the interiors of these hotels were plain and simple, with one-room cubicles. The better residential hotels often had rooms arranged around an atrium illuminated by a skylight (as did some early office buildings), while the cheapest ones featured dark rooms with only an air shaft or "light well" connecting them with the outside world.

There was much confusion concerning the differences between hotels, apartment buildings, and tenements during the latter years of the nineteenth century. One New York City court ruled that an apartment building could be differentiated from a tenement on the basis of centralized services—that is, such amenities as an in-house telephone switchboard, a restaurant, laundry facilities, and a doorman. A tenement was simply a building subdivided into residential cubicles. Tenements, as purpose-built buildings in contrast to subdivided houses, came along in the 1840s, just as hotels were gaining popularity. Apartment buildings were not introduced into the American city until the 1860s.

Thus, at least until the early decades of the twentieth century, there were two distinctive types of residential hotels: those combining a

suite of rooms with a full range of services (a cousin of the luxury apartment) and those containing one-room cubicles and a minimum of services (a cousin of the tenement).

According to Paul Groth, the main differentiating feature of the cheaper residential hotels was the number of rooms per toilet. Groth argues that in 1910 there were four distinctive "classes" of residential hotel, each catering to a different type of downtown resident and each with its own plumbing standard.[4] He called them "lodging houses," "rooming houses," "mid-priced hotels," and "palace hotels." In San Francisco in 1910, for example, cheap lodging houses were supposed to provide one toilet for every 12 rooms, but as late as 1930 a ratio of 1:18 was common. Rooming houses usually had a ratio of between 1:5 and 1:9. Mid-priced hotels were usually 1:2, while palace hotels had private facilities. Plumbing standards were more important to residents than location or room size, especially at the lower end of the scale.

During the 1920s, the skyscraper office tower and the suburban apartment building combined to diminish the status of downtown hotel living. Just as the office towers sucked the life out of the older commercial buildings in the vicinity of the old hotels, so too did apartment buildings cream off the most affluent (and respectable) of those who, for whatever reason, did not occupy single-family houses. In addition, the rise of housing reformers and of city planning during the Progressive Era led to planned eradication of hotel living as a condition unsuitable for American life. From the 1920s through the

Single-room-occupancy hotels: left, *San Francisco;* right, *San Diego*

1960s, city plans and policies aimed at eliminating the blight of single-room-occupancy hotels (SROs). By the 1960s, housing subsidies were available only for units with private kitchen and bath, thus providing another dimension of discrimination against the residential hotel. Hotel living was seen as the housing of last resort from which people had to be saved. Residential hotels and the support uses associated with them, such as restaurants, bars, barbershops, second-hand clothing stores, and pool parlors became synonymous with skid row in the eyes of the city and most Americans. After all, people were meant to live in homogeneous residential areas in proper houses or, if absolutely necessary, in homogeneous residential apartment buildings. If you lived in a downtown hotel, you were a bum or maybe even a communist.

Residential hotels were no longer built by the 1930s, and by the 1950s they had become "invisible housing." Since hotels were supposed to house transients, all residents, even those who had lived in one building for decades, were called "transients" and declared to be ineligible for housing or relocation subsidies. Urban renewal programs were carried out during the 1950s and 1960s as though no buildings and no people were there. In reality, even today, after decades of eradication, residential hotels in American skid rows are still important residential structures. Somewhere between 750,000 and 2 million people live in them. According to Groth, over half of San Francisco's 51,000 hotel rooms were permanently occupied in 1981. Over 20,000 people—three times the number in public housing in the city—lived in SROs, yet as a housing class they remained invisible.

The Economic and Social Function of the Classic Skid Row

The zone of discard, or skid row, came to play an important role in the functioning of the American city. Above all, it was the one place where low-cost, nonconforming housing could be obtained. As American cities were zoned into single-family neighborhoods and as

The zone of discard in Boston before the renovation of nearby Quincy Market

the practice of "letting rooms" declined during the prosperous 1950s, it became increasingly difficult to find cheap, furnished housing units. The apartment boom which began around 1960 concentrated on the provision of unfurnished lower-middle-and middle-income one- and two-bedroom units complete with kitchen and bath, usually at substantial rents. After 1962, most apartments were built in remote suburban locations as developers assumed that residents would own automobiles.

While there are some problem hotels (called "street hotels") on skid row where drug addicts, prostitutes, and the mentally unstable abound, the vast majority of SRO residents are stable, working, or retired blue-collar people. Many have chosen an SRO as the best of a limited number of options, such as living with relatives or sharing an apartment. For others, such as the physically and mentally disabled, there are no options other than institutionalization, so as hotels are closed and cleared, and as cutbacks in mental health facilities increase, they simply hit the streets. Ironically, many cities have closed SROs as health and safety hazards and then wonder why so many people are sleeping in cardboard boxes and doorways.

In addition to cheap housing, skid row has traditionally offered a full range of services to its residents. For many hotel residents, the "house" is scattered up and down the street, with the bedroom in one building, breakfast room in another, laundry facilities next door, and perhaps a "living room" in a friendly bar or cafe. Since nearly everyone eats out all of the time, a wide variety of cheap cafes exist. In San Diego, one study showed that skid row residents ate better meals than low-income people elsewhere because long-time waitresses and bartenders tended to look out for them and steer them toward a balanced meal, in contrast to workers at a fast-food or doughnut shop. Skid row is often a type of community; there are even places to get "just a little" work sweeping floors, taking out trash, delivering messages, and cleaning windows.

The zone of discard has traditionally been a major point of entry for immigrant groups. Under the name "Chinatown" or "Little Italy," run-down districts next to the CBD offer cheap lodgings and a place to learn the ropes for people "just off the boat." Hotels provide most of the housing in San Francisco's Chinatown, and the Tenderloin hotels are filling up with Southeast Asians. There is plenty of menial work and lots of opportunities to learn English. Proper suburban apartments might not be appropriate. Accessibility is important. Skid row provides a sort of ecological niche for certain types of people at certain times and for certain types of economic activities. It can be a place to get started—an incubator.

Skid Row Becomes "Old Town": Problems and Prospects

The zone of discard is changing dramatically, and skid rows are rapidly disappearing. During the 1950s and 1960s, government-sponsored urban renewal projects were responsible for the elimination of many skid rows, often for the construction of sports arenas and cultural centers. By the 1970s, most city governments had become aware of the importance of the zone of discard, either as cheap housing or as a historic tourist attraction, and clearance stopped. By this time, however, the real estate market had become overheated and the office boom was in full swing. In high-demand cities such as San Francisco, SRO owners began to convert their buildings to offices, apartments, condominiums, and tourist hotels. Demand for the space was there. They could now afford to bring them up to code. Older office buildings and even warehouses became sought after as "exposed-brick" quarters for architects and interior decorators.

During the 1970s, the skid row housing picture changed. Groth reports that between 1970 and 1978, Portland, Oregon, lost 2,400 downtown housing units, most of them SROs, while between 1976 and 1981, downtown Denver lost 28 of its 45 cheap hotels. During the same years, San Francisco lost 6,085 units, nearly 20 percent of its SRO stock. Moreover, the trend was not limited merely to large cities. In one year, Eureka, California lost 262 SRO units. And by the early

1980s the homeless problem was beginning to attract national attention.

The French Quarter: Role Model for Revitalization

The earliest and still the best example of a shifting CBD, emerging skid row, and skid row revitalization is provided by New Orleans. While it is far from a typical example, it did provide a kind of role model for many later developments. After the Civil War, New Orleans ceased to be one of the largest cities in the nation as it failed to prosper during the era of railroads and heavy industry of the late nineteenth and early twentieth centuries. Since the city grew slowly, redevelopment of the older sections was never really worthwhile, and so the CBD moved away from the old core along the Mississippi. It crossed Canal Street, the widest in the city, and then moved away from the river, leaving the Vieux Carre, or old quarter, behind. The Vieux Carre, or French Quarter, was a classic mixed zone of stores, houses, warehousing, and light manufacturing roughly conforming to the boundaries of the original city laid out around Jackson Square in 1721. In the early "jazz age" years of the twentieth century, it was mostly poor and largely black. It was leftover space.

Tourists began to discover the French Quarter while in search of the exotic during the 1920s. In 1933, the French Quarter became the second historic district in an American city, preceded only by the establishment, in 1931, of the central Charleston historic district in South Carolina. During the Depression and World War II, there was little pressure for development and change in the district, so it was not until the 1950s, when tourists once more arrived, that urban design guidelines became increasingly important.

Although the French Quarter was saved because it was thought to be unique historically, architecturally, and culturally, it has, in recent years, become the model "old town" for other cities to emulate. New Orleans demonstrated over a period of several decades that the CBD and a revitalized zone of discard could develop a synergistic relationship, with the whole being greater than the sum of the parts. Offices, for example, located in the CBD so that office workers and their clients could have dinner and listen to music in the French Quarter. Hotels and restaurants thrived in the French Quarter because of close access to the CBD work force. New Orleans developed a strong and lively downtown which was, by the 1960s, a major tourist and convention destination. Other cities wanted to have an "old town" too. The issue of historic preservation was on the rise.

For many cities it was too late. In Columbus, for example, the entire skid row, which focused upon a "Tudor" combination market

The French Quarter in New Orleans is a classic example of a zone of discard that has been renovated as a tourist district.

building and city hall from the early 1800s, was cleared in the early 1960s, just as interest in historic districts was emerging. St. Louis had long since leveled most of its historic waterfront in order to make room for the Gateway Arch, and Cincinnati had followed suit for a stadium. There were, however, still a lot of cities with potential.

Preservation Planning in the Zone of Discard: Old Sacramento and Pioneer Square

Two very different procedures for dealing with skid row revitalization emerged during the 1960s and early 1970s: quick and total revitalization, as epitomized by Old Sacramento, and slow and partial revitalization, as epitomized by Pioneer Square in Seattle.

Old Sacramento was an attempt to recreate the ambiance of the gold rush era of the 1850s through the complete revitalization of a classic skid row. By the 1950s, the West End, as it was known then, was perceived as a classic slum. With 167 bars in a 12-block area, the district accounted for 42 percent of the city's adult crime, 76 percent of the tuberculosis cases, and 26 percent of the fires. The buildings dated largely from the period between 1850 and 1880, with the modern CBD located further away from the once flood-prone river. Interest in redevelopment began in the 1940s, but a plan emphasizing historic preservation did not appear until 1963. The West End became a state park known as the Old Sacramento Historic District. During the late 1960s and early 1970s, nearly all of the district was leveled and reconstructed. While a few buildings were rehabilitated, it was often easier to build newer and safer replicas. In some cases, the new buildings were copies of what had been there originally, before a disastrous fire in 1852, rather than what had been there during the century that followed. "Newer" buildings from the 1900s were usually not restored or reconstructed, since they did not have the same historic appeal. In addition, museums and riverboats were built as further attractions.

All of this redevelopment in Sacramento meant that the people and the businesses in the West End were suddenly displaced. While there is some controversy over the level of relocation efforts on the part of the city, it soon became obvious that more could have been done. According to one newspaper account, "A hobo jungle of shanties sprang up to house people driven from their homes. . . . Others sought shelter under bridges, in basements of old houses and by burrowing under the sidewalks."[5]

By 1980, over $33 million had been spent on 58 buildings and 22 more were in the planning stages. The district is pleasant and attractive if somewhat sanitized. There are over 100 retail shops, 50 offices, and 18 restaurants and saloons, but housing and light manufacturing have been largely zoned out. Old Sacramento is a park—a sort of "Disneymento." Still, it provides a reason for both tourists and residents to go downtown.[6]

Pioneer Square in Seattle, the original skid row, illustrates a different, more gradual approach to revitalization. In the early 1960s, plans were afoot to demolish much of the area, and so the classic problems created by redlining and avoidance were abundantly evident. The number of businesses and residents plummeted during the 1960s as hotels were closed for safety violations and as offices moved to the new, towering CBD. Many people were sleeping on the streets, and the 25-block area accounted for over 15 percent of the city's crime. Loans for maintenance and mortgages were not available, and so interest in renovation was stymied, though it was still there.[7]

In the mid-1960s, perhaps inspired by what was going on in San Francisco, where Jackson Square and Ghirardhelli Square were being revitalized, a few architects began to express interest in Pioneer Square. The price of unrenovated office buildings in Pioneer Square had dropped so low that in 1966 private investors were able to obtain a major four-story building for $30,000. Architects interested not only in preservation but also in demonstrating their renovation skills with a showcase quarters led the way. As enthusiasm for urban renewal and

Old Sacramento State Historic Park, a historic skid row in the state capital of California

unlimited parking waned in the late 1960s and as interest in historic preservation increased, the status of Pioneer Square changed. The city of Seattle declared the area a historic district in 1971 and eliminated planned clearance schemes. By 1972, loans for major renovation jobs became available at least at one institution, Seattle Trust, and things began to happen.

In 1973, the district was enlarged, and additional controls over the kinds of land use changes that could take place were added. In 1974, a "minimum maintenance ordinance" was passed in order to stop demolition by neglect. The ordinance allowed the building department to issue a work order when a building deteriorated to the point that safety or preservation efforts were endangered. If the order was not overturned by an appeal and the owner refused to comply, the city could do the necessary repair work and recover the cost from the owner. This was the second such ordinance in the United States (the first affected the French Quarter) and is still in effect today.

One of the first things Seattle did was to channel long-awaited capital improvements into the district. A district manager was appointed to work with such city departments as water, lighting, and engineering in order to ensure that Pioneer Square's infrastructure was upgraded and maintained adequately. Streets were repaved, and weeds were pulled. When federal funding was received for three new city parks, two of them were put in Pioneer Square. Both were small, cobblestoned urban parks that added greatly to the amenities of the district. Another federal grant made it possible to create a tree-lined pedestrian mall complete with outdoor restaurants and cafes. A median strip of trees was built down the center of the main through street over the objections of city engineers, who were aghast at the idea of downgrading an arterial road to a nonarterial.

In 1972, the city established the Historic Seattle Preservation Development Authority, creating the first public revolving fund in the country. The $600,000 fund, modeled after the private revolving funds of Charleston and Savannah, is designed to acquire and hold on to endangered or stagnating buildings long enough to find restoration-minded buyers. Sometimes the mere expression of serious financial interest by the Authority was enough to spark restoration, since investors felt that if worse came to worse, the city would take a "failed" building off their hands.

To encourage private interests to renovate buildings, the city developed a policy of putting governmental agencies that had outgrown their quarters into office space in Pioneer Square. By occupying newly renovated buildings for a three-year period, the city could guarantee some immediate return on investment to developers and, at the same time, convince them of the city's commitment to the area.

Once it was convinced that Pioneer Square was worth rehabilitating, the city building department began to interpret codes flexibly and to work with, instead of against, owners interested in renovation. For example, owners were encouraged to work together and to renovate several buildings at once in order to share fire stairs, exits, and structural bracing. It was decided that old buildings did not have to be brought fully up to code standard; they only needed to be safe. A policy of gradual improvement was deemed more effective in making buildings safer than inflexible code requirements that led to total lack of investment and even abandonment.

In the early 1970s, a Skid Row Community Council was set up to develop an action plan for the area's low-income residents. Approximately 1,000 units of federally subsidized housing were created through the renovation of old hotels and apartment buildings and a skid row shelter complete with shared kitchen facilities was set up for transients. The Pioneer Square Health Station provided free or nearly free medical care for local indigents, and special park department contracts paid skid row residents for part-time maintenance work in the area's two parks. A sense of purpose and a higher degree of self-policing cut the district's share of the city's crime to 0.5 percent by 1976.

Changes in federal policy helped as well. In 1970, the Uniform Relocation Act recognized people living in hotels as bona fide residents, thus requiring systematic relocation for them. Wholesale, massive hotel clearance became much more difficult and controversial. It also became more expensive.

By the mid-1970s, Pioneer Square was an economic success. Tax assessments had increased by 450 percent in three years as buildings became fully occupied, while the overall tax base of the district (including sales tax) increased by 1,000 percent. More than 150 new businesses located in Pioneer Square, 75 percent of them from out of town, thus aiding the sluggish economy of Seattle in the early 1970s.

Employment in the district went from 1,000 in 1970 to over 6,000 in 1976. Over 1,000 jobs were created by the rehabilitation process itself, many of them low-skill jobs going to existing residents of the district. By the late 1970s, 80 buildings had been renovated, and rents were rising fast.

Not everyone is enthusiastic about preserving the social diversity of the area. Local indigents still occupy the park benches and search the bushes for discarded treasures. So far, however, the yuppies and the poor have coexisted. Bill Speidel, a Pioneer Square entrepreneur stated: "We're not Newport, Rhode Island; we're an old gold rush town and the original skid row. If we didn't have the bums around, we'd have to hire them from central casting."[8] Still, the area had changed. Between 1960 and 1981, Seattle lost 16,000 housing units, including about half of its downtown SROs. As the Seattle economy has improved and as its downtown office market has heated up, the pressure on Pioneer Square has increased. Compared to Old Sacramento, however, Seattle's skid row has retained some of its functional and social diversity.

Skid Row Revitalization: Conflicting Goals and Interests

In the core of the central business district, there is no doubt about what the consensus goal has been: profit. Developers, corporations, and property owners have all wanted to build the biggest, tallest, most monumental, and most profitable building possible. In the zone of discard, however, several competing ideologies have suddenly replaced total disinterest and avoidance, and nearly every policy and plan aimed at revitalization has become controversial. Most of the plans focusing on the skid rows that have not already been cleared involve somehow the ideology of historic preservation. Even within this ideology, however, there are several competing purposes and goals.

Peirce Lewis and others have identified several recurring themes or

Renovated buildings and street trees in Pioneer Square, Seattle, mid-1970s

arguments that emerge when preservation policies are advocated: (1) cultural memory, (2) successful proxemics, (3) environmental diversity, (4) antique texture, and (5) economic gain.[9]

The "cultural memory" argument asserts that any healthy society needs to have a sense of its own history. It needs to know where it is and how it got there. In order to have a sense of history, we need to have tangible reminders of the kinds of environments in which our ancestors worked and played and lived out their lives. This argument, epitomized by the reconstruction of Williamsburg, and to some degree by Old Sacramento, puts the emphasis on the recreation of historical settings. The zone of discard must be restored and/or rebuilt in order to teach the evolution of the city.

The argument of "successful proxemics" focuses on the importance of the zone of discard as a human-scale environment in distinct contrast to the monumental scale of the CBD core. Jane Jacobs, Herbert Gans, and others have pointed out the relationship between the fabric of the built environment and the fabric of society.[10] Skid row provides spaces (buildings, streets, alleys, etc.) that fit the human body, and while the area may be a bit shabby, we need to save some of these spaces in the name of human sanity. Just as the Renaissance squares were appreciated in the proximate contrast to narrow, claustrophobic medieval streets, so too are skyscrapers best appreciated in contrast to the traditionally scaled city. Skid row has a certain scarcity value in a city full of towers, freeways, and urban renewal projects.

This argument often includes some concern for the existing residents of skid row. Gans's study of the West End of Boston (before it was cleared) pointed out that the shabby nooks and crannies of the district provided a rather successful home for a wide variety of people with a wide variety of needs in distinct contrast to the homogeneously dreary slabs in most public housing projects.[11] People knew how to use the spaces.

A related argument for preservation in the zone of discard is provided by the theme of environmental diversity. Before zoning and automobiles, local environments were diverse because they had to be diverse. People were able to obtain most of the things they needed from nearby sources. The older parts of the American downtown still feature this diversity, with hotels, warehouses, commercial establishments, and theaters often on the same block. Not only is there functional diversity, but there is also architectural diversity, since buildings were inserted over a long period of time. Buildings from the 1870s may be next to those from the 1920s; a high Victorian may be next to a remodeled art deco. A walk down the street can be an interesting experience. The architectural diversity is, of course, inextricably intertwined with the diversity of inhabitants, for a wide range of residential and commercial rents allows for a wide variety of people and functions. This diversity does not and cannot exist in the CBD core, where the rents are all high and the controls are all strict.

Those who desire environmental diversity see the best environments as those where several pasts are displayed on any given block. A palimpsest exists in which pasts are layered one on top of the other. Such environments teach change rather than a particular point in time. Changing scale, architecture, and functional arrangements give us insight into changing economics and cultural values. Some have even argued against the cleaning of smoke stains, since such reminders of the past constitute part of the texture of the place. This is definitely an argument against a sanitized treatment of history.

The fourth argument for preservation, that of antique texture, is often couched in the language of architectural styles and urban design guidelines. Old buildings of a particular style are seen as "precious" because of their beauty, symmetry, detail, and age. Extreme advocates of this position are often antimodern. Old buildings are thought to be much more aesthetic than new buildings, and so it is argued that an entire district of old buildings should be carefully preserved and monitored. Uniformity rather than diversity is admired. A modern tower or a 1930s diner is aesthetically out of place in a "Victorian" district. This argument is often associated with the Renaissance aesthetic view, which culminated in the creation of such cities as Bath, where everything fits together in a pleasing whole.

The final argument in favor of preservation is that it pays. The argument of economic gain emphasizes the role that an old town can play in attracting tourists and businesses to the city and its downtown. A study in the 1950s showed that tourism focused within the French Quarter was second only to the port in bringing money into the economy of New Orleans. Historic preservation became a major component of any plan to save the downtown economy by the early 1970s. Preservation attracts tourists, affluent residents, classy businesses, and luxury hotels, and it will eventually result in higher real estate values and higher property taxes.

The problem is that many of these arguments work at cross-purposes. Those who feel that the district should be historically "authentic" and be useful for the teaching of history must pick one past and erase all others. In Old Sacramento, all traces of the early twentieth century have been carefully removed in favor of the recreation of the gold rush town. One former resident summed up this problem by exclaiming, "Pardon me, my past is missing." Obviously, considerable displacement of both people and businesses will occur in a district designed to remain forever in one architectural era. Allies for this "official past" view are sometimes found among the antique texture crowd, but conflicts sometimes emerge when advocates of historic texture and aesthetics, for example, like old buildings from two or more eras while those seeking to display a particular cultural memory want to emphasize the landscapes of only one era.

Those who are most concerned with environmental diversity and successful proxemics are sometimes directly opposed to the ideas put forth by those with historical and cultural interests even if they are all part of the preservationist camp. People who argue that skid row provides a human-scale environment may agree with those who like old buildings that small is good, but good for whom? The older districts should be good neighborhoods and good places for small businesses to start. Excessive restrictions on architectural change, sign control, and the like interfere with the kinds of dynamic changes that must occur in any real live neighborhood. People and activities come and go. A city is diverse.

Those who feel that historic districts are an economic bonanza argue that rents should go up and that only the "best" businesses should occupy such valued space. The result is often the same type of functional homogeneity that characterizes suburban shopping malls. The French Quarter has lost most of its local businesses and is now filling up with chain restaurants such as Benihana of Tokyo that have nothing to do with the traditional sense of place. Often there is simply too much money chasing too little history as investors all want to be in an officially designated district that tourists know about. The rest of the zone of discard is ignored. In other cases, preservation backfires. Property owners who once lobbied for designation of a district in order to attract investment may later become advocates of looser controls which would allow high-rise hotels or offices once the area becomes fashionable and property values skyrocket. New York City, for example, passed an ordinance making it difficult for developers to destroy theaters in order to try to save the theater district. Theater

CITIES AND BUILDINGS

owners have now sued the city for depriving them of real estate values.

The controversies over revitalization in the zone of discard have led to a variety of new planning solutions. For example, several cities from New York to Denver have modified traditional zoning ideas aimed at separating land uses. Loft living is now encouraged, as residential use, often by artists, and is allowed in converted warehouses and factories. In such cases, building codes are interpreted in a flexible manner so that factories still look like factories rather than new condos. In some cities, including San Diego, several new SROs have been built as cities have finally recognized that this type of housing fulfills an important need. Others have been renovated. Since SRO residents are now eligible for relocation, new government-financed housing complexes are being built downtown for those displaced by growth and change. Indeed, the classic skid row may be a thing of the past —a temporary aberration in the evolution of the North American city.

Waterfront Redevelopment: Opening Up the Zone of Discard

Redevelopment of waterfront segments of the downtown frame has become an increasingly important component of skid row revitalization.[12] Waterfront areas constitute the traditionally uninhabited part of the downtown frame composed of warehouses, factories, and wharves. Once considered to be grimy areas of concentrated disamenity, many have been transformed into gleaming symbols of the urban renaissance.

While many of the cities of Europe, from Lisbon and Venice in the south to London and Paris in the north, had magnificent public buildings and plazas along harbors and riverfronts by the mid-nineteenth century, the situation in North America was far different. The core business and elite residential districts in American cities tended to move inland as quickly as possible as waterfront zones were given over to industrial uses. Manhattan provides a case in point. Although located on an island, Manhattanites have had, until recently, very little contact with the water. The business spine of the city quickly moved northward along Broadway and Fifth Avenue, while elite residential zones focused upon inland open spaces from Gramercy Park to Central Park. The waterfront was to be avoided. For example, in the 1954 film *On the Waterfront* it was strongly linked with hard labor and corruption.

Although a few tentative steps were taken in the early years of the twentieth century to redesign waterfront areas, such as Lakefront Park in Chicago, as late as 1960 most were derelict. Beginning in the 1960s, however, sweeping changes occurred. In cities as diverse as

Boston, Baltimore, New York, Cincinnati, St. Louis, New Orleans, Seattle, San Francisco, and San Diego, to mention only a few, waterfront redevelopment began to play a major role in downtown (especially zone of discard) revitalization.

The primary impact of waterfront redevelopment on the zone of discard has been to change the relative location of the zone from one that was deeply embedded in the most congested part of the city to one that was closely linked, both visually and psychologically, to magnificent open spaces. Laclede's Landing in St. Louis, Quincy Market in Boston, and the Gaslamp District of San Diego are all now gateways to grassy parks and spacious waterfront promenades. In many cases, the battle to link the waterfront and the zone of discard has been hard-fought. The French Quarter in New Orleans, for example, was cut off from the Mississippi for decades by a strip of warehouses, and until recently, plans called for a freeway between the historic district and the water. Only with a change in those plans have the French Quarter and the Mississippi come together for the first time since the early years of the city.

While people in search of recreation once left the congested city for idyllic suburbs, the combination of hypergrowth in suburban areas and waterfront redevelopment in the city has meant that truly "placeful," monumental open spaces are most associated with the latter. In its first year of operation, 1976, more people visited Boston's Quincy Market than went to Disneyland.

With the creation of waterfront amenity areas in many cities, the edge of the former zone of discard has become a fashionable place to live. While much revitalization has focused upon the preservation of a waterfront ambiance, the increasing construction of high-rise apartment buildings and condominiums may soon decrease the traditional waterfront sense of place.

The Zone of Assimilation: A Place for "Dazzling Urbanites"

The zone of assimilation is the area on the expanding side of the CBD, usually the opposite side from the zone of discard. Like the zone of discard, this zone has looked a bit shabby over the past several decades as some houses have been converted to office space while others have been torn down for parking lots. As new office buildings have crept into the area, land speculation and an expectation of change has led to deferred maintenance on existing buildings. Part of the problem is that most American central cities were initially underbuilt. While European cities experienced centuries of gradual rebuilding and now have inner cities filled with multistory structures covering the entire lot, American cities, especially those west of the

Quincy Market, Boston

Appalachians, were laid out as "garden cities" with cottages set in yards. Consequently, the area of higher ground, on the opposite side of the downtown from the waterfront and zone of discard, usually remained low-density residential well into the twentieth century. In many cases, the mansions of the elites lined a broad boulevard leading outward from the heart of the city. Although usually part of the city politically, these areas were "suburban" in landscape, with houses, churches, schools and a few stores. Industry and warehousing were largely absent. Streetcars connected the district with the PLVI.

Since residential growth was concentrated on this side of downtown and since purchasing power was greatest in the area of better residences, the first commercial nodes outside of downtown sprang up here. These were intervening opportunities for shoppers heading downtown on the streetcar lines and were often located where two or more lines came together—a sort of mini-PLVI.

By the early 1900s, the pressure for redevelopment on the "good side" of downtown increased. Unlike buildings in cities such as Paris, the houses in American cities were simply too small and too architecturally inappropriate to be converted permanently to new uses. By the 1920s and 1930s, affluent residents were using their automobiles to move farther out to newly developing suburbs, leaving once fashionable districts to be subdivided and converted. The automobile in league with the streetcar was turning the old boulevards into "strips,"

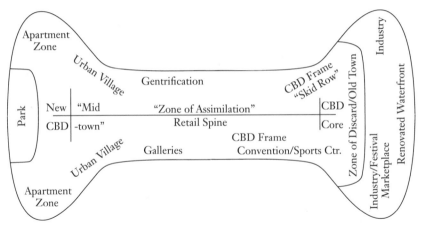

A Model of the American Downtown

As North American downtowns have grown and changed over the years, many have assumed a predictable shape and size. The best model to describe them is a dumbbell with the old waterfront/skid row/central business district at one end and a new uptown/museum/nightlife district (and sometimes a park) at the other. The two ends of the dumbbell are typically connected by a relatively thin spine focusing on a major retailing street. Although there are many variations on the theme, the model describes the nearly universal process of CBD extension and reconcentration.

as motels, gas stations, coffee shops, and doctors' offices appeared along them. In most cases, these changes corresponded with the expansion (extension) stage in the evolution of the CBD. Land uses which had formerly concentrated in the heart of the city were both pushed out by increasing, skyscraper-pegged land values and pulled out by the attraction of automobile accessibility.

The character of change in the zone of assimilation varied from city to city. In some cases, as along Euclid Avenue in Cleveland, old mansions were converted to multiunit housing and automobile dealerships, and the area quickly became a sort of slum with at least some of the characteristics of a zone of discard. Skid row thus emerged on all sides of the CBD. In other cities, such as Los Angeles, streets like Wilshire Boulevard were known as "miracle miles," as classy office buildings, department stores, and theaters sprang up along them. The unanchored Los Angeles CBD simply chased affluent residents to the west, and today, some would argue that "downtown" Los Angeles is really a 20-mile corridor from the old plaza at Olvera Street to the 40-story towers at Century City.

In other cities, the downtown was completely or very nearly replicated somewhere in an extended zone of assimilation. This was especially true in cities with a major park, lake, or other amenity located within the zone. In St. Louis, for example, a new downtown first emerged in the Central West End neighborhood on the east side of Forest Park. By the 1960s, geographers were writing about a new St. Louis downtown in Clayton, to the west of the park.[13]

Perhaps the best example of a dominant zone of assimilation is provided by Phoenix, where the zone of assimilation is the downtown. The old CBD of the city has languished as office and hotel towers and a major regional shopping center have been built along Central Avenue, a mile or two north of the historic center of town. Along this corridor, crumbling bungalows sit in the shadow of 20-story towers awaiting their conversion to higher and better uses.

The Zone of Assimilation and the Revival of Urban Culture

Like the zone of discard, the zone of assimilation has been "discovered" by those wishing to partake of urban culture and by entrepreneurs seeking a near-downtown ambiance for upscale shops and restaurants during the past decade or so. While there are no role models quite as important as the French Quarter was for the zone of discard, there are a number of very good examples. The Yorkville section of Toronto, centered on the University of Toronto and only a mile or so from the CBD, typifies the emergence of "urbanity" in that city. Famous urban advocate Jane Jacobs left Greenwich Village to live there. The Back Bay section of Boston, with its towering Prudential and John Hancock buildings juxtaposed against expensive art galleries located in renovated townhouses, provides a similar ambiance. The North Side of downtown Chicago along Rush Street has become "the place to be," similar to Nob Hill in San Francisco. North American downtowns without such zones generally have a much tougher time attracting both residents and nightlife back to the city.

Over the past two decades, the zone of assimilation has seen several waves of new construction. By the time zoning arrived in the 1920s and 1930s, the zone of assimilation was no longer homogeneously residential, and so a patchwork of "after-the-fact" land use districts evolved. Much of the area remained single-family, while multiunit structures and commercial establishments were permitted on the main streets. By the 1950s and early 1960s, some houses had been converted and others had been removed for parking lots. The zone was generally underutilized. In the past two decades, at least in cities with strong downtowns, this situation has changed.

Mid-rise office buildings—especially medical complexes and insurance companies, condominiums and apartment buildings, large houses both converted and unconverted, hotels, and "art" theaters—typically share space in the zone of assimilation of the 1980s and '90s.

Yorkville, in Toronto: shops and restaurants in the zone of assimilation

Since the near-downtown streets are smaller scale than those in more
recently developed suburban districts, the ambiance is right for sidewalk cafes, boutiques, and a sense of street life.

Part of the attraction, from both an aesthetic and functional standpoint, is architectural diversity. In most cases, the zone of assimilation
is the most diverse area in the city. Not only is there a wide variety of
architectural styles and building types, but also, because of both new
buildings and old buildings in various stages of renovation and conversion, there is a good mix of rents and types of spaces. Students and
executives, used bookstores and boutiques, cafes and coffee shops,
garages and optometrists, all share space along the early streetcar
strip. Because the architecture is so diverse and because much of it is
so recent, there are relatively few preservation issues. Most concerns
focus on individual houses or groups of houses rather than on the
district itself. In St. Paul, a number of old mansions have been preserved by carefully and tastefully converting them to condominiums.

The question is, Can diversity continue in the face of new development? In cities where housing demand and housing prices are high,
apartment building construction has boomed on the fringes of downtown. In San Diego, for example, the city has placed a moratorium on
new construction in several neighborhoods close to downtown as a
result of neighborhood concerns over parking, traffic, and change in

Nob Hill, San Francisco: luxury hotels, clubs, and apartments in the zone of assimilation

general. The city is trying to shift housing demand to revitalization efforts in the zone of discard.

Linking the Parts: Toward a City of Architectural Realms

One of the major problems with the American downtown is its isolation from surrounding neighborhoods, both physically and psychologically. The physical separation results largely from massive clearance schemes for freeways and related automobile uses such as on-ramps and parking lots. It is rarely possible now to walk downtown from nearby neighborhoods without crossing what Grady Clay refers to as a DMZ, or "dangerous movement zone."[14] The CBD core is not only physically separate from the rest of the city, but visitors must cross a sometimes ominous and chaotic zone of discard or assimilation in order to get to the gleaming towers beyond. Everything from sprawling parking lots full of blowing trash to massive medical complexes to decaying buildings with sleeping winos in the doorways stick in the minds of many who visit downtown. As people spend more and more of their time in suburbia, downtown landscapes become increasingly foreign and psychologically remote. The trick to making the downtown seem more attractive is to link the parts and to make each part of downtown accessible to the other parts.

A good downtown has certain Disneyland characteristics. There are distinctive architectural and functional zones, each with identifiable and memorable images à la "Adventureland," "Main Street," and "Tomorrowland." Exploration is more fun when there are different "places" to visit. The sense of place of each district can be enhanced by its having a different sense of time as well; we can thus move from the present to the past or the future. Kevin Lynch argues: "The best environment is one in which there are both new stimuli and familiar reassurances, the chance to explore and the ability to return."[15] Preservation districts, for example, can act as aesthetic foils to new development. A definite collar of familiar settings around land cleared for new structures can serve as a reassuring boundary, making change both more exciting and less threatening. In addition, the continued use of old buildings during construction can keep areas alive and the existing sense of place intact over often unexpectedly long development periods. Boundaries which are both tight and clear help to delimit different worlds of scale, texture, and detail in the city.

The renewal experiences of Boston and St. Louis during the past few decades offer contrasting examples. St. Louis destroyed too much, and by the 1960s its downtown was separated from the rest of the city by vast, empty fields awaiting future development. About two-thirds of what was downtown St. Louis had been leveled. Clearance of the historic waterfront began during the 1930s for the Gateway Arch, a project that was not completed until the mid-1970s. Other projects leveled huge spaces for Busch Memorial Stadium and a convention center. Freeway projects and slum clearance added to the "openness" of the central city. When a public housing project (Pruitt-Igoe) built in the 1950s was blown up in 1972 because it was uninhabitable, the fields became larger. The increasingly remote CBD languished.

Downtown St. Louis had to be completely rebuilt on all four sides. The potential for architectural variety and functional diversity in renovated zones of discard and assimilation has been largely lost. Although some very nice preservation projects have been carried out, such as the rehabilitation of the train station, there are still few connections with the city beyond.

Boston, equally dreary before redevelopment began in the 1960s, took a different approach. While some valuable neighborhoods such as the West End were cleared, others such as the North End were gradually renovated. Similarly, parts of the waterfront were cleared for a small park while several old warehouses were converted to housing. "Sacred" districts such as Beacon Hill and the Boston Common were protected, while Scollay Square was leveled for a new government center. Central Boston thus contains a series of distinctly differ-

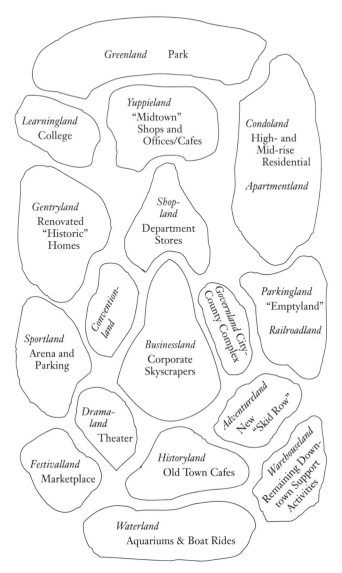

The Central City as Disneyland

Over the past century, the typical North American downtown has been extremely dynamic, with some land uses expanding rapidly at the expense of others. Architectural changes have been equally noticeable, with continuous adjustments in building size, style, and function. Recently, a certain stability has begun to set in as particular areas have been given over more or less permanently for use as office towers, recreational waterfronts, convention and sports arenas, historic districts, residential districts, and the like. A combination of the large scale of new development and urban design ideologies has brought about a new kind of central city: a city of separate worlds.

ent architectural worlds. Its districts are "imageable" in that there is no mistaking the North End and Beacon Hill or South Cove and Financial District. Tight boundaries around each of the districts have helped to control speculation and the expectation of change, since older neighborhoods are protected from the invasion of bigger structures.

While much of the close-grained vitality of Boston is due to its restricted site and historical compactness, in Seattle the various downtown zones have been linked through careful planning. Pioneer Square, on the southern edge of the CBD, was made even more accessible with a "Magic Carpet Ride," or free bus service throughout the downtown. In this way, CBD workers were encouraged to go to Pioneer Square for lunch or bookstore browsing during the day. A major addition to the revitalization of Pioneer Square occurred in the mid-1970s when the Kingdome—a huge, domed stadium used for professional football, baseball, and basketball—was built in a former railroad and industrial area just south of the historic district. Fans could easily have lunch in Pioneer Square, see a game, and then return to Pioneer Square for dinner and music. A symbiotic relationship was developed between sports and skid row which, by encouraging people to come early and stay after the game, helped to alleviate traffic snarls.

To the north and east of the CBD, in the zone of assimilation, other projects helped to connect downtown districts. The former World's Fair complex, built in 1962, was revived as a permanent park and exposition focused upon the 600-foot Space Needle with its observation deck and restaurant. The park is connected to the CBD by a monorail. Nearby, old houses and commercial buildings have been restored and serve a variety of visitor-related purposes.

Capitol Hill, a high-density residential and commercial zone east of the CBD, provides an excellent example of an uphill zone of assimilation with views of the waterfront below. During the 1960s, Interstate 5 (a freeway) was built between the CBD and Capitol Hill, creating a physical and psychological barrier. To link the two zones, Seattle created the nation's first "freeway park," a landscaped shelf covering a section of the highway. The park was paid for partially by assessing new office and residential towers that went up around the new, centrally located amenity. It is now possible to stroll from the condos of Capitol Hill to the office towers of the CBD along pleasant, green walkways without experiencing a bleak and noisy DMZ.

To the west of the Seattle CBD, the waterfront has been revitalized through the restoration of old piers for shops and restaurants and the construction of a major aquarium and several fountains and miniparks. In addition, Pike Place Market (a huge, rambling, turn-of-the-century food market) and the old hotels and warehouses that have historically supported it have been restored. The market continues to be an excellent place to purchase food, as there are limits on the amount of space which can be used for trendy, nonfood items. Several of the old hotels have been restored to serve as low-income housing.

The Seattle CBD is well-connected to the downtown frame in all four directions. Rather than being a cluster of towers set apart from the rest of the city by parking lots, freeways, and cleared fields, downtown Seattle contains a series of very different but complementary architectural and functional worlds. It is fun to explore the downtown.

Other cities have different architectural traditions and different spatial arrangements, but the idea of creating symbiotic relationships by linking and connecting different "worlds" is gaining acceptance. By encouraging a pedestrian flow and exploration throughout the downtown, a city can make both gradual renovation and new construction profitable over a large area and thus lessen the trend toward a concentrated, vertical, enclosed core.

The city of San Diego is working toward this goal. Until redevelopment efforts began in the mid-1970s, downtown San Diego had three classically distinctive districts—a CBD, a zone of discard, and a zone of assimilation. The PLVI had wandered northward over a period of seven decades, leaving the older nodes several blocks behind. The CBD tended to migrate uphill toward the attraction of Balboa Park and the residential neighborhood around it and away from the industrial waterfront. Fifth Avenue became a temporal collage, with buildings from the 1880s on one block and the 1890s on the next, on up to the 1970s. No major tower had ever anchored the financial core. The zone of discard included warehouses, small factories, and a classic residential and commercial skid row.

The section of the zone of discard between the CBD and the waterfront, including the heart of skid row, has been partly renovated as the historic Gaslamp District and partly redeveloped for luxury and middle-income housing and for a major shopping center and hotel complex. In order to encourage movement into and through the once infamous zone, a quaint shopping area (Seaport Village), a park, and a marina were built at the old industrial waterfront. A convention center and several new hotels have opened there as well. Visitors and professionals from the CBD can hop a cute trolley along Fifth Avenue and ride to the convention center at its lower end. The convention center is the San Diego version of the Kingdome.

In the process, perhaps thousands of low-income people have been displaced, as about half of the city's SROs have been destroyed. Skid row has moved into the eastern part of the zone of discard, and, belatedly, new service centers and new SROs are being built. We have yet to learn how to build really mixed yet vital urban areas.

Conclusions: The Importance of "Place" in the Downtown Frame

Throughout the 1960s and 1970s, most cities concentrated on facilitating an office building boom in and around the CBD core. While the business district grew vertically, it often became smaller in area, and much of the downtown frame suffered as building maintenance was deferred and demolitions for parking lots increased. Recently, many cities have come not only to appreciate the architectural character of the older office buildings and hotels but also to better understand the vital social role played by SROs and associated land uses in serving low-income communities. A combination of renovation for upscale uses in the zone of assimilation and renovation for continued low-income uses in the zone of discard characterizes the most enlightened planning for the downtown frame today.

In addition, planners and developers are beginning to pay more attention to the spatial arrangement of various projects. The best downtowns are those that not only have a variety of interesting and different districts but have linked them together successfully. By accentuating existing architectural regions within the downtown and supplementing them with new ones, the entire downtown—both core and frame—can become an integrated economic unit.

With a few exceptions, most American downtowns are simply too big—that is, too extensive in area—for the functions that concentrate there. While office and hotel space have concentrated in high-rise buildings in a small core area, depopulation and deindustrialization have left much of the frame underutilized. Vast areas of parking lots and vacant structures have diluted the sense of city. The selective preservation of old uses and the creation of new uses in the downtown frame serve to fill up the downtown and give it greater permanence as well as variety. In the best cities, the frame is no longer in transition: it has arrived.

3 Places to Shop

Arcades, Bazaars, and Festival Centers

The city has always been a place to shop. Indeed, at least until quite recently, a market town was what most people imagined a city to be. The search for successful architectural solutions and spatial arrangements for retailing has been going on for at least 500 years in the Western city, and the demand for new and novel shopping environments still plays an important role in urban design planning and policies.

Shopping for day-to-day needs such as food and soap can be drudgery, but major shopping excursions for special and especially nonessential goods have always been major events associated with fun and festivity. Medieval and Renaissance fairs attracted jugglers, clowns, musicians, and jousters. These fairs were places for aggressive hawkers and traveling merchants to display and sell their wares amidst a jolly crowd of fun-seekers. The town market was more controlled and regulated, but there was still a sense of excitement and life. The market square was where everything happened. It was also where the architectural and symbolic splendor of the city was displayed, since the cathedral and town hall were usually at or near the market square. In this chapter I deal with the evolution of a variety of shopping environments. The focus is on the center of cities (thus rounding out the discussion of "downtown" in the two previous chapters) and thus slights such things as the development of suburban malls.

The Market Square and the Emergence of the Shop

While there was no doubt during the Middle Ages and the Renaissance that the market should be central, there was growing controversy about the proper architectural arrangement for shopping. The noun *shop* was applied initially to any place where goods were sold even if they were simply laid out upon the ground. Gradually, only a booth or stand was a proper shop. While shops became associated with buildings, and while a definite and predictable market square evolved, pedestrian access remained essential in order for them to function. Buyer and seller haggled over prices as they faced each other through a small opening. Shops were basically stalls with wooden double doors so that the upper part could be raised and goods hung from it while the lower part was raised as a counter. The seller stood in the stall while the buyer stood in the street. At night, the wooden doors were closed, and the street facade was blank and forbidding.[1] Shopping was a daytime activity.

In the multipurpose medieval building, the shopkeeper lived above the shop, and goods were stored in the cellar. In some cases, artisans made the goods there as well. The idea of having a shopping district set apart from the residences of the owners was incomprehensible. Solid, fortress houses where goods could be made, stored, and sold under the careful watch of the residents were the norm.

The above arrangement was not entirely pleasant. Streets were usually muddy, noisy, and crowded with people and animals. Shopping was not something to do in your best clothes. In the Islamic city, shopping districts were more carefully designed. In cities like Isfahan, Jerusalem, Cairo, and Fez, covered souks, or bazaars, evolved to provide protected and relatively organized space for shopping. Narrow streets lined with small shops were covered with vaulted ceilings to protect those below from wind, sun, and rain. These shops often had back rooms for storage and upstairs rooms where major purchases could be discussed in relative serenity over tea. Then as now, making a deal often took a long time. Streets specialized to a very high degree, and in some, because of the presence of mosques or madrasses (Islamic universities), animals were prohibited.

The Islamic souk was the first designed area for shopping, or at least the first since the Greco-Roman market square. Some of the bazaars (essentially vaulted or otherwise covered systems of narrow shopping streets) were monumental in scale and design. European travel accounts from the time of the Crusades until well into the nineteenth century were full of references to the huge, exotic bazaars in cities such as Constantinople and Cairo. There was nothing comparable in Europe.

In European cities the idea of having a special place for shops evolved with the development of the town hall/market/exchange discussed earlier. A key element in these structures was an arcaded lower level facing either a courtyard or the street. The idea of a covered arcade was a classical one that was revived during the Italian Renaissance although the inspiration for doing so probably came from Constantinople.

Constantinople had not only impressive bazaars but also colonnaded facades called *emboloi* in fancy residential districts. During the fifteenth and sixteenth centuries, arcaded streets appeared in such Italian cities as Bologna and Padua. At roughly the same time (1419), Brunelleschi used a grand colonnade to enhance the sense of beauty and spaciousness in the Foundling Hospital in Florence. Impressive arcades soon sprang up around the Piazza San Marco in Venice and in the Palladian buildings of Vicenza. The arcaded street gradually diffused northward to Switzerland and Austria. Bern provides the best example of an arcaded city, although cities from Innsbruck to Annecy accepted the innovation. While the origin of "The Rows" in Chester, England, is independent of this diffusion, probably having been the result of medieval attempts to build over Roman ruins, the rebuilding of these upper-level covered walkways in 1591 represents a breakthrough in urban design in northern Europe. Strolling in the center of the city was becoming more pleasant.

While arcaded streets made the Renaissance city more comfortable, they were not special shopping districts per se. A wide variety of urban activities continued to cohabit even the best arcaded streets at least until the seventeenth century, when the English residential square and the Spanish *plaza mayor* became more specialized.

The Shopping Arcade as a Building Type

The true shopping arcade did not develop until the eighteenth century. During the late 1700s and early 1800s, a variety of social, economic, and architectural changes made a new kind of shopping district possible. The eighteenth century was a time of relative peace and prosperity. European colonization and trade were bringing exotic goods and ideas to cities like London and Paris, and a wealthy class of bourgeoisie merchants, traders, and builders was emerging to enjoy a new urbane lifestyle. Cafes, salons, and specialty shops evolved to cater to the new affluent classes. Where to locate these shops was the question.

Equally important was the new preoccupation with promenading. As leisure time increased for the affluent classes, pleasure gardens, assembly rooms, and riverside boulevards evolved to provide a place to stroll and to see and be seen. Pleasure gardens—parks filled with places for eating, dancing, strolling, and purchasing treats—such as Ranelagh Gardens in London and Tivoli Gardens in Copenhagen were, in fine weather at least, the places to be.

The French were the first to sense the commercial possibilities of putting luxury shopping and eating establishments together in a special environment made for promenading and socializing in all kinds of weather—the shopping arcade. The prototype for what is generally assumed to be the first shopping arcade was constructed in 1781–86 in the Jardins du Palais Royal in Paris. The shops, cafes, and restaurants were designed to provide extra money for the royal family. The French Revolution changed this financial arrangement but not the basic idea, for the newly emerging middle class delighted in having a place to meet, sip coffee, and talk politics. The arcade caught on, and between 28 and 40 (records are sketchy) were built in Paris around the turn of the nineteenth century.

The popularity of the Parisian shopping arcade was directly related to the character of the typical Parisian street. Not only were the streets narrow and filthy but there were no sidewalks. As horse-drawn carriages increased in number and velocity, streets became dangerously congested. In addition, runoff, of a variety of kinds, was accommodated by one drainage ditch in the center of the street, which, in times of heavy rain, was usually inadequate. The streets became rivers. It was not until the street-widening and sewer-building projects of Haussmann during the mid-1800s that Paris gained sidewalks and an adequate drainage system. In the meantime, the elites needed someplace to shop. The shopping arcade allowed them to escape the chaos of the street and to stroll happily among their peers.

Paris soon became famous for its shopping environment. The garden of the Palais Royal was famous as the shopping center of Europe and, for a while, was one of the most memorable and enjoyable places ever to have been created in a European city. Thiery's 1787 guide to Paris described it as "a kind of perpetual fair." According to Girouard, "It was as though the Piazza San Marco in Venice had been amalgamated with Vauxhall, Ranelagh (pleasure gardens) and the best shops of London. Shopping at its most luxurious and entertainment at its most enjoyable were concentrated into one highly decorative ensemble right in the center of Paris."[2] Puppet shows, Turkish baths, theaters, cafes, and waxworks shared space with the shops and added variety to the scene.

London was experiencing the same demand for luxury shopping areas but was less in need of special arcades. Because the city had been rebuilt after the fire and luxury shopping had moved to the new West End, the streets of London were wider and had sidewalks. While streets such as Bond became famous for luxury shopping without arcades, by the early 1800s London too had shopping arcades. The

Burlington Arcade, perhaps the most famous, remains synonymous with luxury shopping even today.

The Perfection of the Arcade: Building Technology and Urban Morphology

Innovations in architecture and building technology along with changing attitudes toward urban real estate were also important in the development of the specialized shopping arcade. Since northern Europeans were rarely faced with the prospect of escaping a blistering sun, the dark passages of the Islamic souks were not desirable. The development of light and airy covered arcades depended upon the utilization of iron and glass. Of these, glass was the most important.

When shops were enclosed with wooden shutters, there was no way to see inside the shop when it was not open. Glass windows allowed an entirely new recreational experience—window shopping. Until the late 1600s, glass was very expensive and could be made in only very small, thick panes which were not particularly good for displaying the wares of a shop. In 1688, the invention of cast glass by Frenchman Lucas de Heheon made it possible to manufacture larger, more transparent glass plates. But glass was still very expensive, especially in England, where a "window tax" was imposed in 1691 and not repealed until 1851. Cast plate glass was developed in 1773, but it was not until 1832, when broad or sheet glass was invented, that really large, thin glass windows and coverings were possible. It then became possible to window shop through large panes of glass even at night, since gas-lit shops could display goods well after closing time.

Glass could also be used for skylights. Instead of arcaded streets in which all of the light came in from the open side, there could now be narrow arcades in former alleyways made bright and usable in all weather by glass coverings overhead. As long as skylights were made of wood and small panes, they tended to be dark and to leak a lot. The combination of iron and plate glass made glass roofs possible. By the 1850s, the Crystal Palace had demonstrated the practicality of glass buildings, and everything from conservatories to railway stations were soon following suit. The huge shopping arcades that were built throughout Victorian England were a mid-century status symbol—a sign that a new industrial city had arrived. [3]

Shopping arcades benefited real estate speculators as well as shoppers. Narrow, dark alleyways that had previously been used only for residences and artisan quarters of the cheapest kind could now be opened up to profitable enterprises. Bigger, deeper lots could be utilized with interior arcaded passageways. Obviously, profits were even higher if an arcade became the place to meet for elite shoppers and cafe-goers.

There were some other problems to be worked out. Sometimes shop owners were not excited about having shops in a nonresidential specialty district because they were not able to be there at night to watch over their property. Resolving this dilemma involved developing strict controls over access (only the best people were allowed in some arcades) and use of locked gates guarded by a beadle (a sort of all-purpose watchman/doorman) at night. Then as now, the trend toward privately controlled "public spaces" was controversial. There were also plumbing and sanitation problems in the early years, since even luxury retailers were not used to occupying such a confined and controlled space. Heavy fines were levied on those second-floor tenants who emptied chamber pots on the elite below. Prostitution was also a constant problem. Some arcades prohibited all women employees from the upper floors of the building.

The Diffusion of the Arcade

Shopping arcades soon diffused to the American city. John Haviland, an English architect, built the first American arcades in New York and Philadelphia in 1817. American, as well as later English Victorian arcades, never included housing but, rather, had two or more floors of rentable shops. The multistory, special-purpose shopping arcade may have been invented in America. The Weybosset Arcade in Providence (1828) still stands as an example of this early development.

Just as a specialized financial district emerged in European and North American cities in the early 1800s, so also did the specialized retailing district, and as we have seen, it too had its own building type. Pushed outward by the higher rents that offices could pay, retailing had a tendency to migrate outward from the core of the city even during the early 1800s. This was sometimes a push-pull situation, as luxury retailing often chased after the elite shoppers, as in London's West End or New York's "Ladies Mile."[4]

The shopping arcade, in a newly gigantic form, made a final nineteenth-century attempt to occupy the core of the city from the 1860s to the 1880s. Perhaps the most famous shopping arcade of all, the Galleria Vittorio Emanuele, was completed in Milan in 1867. Built on the cathedral square near the La Scala opera house, the Galleria was truly monumental in scale and design. The cities of the newly independent country of Italy were actively competing to be the center of the nation's business and culture, and a first-class shopping arcade was seen as one way to attract attention. The Galleria in Milan was built by an international consortium that included an Ital-

Piccadilly Arcade, London: sidewalks, plate glass, gaslights, and arcades made shopping a genteel activity in the early 1800s

ian designer, a French engineer, and a British builder; and it immediately attracted world attention as the epitome of a nineteenth-century shopping center. Turin, Naples, and other Italian cities quickly followed suit, but Milan got the lasting fame.

Perhaps significantly, the two largest shopping arcades in the world were built simultaneously in Russia and the United States during the late 1880s. In Moscow, Red Square had been the traditional place for market stalls since the sixteenth century. In the mid-1800s plans were made to clear the square for ceremonial purposes and to build a special shopping arcade for the market. A monumental arcade building with three linked three-story galleries was completed in 1893 and was known as Torgovye Ryadi. Although even today it is made up of hundreds of separate stalls, after the revolution its name was changed to GUM, the state-owned department store. It was closed by Stalin during the 1930s as a symbol of capitalism and used as a military hospital during World War II. It was reopened as GUM in 1953 and is once again teeming with shoppers and 7,000 attendants. While there is none of the cafe life of Milan, the building does provide spaces for viewing up close the pace of the city.

The largest shopping arcade in North America opened in Cleveland in 1890. Built in the heart of the city (between two office buildings), linking the two busiest commercial streets, the Cleveland Arcade included five stories of galleries with 100 shops. Although it

has been renovated and slightly redesigned, the arcade remains today very much what it always has been, a major place to shop and promenade in downtown Cleveland.

By the late 1800s, the shopping arcade was beginning to lose favor. The novelty was wearing off as new innovations such as elevators, escalators, electric lights, and skyscrapers were attracting people's attention. The main problem, however, was that the nature of retailing had changed. Small, independent specialty shops were thought to be anachronisms. Mass production and mass distribution was what the future was all about. For this, department stores were needed.

The Department Store: Corporate Ownership and Mass Consumption

Like the evolution of the shopping arcade, the invention of the department store was more than just a change in retailing. A variety of social, economic, architectural, and political changes were necessary to make the department store the key to a big city shopping district. A department store is essentially one very large store under single ownership having a wide range of goods available in separate departments. While most early department stores started out with an emphasis on clothing, by the mid-1800s they were known as places to get everything from food to furniture. Shopping arcades symbolized eighteenth-century requirements for small, tasteful shops selling limited quantities of luxury items; the department store represented the nineteenth-century emphasis on mass production and mass consumption.

Far left, *the Cleveland Arcade (1890s), still one of the largest in the United States;* near left, *Eaton Center in downtown Toronto, a modern version of the arcade*

It is hard to say exactly where and when the first department store appeared. Girouard maintains that the idea of grouping a wide variety of commodities for sale under one roof came from colonial contexts such as that found in Calcutta in the late 1700s.[5] There, ships occasionally arrived with vast supplies of assorted European products. These products were arranged by type in a large "European store" so that colonial administrators and their families could shop easily. This was relatively easy to pull off, since colonial cities usually did not have the cumbersome guild-inspired regulations affecting retail shops in cities such as London and Paris. The best known of these European shops was Dring's Long Rooms in the Lall Bazaar in Calcutta. The rooms were 200 feet long and contained everything from saddles to silk stockings.

Inspired perhaps by both Islamic and colonial models, European cities began to develop shopping arrangements called "bazaars" in the early 1800s. Meant to recreate the wide assortment of goods and the colorful excitement of the Middle Eastern market, the first bazaar appeared in London's Soho district in 1816. It was Paris, however, which led the way in the invention of the department store—an organized and carefully planned version of the bazaar with variety of separate "departments" all under one roof.

The French Revolution in 1789 did away with most of the guild regulations that limited retailing by keeping the range of goods available in a particular type of shop very narrow. In addition, the muddy, narrow streets of Paris prevented the English custom of strolling and window shopping from becoming popular. The best shops were off the street, protected from the chaos of the city. The large bazaar seemed like a viable option to the merchants of the early 1800s.

The first Parisian bazaars were intermediate between shopping arcades and department stores in that, although everything was under single ownership, large, skylit galleries were built which were organized into individual stalls in the manner of GUM in Moscow. By the

The Lit Brothers Department Store in Philadelphia exemplifies growth by acquisition of adjacent buildings.

1830s, the architectural plan of a multistoried gallery organized around an open nave had become the norm. While shopping arcades emphasized exclusivity, these new *magasins des nouveautés* emphasized bulk buying, big stocks, low prices, and quick turnover. Fixed prices had been pioneered in some of the better arcades and became standard practice in the protodepartment store. Advertising to attract customers was also introduced.

From the 1830s through the 1850s, the department store idea diffused rapidly, especially in North America and Britain. The vast majority of department stores, however, were not specially built as such but rather evolved ad hoc. Typically, a successful haberdasher or draper would buy the shop next door in order to expand. Gradually, an entire street of shops or houses would come under single ownership as space for storage (necessary for big stocks and quick turnover), clerks, and display. Sometimes shops of a different type would be bought and new lines would be added to the original store. Harrod's of London accreted over time in just such a manner until an entire terrace of houses along Brompton Road had been acquired. These stores catered to the gradually increasing buying power of the middle classes during the industrial and commercial revolutions of the mid-1800s. They would not have been possible without mass production (some would say overproduction) of items such as textiles and, later, ready-made clothing requiring quick distribution. At what point a series of shops became a department store is a matter of question, and so it is difficult to say when the first department store came into existence.

While the protodepartment store had been evolving for some time, the true, purpose-built department store first appeared in Paris in the 1860s.[6] There were several reasons for this. The grand exhibitions of the 1850s, such as those at the Crystal Palace in London and the Industrial Exhibition in Paris, demonstrated an entirely new scale of displaying products. Transportation innovations, especially railways and horsecars, made it possible to bring unprecedented numbers of people together in one place for exhibitions. Wise merchants realized that they could also be brought together in one place for shopping. The PLVI was emerging as an important place that needed to be developed to its full potential. The construction of railway stations, exhibition halls, prisons, museums, and office buildings at a new, monumental scale, along with the invention of such things as the elevator and gas lighting, meant that larger stores were also a possibility.

The first truly large building built to be a department store was the Bon Marché in Paris. Merchants Boucicaut and Videau owned an expanding series of shops during the 1850s and 1860s and worked out some new business principles that came to be associated with the department store. Not only were fixed prices the norm, but also customers were given free inspection of goods, the possibility of exchange, reduced prices for slow-moving goods (at one point in 1862 Bon Marché had a sale on 1,500 parasols), and a wide variety to choose from. Boucicaut and Videau also required cash payment. Their store was a success, and in 1870, a monumental new Bon Marché Department Store was completed. The new store covered an entire city block and had continuous show windows (Eiffel was the engineer on the project.) The interior was glass-covered, with a series of three-story, inward-facing galleries inspired by the shopping arcades. Enormous, free-hanging staircases provided access to the upper floors. The Bon Marché sold everything from Oriental rugs to stationery. In 1872, even a special travel accessories department was added.

The Bon Marché was a city within a city. Not only was it a massive shopping center, but it was also the site of concerts, English and fencing lessons, kitchens and dining halls for employees, and office and storage space (which occupied less visible parts of the structure).

The protodepartment store also evolved in New York and other American cities from the 1820s on. Lord & Taylor, for example, opened a store on Park Row in New York City in 1826. As in Paris, however, it was not until the later decades of the century that the true

Harrod's Department Store in London, a Victorian special-purpose building.

department store came into being. During the late 1850s and early 1860s, impressive new five-story department stores appeared. They looked very much like the office buildings of the era, and in fact, many have since been converted to office space. Gradually, bigger buildings, which featured the interior panache of the Bon Marché were constructed in American as well as European cities. By the 1930s, Macy's in New York City was the largest department store under one roof in the world. Macy's had been founded in 1858 and had grown and moved several times before occupying its new 20-story building on 34th Street in 1924. By 1931, additions to the structure gave the store over 2 million square feet of floor space. It was truly "a miracle on 34th Street."

The Department Store as a Building Type

During the later years of the nineteenth century, the department store evolved as a building type and achieved an identity separate and distinct from the shopping arcades and bazaars that preceded it. The development of a large building for retailing represented a significant shift in the way cities were perceived and used. Buildings took precedence over outdoor spaces. No longer were streets, lanes, alleys, squares, and arcades the settings where the life and commerce of the city was conducted; it now took place inside buildings. Outside, there was only leftover space. This inward movement was due both to the

*Macy's in New York City is the world's
largest department store.*

pull of architectural and economic innovations and the push of increasing
zoning and code regulations.

With the advent of electric lights,
elevators, escalators, cafeterias, indoor plumbing, central heating, and a
variety of other innovations after the
1880s, department stores could become larger and more self-contained.
A single ten-story building covering a
city block could contain an endless
number of worlds to visit, from Santa's Toy Shop to a rooftop cafe. Outside, it was becoming more and more
difficult to use the street, as fire
codes, sanitation regulations, rules concerning sidewalk access and
fire exits, and so on led many cities to prohibit the construction of
shopping arcades by the 1890s. Everything moved inside. Geist argues that greater symbolism was involved. Around 1900

> the city became suspect; its social, spatial, and hygenic condi-
> tions were subject to criticism, and the garden city was pro-
> claimed as the escape from this misery. . . . The individual
> building became an independent entity and no longer played a
> subservient role. The city as a system of spaces was replaced
> by a system of separate entities. The distances between build-
> ings were based on fundamentally different criteria from those
> used in the nineteenth century. The arcade had no place in this
> new spatial system, which still plagues us today.[7]

By the turn of the century, the department store as a building type
had become standardized. A combination of fire and building codes,
coupled with the need to make every inch of space profitable, discouraged the construction of open galleries and skylights. Department
stores became big, rather ordinary-looking buildings with different
products on different floors.

The internal "geography" of the department store was characterized by certain regularities. First, compared to office buildings,
department stores could not be very tall. While some department
store buildings exceeded 20 stories, the number of floors actually

devoted to retailing was usually less than 10. The problem of enticing and moving large numbers of shoppers to the thirtieth floor was insurmountable even with modern elevators; department stores needed a large amount of horizontal space. Second, the location of goods within department stores came to be predictable and based on consumer preferences. Everything had to be in a convenient location. The first floor contained relatively low-priced articles that were often purchased on a whim—gloves, ties, socks, perfume. Men's clothing might also be on the first floor, based on the idea that men were less willing than women to venture too far into the world of shopping. High-fashion articles were typically located on the second and third floors, while larger household items such as rugs and furniture were placed on upper floors. Sometimes, children's toys occupied the top floor, based on the idea that young shoppers could not be deterred. Cafeterias and restrooms also occupied the upper floors. The bargain basement—a place for things that could not be sold elsewhere—also became the rule. As department stores became predictable, they also became a bit boring.

As more department stores became the norm, they could no longer count on novelty to attract customers, and so a variety of special events were initiated in addition to advertising and special sales. Some stores had rooftop gardens and even amusement rides (still common in Japan) to get customers to move upward through the store. Others sponsored concerts and special events.

The Impact and Location of Department Stores

One of the major problems facing those who would invest vast sums of money in a giant retail establishment was where to put it. Locating a department store was trickier than locating an office building. If a large office building became slightly off-center as the PLVI moved, it might suffer a loss of prestige and no longer be able to attract the highest-paying occupants. If a department store had a poor location, it failed. The goal was to locate in a very good, prestigious location, but one far enough away from the office core to avoid high "skyscraper" land values. Access to transportation nodes was essential, and there could be no "bad areas" between the subway or streetcar stop and the store entrance. A park or other amenity was desirable as long as it was not so large that it gave the store a sense of isolation or so poorly supervised that it attracted unsavory characters.

In some cities, such as New York and Los Angeles, major department stores moved several times in search of the right location. The first (proto-) department stores in New York City were located just north of the CBD in lower Manhattan. By the 1870s, they were concentrating near 23rd Street between Fifth and Sixth. By 1902, Macy's was up to 34th Street, where it was soon joined by Gimbels. Eventually, Fifth Avenue between 34th and 42nd became Manhattan's prime retail district. Today, this elongated retail spine serves to connect the lower Manhattan and Midtown office centers. It is thus more of a frame than a CBD core location, almost a zone of discard for the Midtown district centered around 50th Street. An attraction for this location was access to Manhattan's huge garment industry. Department store buyers could not only watch what was being wheeled down the street but could also order "spare parts" for in-stock items and get them immediately. Department stores, some argued, needed access to light industrial districts as well as to elite office and residential zones. Bloomingdales and Bonwit Teller, on the other hand, seemed happy to occupy a zone of assimilation north of the Midtown core and close to the swank Upper East Side.

In other cities, such as Boston and Cleveland, department stores stayed closer to the original commercial core. Mona Domosh attributes this to a greater sense of community attachment and continuity in Boston as well as a greater respect for close-in residential neighborhoods.[8] Also, the Boston Common provided both an amenity and an obstacle for migrating department stores. In Cleveland, the Cleveland Arcade was a continuing attraction downtown, but the main draw factor was created by the building of Higbee's Department Store directly over the railroad station as part of the Terminal Tower Complex. In San Francisco, department stores drifted down Market Street until settling comfortably around the amenity of Union Square.

As department stores got bigger, they anchored their own commercial district. By the time Macy's became the largest store in the world, it was simply too big to be abandoned—just as the Empire State Building and the Woolworth Tower were. In Chicago, a group of large department stores on State Street has provided that address with a sense of permanence. In smaller cities, the department store has had even greater impact.

By the 1950s, if not before, the F&R Lazarus department store was synonymous with downtown Columbus retailing. This store evolved from a small shop specializing in men's and boys' clothing opened by Simon Lazarus in 1851; 100 years later it was the fourth largest department store in the world. A new main store was built in 1909, and through 1958, expansion was continuous. By the late 1950s, the store occupied 28 acres, with a complex of six- to ten-story buildings. In addition, three parking garages with space for over 6,000 cars occupied the blocks nearby. Shoppers did not just go downtown; they went to Lazarus. Small department stores and specialty shops could not compete: Lazarus carried *everything* at good prices, and you could always return merchandise.

The huge and successful department store completed the process of internalizing downtown shopping. Parking, eating, hairdressing, shopping, were all in one complex, and there was no reason to go elsewhere. By the 1950s, air-conditioning had made windows obsolete, and there was no longer even visual contact with the rest of the city. Just as the skyscraper office building had led to a more compact CBD core, so too did the department store reorganize the retail frame. As the life of the city moved inward, city streets remote from the new stores became lifeless, empty, and dangerous. The downtown became less attractive and, as suburban options appeared, less successful.

Beginning in the late 1940s and gaining momentum in the 1950s to the 1970s, downtown retailing lost momentum. No new department stores opened in most downtowns after World War II, and additions and expansions generally stopped during the 1950s. Downtown department stores lacked the excitement and novelty so important to fickle consumers. Predictable and convenient gradually changed to boring and inconvenient. Shopping centers were the new rage. By 1960, consumers were once again about ready to change allegiance.

At first, suburban shopping centers were simply streetcar strips curved into a crescent and dominated by grocery and hardware stores. They offered convenience goods but were no threat to downtown retailing. While there were some important exceptions to this generalization, such as the planned shopping and apartment complex known as the Country Club District built in Kansas City in the early 1920s, it was not until the late 1950s that competitive suburban centers became commonplace. Department stores, now increasingly organized into multistore chains with headquarters in one city making decisions affecting many others, decided to join the suburban boom.

Suburban department stores were not entirely new. In Los Angeles, Bullock's Wilshire opened in 1929 in a location designed to serve the film stars of Hollywood. By 1932, there were stores in Westwood, Pasadena, and Palm Springs. However, that was typical Los Angeles. Elsewhere, things happened more slowly. A seminal event occured when J. L. Hudson promoted, helped develop, and then located a store in Northland Shopping Center on the outskirts of Detroit in 1954. This was the first time that *the* major downtown store had built a facility in the suburbs large enough (four stories) to compete with many main store departments. By the mid-1960s, most major department stores had suburban versions. Although the suburban branches were not as large as the downtown stores, they were newer, brighter, and more convenient for those traveling by car from the suburbs. Moreover, they were literally surrounded by acres of free parking. Fountains, greenery, and Muzak added to the novelty. In 1985, the J. L. Hudson Corporation closed its downtown store—at one time one of the largest in the world.

It was during the late 1950s and early 1960s that suburban shopping centers began to seriously compete with downtown retailing. Part of the attraction of the suburbs involved the invention of the shopping mall, as opposed to the earlier shopping center. The word *mall* evolved from the game pall-mall, a variation on croquet, which was played on grassy fairways in England beginning in the seventeenth century. The open spaces themselves soon came to be known as malls (as in London's Pall Mall) and often were reserved for pedestrians. The Mall in Washington, D.C., is perhaps the most famous example of such a thing in America. However, there is still some confusion about just what a shopping mall is.

Until the late 1950s, shopping centers were little more than linear commercial strips bent into the shape of a half-moon and separated from the street by a large parking lot. They had grocery stores and hardware stores but rarely did they have a major department store. They were convenient places to shop rather than places to hang out. In 1950, the Northgate "mall" in Seattle introduced the idea of shops lining both sides of an open pedestrian way, with a branch of a major department store "anchoring" the project. In 1956, the idea was repeated in the Southdale Mall outside of Minneapolis-St. Paul, and the entire project was enclosed to protect it from the elements. The shopping center had become a kind of combination galleria/Main Street. During the 1960s, the shopping center/mall became more and more enclosed and inwardly focused. Fountains, skating rinks, and theaters were added so that urban life could take place completely apart from any contact with a public street. The process of the internalization of retailing that had begun with the galleria and department store was perfected in the suburban mall. No longer was there any contact with the outside world.

Meanwhile, in many cities the downtown department store has fallen upon hard times. In struggling, unsuccessful downtowns, there is no one there to shop. The downtown is seen as ugly, bleak, and dangerous. In successful and vital downtowns, the pressure from expanding office uses sometimes forces retailing and associated activities further from the core. In London, for example, Saville Row, synonymous with high-class tailoring, is being forced out of its Bond Street location by offices that can pay several times more for the precious West End Space. Department stores are often caught in the middle, since they are close enough to the core to experience high costs and congestion but too far from parking and transit lines to be accessible to customers. By the 1960s, downtown retailing was in need of a new "shtick"—a novelty to attract customers from the increasingly remote suburbs.

Several cities tried creating pedestrian malls along the major downtown thoroughfare, but many retailers and office workers opposed the idea because it would make downtowns even more inaccessible for those in automobiles and delivery vans. For a variety of reasons, malls did not work very well. Most mall designs emulated the suburban shopping center by adding plants, benches, and fountains to the once auto-filled streets. Suburbia was brought downtown on the assumption that people liked suburban designs better. The mall failed to provide a novel attraction to shoppers, and some have been removed. Perhaps the idea was premature, since it preceded the office and condominium booms of the 1970s that brought increased numbers of workers and affluent residents to many cities. Where pedestrian zones have worked in Europe and Japan, the nearby population densities are much greater than in the typical American city. The basic problem was lack of sufficient novelty to bring people back downtown. After the new downtown malls were completed, they were still lined with the same old department stores, office buildings, and coffee shops. Suburban malls were seen as both more exciting and more convenient.

Industrial Chic Retailing: An Urban Design Opportunity

Just as special-purpose buildings emerged during the mid-1800s for offices and retailing, so too did large special-purpose buildings evolve for manufacturing and warehousing during the railroad/industrial era following the Civil War. Unlike most European cities, which were already quite large by the time heavy industry developed, American cities grew up around the factory. While Paris and London had industrial suburbs, New York, Cleveland, Chicago, and San Francisco all had massive industrial complexes along the railroad lines and harbors just beyond downtown by the turn of the century. In American cities, and in some "new" industrial cities in Europe such as Manchester, industry took the best sites. From the Inner Harbor at Baltimore to the San Francisco waterfront, factories and warehouses hugged the shoreline.

It soon became apparent that the central city was an inappropriate place for heavy industry. As early as the 1920s, scholars began to write about the inevitable and desirable dispersion of industry to more spacious quarters in suburban locations. The noise, pollution, and congestion associated with industry led cities to use zoning to "keep industry in its place" during the early decades of the 1900s.

Of all the activities in and around downtown, industry has declined the most rapidly. This has been due to an absolute decline in industrial employment in most American metropolitan areas over the past four decades, coupled with the decentralization of successful industries to suburban industrial parks. The declining importance of water and rail transportation and the increasing reliance on trucks (and freeways) has necessitated moving to peripheral and satellite locations. As products and resources have become more standardized and as the labor force has become more mobile, there is less need for a location in the center of the city.

While people tend to grimace at the mention of the words *heavy industry* and to conjure up images of belching smokestacks and piles of slag, many of the Victorian factories were monumentally picturesque. The exaggerated opulence that characterized offices, hotels, department stores, and apartments during the late 1800s was also applied to many large factories and warehouses. Breweries in the form of castles and warehouses in the form of palaces were not unusual. As industrial uses folded or moved from these premises, the initial response was to clear away the grunge and to eliminate the industrial image from the urban landscape.

From the 1940s to the 1960s, American landscape tastes demonstrated little interest in the care of older buildings. The hiatus in construction caused by the Depression and World War II, followed by a sort of techno-euphoria associated with the seemingly endless stream of new gadgets emerging in the affluent postwar world, led many to see urban renewal as the way to achieve a new urban slate. Americans wanted shiny new modern landscapes, not dirty old ones. Things began to change, however, during the 1960s.

Perhaps the shock of seeing so much of the city leveled for freeway and urban renewal projects coupled with a new sense of urban maturity led to an increasing interest in historic preservation as an important component of urban design planning by the mid-1960s. Just as this new awareness brought increasing attention to former skid rows in cities such as Seattle and Sacramento, so too did it begin to focus attention on former industrial buildings.

The earliest and perhaps still most famous example of an industrial complex that was preserved and recycled for other uses is Ghirardelli Square in San Francisco. The Ghirardelli operation, specializing in the business of importing chocolate, mustard, coffees, and spices, began in Jackson Square near the heart of downtown San Francisco in 1849. In 1867, Ghirardelli discovered how to make ground chocolate,

This festival marketplace in Ghirardelli Square, San Francisco, is a renovated factory complex.

and the manufacturing dimension of the firm grew rapidly. In 1900, the factory sought more spacious quarters away from the growing CBD and built a red-brick complex of industrial buildings complete with an ornate Victorian tower on the northern waterfront of the city. The waterfront was an industrial zone with canneries, warehouses, and wharves. In the early 1960s, as Fisherman's Wharf was beginning to become a major San Francisco tourist attraction, the company once more sought more spacious quarters and moved out of the city to suburban San Leandro. At that time, the buildings seemed ripe for clearance. Highrise apartment buildings had gone up next door, and the old factory buildings stood in the way of further "progress."

Concerned that the picturesque buildings would be destroyed and replaced with view-disrupting high-rises, the Roth family purchased the property in 1962 and began restoration work. In 1964, the first phase of Ghirardelli Square was opened to the public. Completed in 1967, the square became a great success as both a retail center and an architectural showpiece. With 75 shops and restaurants on three levels occupying nearly 340,000 square feet of space, Ghirardelli Square became one of the places to be for both tourists and locals during the late 1960s and early 1970s. Soon there were several spin-offs. The nearby Cannery opened in 1968 in, as the name suggests, a complex of renovated red-brick cannery buildings. Art galleries and cafes occupied the remaining industrial landscape on the northern waterfront. Old factories became so popular that there was considerable talk of building new "old factories."

Ghirardelli Square was truly different from suburban shopping centers in a variety of ways. It was different in terms of both design and location. Because the complex was a set of industrial buildings—a chocolate factory, a mustard factory, a woolen mill, and a (rebuilt) box factory—tied together with an interior courtyard, the spaces in the complex were more like a slightly mysterious medieval city than a standard shopping center. It was a complex complex. There was also a sense of history. Buildings from different eras (the woolen mill dated from 1862) with historically different functions connected the visitor with a rich and varied past. Finally, the success of the project was partly just a matter of good design. Instead of using "shopping center plan number six," every effort was made to create something wonderful out of the historic place.

From the standpoint of retailing, Ghirardelli Square broke all of the rules. No one considered it to be a model of efficient selling. Common wisdom called for high visibility shop fronts on a maximum of three levels arranged in a simple and recognizable pattern. Anchor stores were thought to be a must, along with plenty of free parking. Ghirardelli Square was more like a maze spread over eight levels with no single level reaching all the buildings, complete with dead ends and shops along single loaded corridors. "There was high adventure even finding some of the upper floor enterprises," wrote one surprised architect.[9]

Ghirardelli Square was not just a place for shopping. Clowns and jugglers, mimes and comics, puppet shows and tap dancers—all were encouraged to entertain in and around the shopping and eating areas. A small park created between the Cannery and the Square allowed people to sit on benches or lie on the grass and absorb the atmosphere and life of the setting. The waterfront became a place to go for a cappuccino if nothing else.

The location was also different. Set on a slope with the industrial waterfront and presenting a sweeping view of the bay below and residential neighborhoods climbing the hills above, the complex had a strong sense of connection with the city. Ghirardelli Square was some place—it was in "Old San Francisco." That it was also at the end of the Hyde Street Cable Car Line meant that people could get there easily from downtown hotels without using automobiles. The trip to Ghirardelli was fun.

Ghirardelli Square was famous almost as soon as it opened. In 1965, architect Charles Moore praised the project: "It came about at the turning point when it seemed downtowns had died and everybody was lost in grim and disgusting shopping malls. With Ghirardelli Square, people began to think that the public environment could in some way reach out and touch people."[10] Ghirardelli Square was the first of what has since become known as the "festival center."

Adaptive Reuse: Shopping as an Urban Adventure

Adaptive reuse became popular throughout North America as property owners, cities, and developers everywhere hurried to cash in on the "industrial chic" dimension of historic preservation. Industrial buildings were typically located beyond the congestion of the CBD where parking was often available. As factories closed and smoke-stacks stopped belching, buildings could be cleaned up and made to look nonthreatening for suburbanites. Tax credits for historic preservation projects also encouraged adaptive reuse projects. It has been estimated that between 1981 and 1986, the 25 percent investment tax credit that allowed for the rehabilitation of buildings listed on the National Register of Historic Places or located within a historic district has generated over $5 billion in private investment on projects involving more than 6,800 buildings.

In New Orleans and Denver, massive breweries have been converted to shopping and entertainment complexes. The Jackson Brewery near the French Quarter in New Orleans closed in 1974 after 83 years of service (local beers everywhere have had a very tough time competing with the national brands, at least until the recent popularity of micro-breweries), and in 1983 work commenced on its renovation. Its Romanesque turreted-castle exterior was thought to be a landmark worth preserving. The interior was rebuilt with six levels and a 100-foot-high glass atrium. When it opened in 1984, this "festival marketplace" was already 100 percent leased, and an expansion project was soon under way. Of course, it helps to be close to the French Quarter.

In Denver, the Tivoli Brewery near Larimer Square (a revitalized skid row) has been renovated as a complex of 12 theaters, shops, and restaurants. The list of similar projects is a long one.[11] In Minneapolis, the former Munsingwear complex of factories has been completely renovated for a regional design center and trade mart. In San Diego, a Bekins warehouse has become a fancy waterfront restaurant. Perhaps the largest restoration project to date has been the conversion of Union Station in St. Louis into an Omni Hotel and shopping complex.

When it opened in 1891, Union Station was the largest single-level passenger terminal in the world, and its 11.5-acre train shed was the largest ever built. Through the first half of the twentieth century, the station was the busiest in the United States as well as one of the most architecturally monumental. By the 1970s, however, the station was dreary and largely abandoned. The last train pulled out in 1978. Although the station cost $6.5 million to build in the 1890s, the property sold in the overheated real estate market of 1979 for only $5 million. A 550-room hotel now occupies the main building, while the arches of the former shed cover three levels of shops and restaurants. Over $135 million was spent on the project.

The most famous developer of festival centers is James Rouse. A

A festival marketplace at Covent Garden, London

long-time resident of Baltimore, Rouse became famous in the realm of urban revitalization with the 1976 completion of the Quincy Market–Faneuil Hall renovation in Boston, which coincided with that city's celebration of the Bicentennial. Attracting more visitors during its first year of operation than Disneyland, Quincy Market proved that downtown reuse projects and lively urban centers were inextricably intertwined. The success of that project and the many projects that followed even led to new words such as "Quincification" and "Rousefication" to describe the banner-filled fun zones emerging in cities across the nation.

The successful renovation of the Covent Garden market buildings in London demonstrates that a successful reuse project can revitalize an entire neighborhood. It also illustrates that the evolution of cities sometimes involves an ironic twist of fate. Covent Garden was developed in the 1600s as an exclusive residential square on land once belonging to a monastery (thus "convent garden"). The exclusivity attracted other emerging uses, such as the Royal Opera House. The posh character of the district did not last long, however, since property owners decided that greater profits could be gained by using the square as an open market. Soon the buildings around the square were used for storage and wholesaling. In the early 1800s, market buildings were constructed in the center of the square.

When it was announced that the wholesale food market would move to the suburbs in 1967, many redevelopment proposals were put forward. Finally, preservationists won out, and the market buildings were rehabilitated for retail space and associated wine bars and restaurants. Since the opening in 1980, the project has been an immense success (in spite of the fact that the market building itself has only about 50,000 square feet of rentable space), and buildings for many blocks around have also been rehabilitated. The wholesale-industrial look of the place now attracts shoppers and diners to the London theater district and opera. Thanks to the renovated market, the area finally has the "class" it was intended to have when first designed by Inigo Jones in the 1600s.

Perhaps Americans were starved for fun zones by the 1970s. The amusement parks that had grown up at the end of trolley lines in the early years of the century had long since closed, and downtowns were empty. Suburban shopping centers were convenient, but their novelty was wearing off. Besides, suburban locations at freeway interchanges somehow seemed isolated and disconnected. There was no "there" there. Once again, consumers were in search of novelty. Just as markets, shops, arcades, department stores, and malls were attractions in their day, until the novelty wore off, standard shopping centers were becoming a bit passé by the 1970s.

The problem was that retailing environments had become overspecialized. European-style street markets offered excitement but a limited selection. Department stores offered a vast selection but were predictable and lifeless. Shopping arcades had provided a place to promenade and be seen, but shopping only got in the way. Renovated factories provided a sense of place and time, but often the spaces were not quite right and anchor stores did not fit in. By the late twentieth century, it seems that we were beginning to understand what the urban shopping experience is all about and to design accordingly.

The examples of projects such as Ghirardelli Square and Quincy Market helped to distill what shopping complexes needed in order to combine all of the attractions required by the new generation of urban shoppers. As people demonstrated a willingness to get to "inconvenient" places with "inadequate" parking such as downtown in order to simply *be* in Quincy Market or Ghirardelli Square, old attitudes toward downtown retailing began to change. Projects moved inward from the industrial zone in order to connect with the CBD, and new projects that were constructed included some characteristics of the renovated industrial buildings. Of these, perhaps Harborplace in Baltimore is most famous.

Until it was cleared in the early 1970s, Baltimore's Inner Harbor was a 250-acre wasteland of rotting wharves, railroad yards, ware-

Baltimore's Harborplace is a new festival marketplace on the city's revived waterfront.

houses, and factories. Today, it contains a park, a national aquarium, a world trade center, and a festival marketplace. Developed by the Rouse Corporation, Harborplace consists of multilevel shopping arcades in a style of architecture evocative of nineteenth-century wharf buildings. The 3.2-acre site includes only 140,000 square feet of rentable space, but in 1980, its first year of operation, it attracted 18 million visitors (more than Disney World). It also created 2,300 jobs, earned $42 million, and paid the city over a million dollars in taxes.

The often-quoted comparisons of attendance figures between festival centers such as Quincy Market and Harborplace and attractions such as Disneyland and Disney World are appropriate. In order to be successful, urban retailing must include an amusement-park dimension. It must provide more than a place to shop: it must be "where the action is" for the entire metropolitan area.

Learning from the Past: Shop Location and Design

After a century or so of experimentation, American cities are now discovering what makes downtown retailing work. Although only a small percentage of a metropolitan area's total sales can be expected to occur downtown, since convenience shopping will continue to take place in the suburbs, downtown can nonetheless be an important node of activity if its festival centers are properly located and designed. The following is a partial list of several criteria for successful downtown centers:

- *Festival centers must be centrally located, in highly-visible, symbolic settings.* It has been suggested that cities will never die because they occupy the very best settings; festival centers must take advantage of this. The Boston and Baltimore harbors and the San Francisco waterfront are *places* unlike any in the suburbs. Nestled between an imposing modern skyline and a historic waterfront, a festival center can offer an important sense of connection with the city's past, present, and future.

- *Festival centers must have a symbiotic relationship with other downtown activity centers, such as convention centers and hotels, office towers, and revitalized zones of discard.* Urban designers must return to the idea that cities are made up of a series of spaces rather than of individual buildings. Pedestrians must be encouraged to wander; activities must flow. The internalization of the city into self-contained mega-structures may no longer be the way to go.

- *Festival centers should emphasize the full diversity of urban life.* They should not only include places for shopping, eating, and drinking, but also be entertainment centers both in the formal sense of having theaters and concert halls and in the informal sense of having places for street singers, jugglers and clowns. They must also be places to promenade, relax, or watch the world go by.

- *Festival centers should be mysterious and unpredictable places providing a sense of magic and adventure.* People do not go downtown for convenience: they go for excitement. Many of the recycled industrial buildings contain unexpected and unorthodox charm because of confusing spaces and interesting design contrasts.

- *Festival centers should have a sense of openness and connection with the outside world.* Open or partially open markets like Ghirardelli Square or Covent Garden help to relieve some of the claustrophobia of hermetically sealed, clinically clean, air-conditioned, and increasingly windowless office, school, and shopping complexes. The skylit Victorian arcades have been models for many successful festival centers.

- *Festival centers should provide a sense of psychological connectedness to the city's history and past architecture.* Festival centers need not be replicas of past architecture, but they should give the visitor a sense of being in a particular place and time. Pike Place Market in Seattle should not be altered to look more like Harborplace. The awful sameness of modern shopping centers should be avoided.

Shoppers constantly seek novelty and entertainment. Because of increasing affluence and leisure time and the trend toward deferred marriage and smaller families, many people spend a considerable amount of time searching out places to shop (and be). With increasing numbers of downtown office workers as well as tourists and conventioneers, downtowns are well located to benefit from this activity. In addition, there appears to be a sincere need on the part of many Americans to participate in the life and sense of place of the city. Festival marketplaces have nearly always been successful. In spite of the obvious demand for them, such marketplaces have not always been easy to design and build. This is especially the case when planners have sought to locate retail excitement in the heart of the CBD. San Diego is a case in point.

The Festival Marketplace as City Center: Retailing in the CBD

San Diego, like many of the younger cities of the West, had a very weak, underdeveloped downtown in the early 1970s. There were no major department stores and only a few moderate-sized office towers. The southern section of the downtown, the zone of discard south of Broadway, was especially decrepit. There had been no major construction there for nearly 60 years. In 1985, the Horton Plaza Shopping Center opened there, an unusual 900,000-square-foot multiuse complex designed to look as though it had accreted over time rather than having been designed all at once. With its use of postmodern architectural forms, bright colors, Mediterranean courtyards, narrow passageways, and a confusing maze of stairways, Horton Plaza has become a major attraction for locals and visitors alike. It took a long time to work out the details.

Since land near the CBD is priced as though office towers will be built there, retailing space has been difficult to build in most cities without some sort of public assistance. In San Diego, a 15-block redevelopment district was delimited in 1972, and over the next few years the city spent more than $33 million acquiring and clearing properties and improving the infrastructure. In 1974, shopping center developer Ernest Hahn won a design competition for Horton Plaza (the Rouse Corporation dropped out), and planning began. Nearly everyone was skeptical about whether downtown retailing could work in a sprawling city like San Diego. Although Hahn had had no problem attracting major tenants for his suburban San Diego projects, attracting anchor stores downtown was another story. Hahn even suggested that the project wait for the development of a downtown convention center and more housing.

No one was sure how to attract major tenants. In 1975, Hahn

unveiled a design plan that featured an inward-facing megastructure reminiscent of many large suburban malls. His principal justification was that "the retail industry is a very traditional and conservative industry and therefore any success that we might have in re-establishing retail shopping in downtown San Diego would depend on our ability to produce a center that has at least some of the characteristics that are found to be comfortable, familiar, and economically viable in the suburban centers."[12] Hahn and others were also convinced that lots of free parking would also be essential if the project was to succeed.

Public outrage with the originally planned megastructure coupled with proposals to demolish several historic structures caused the project additional delays. Gradually, a new type of center evolved. In 1977, Jon Jerde, an architect with an interest in restoring old buildings, was hired to redesign the center. He advocated something very different from a suburban center—"the antithesis of prototype." By 1982, Hahn was convinced: "This damn place should have as little resemblance to a typical shopping center as possible."[13]

When completed in 1985, the center was indeed different. Although there were the usual four anchor stores along with 190 small retail and food tenants, two live theaters, and a cinema seven-plex, the spaces were unique. Three historic buildings, including an SRO hotel, had been preserved and visually linked with the center, and new structures were designed to relate architecturally with older buildings in the neighborhood. Views of the bay and the city skyline were well-planned, and the five-level interior was left open to the sky. The march toward ever more enclosed and hermetically sealed shopping centers was at least temporarily detoured in favor of visual linkage with a sense of place. Parking requirements were scaled down (2,800 spaces), and the main entrance was designed to face the once (and some would say still) seminotorious Horton Plaza "skid row" park. The center was eventually designed to look like a series of haphazard and very urban spaces that had simply evolved with the neigborhood around it. Horton Plaza has become a major success. Design matters.

The revitalized Gaslamp District adjacent to Horton Plaza offers a symbiotic relationship, as do the office and hotel towers just to the north. Thousands of units of housing are under construction close to Horton Plaza; it has become a place worth locating near. A system of trolley lines focuses on the CBD and accentuates the once-fading idea of a PLVI.

Throughout the nation, from South Street Seaport in New York to Pike Place Market in Seattle, downtown festival marketplace shop-

Horton Plaza, San Diego, a downtown shopping center designed as a festival marketplace

ping is turning away from isolated and enclosed buildings to a concern for the totality of the place. The frame supports the core. Perhaps we are coming around again to the market squares of Renaissance Europe.

Packaged Landscapes: A Skeptical View

While many feel that urban festival marketplaces represent the distillation and successful replication of many of the key elements that have made cities viable and exciting places over the centuries, there are those who are less sure. Robert Riley is concerned that festival centers represent our increasing total reliance on commercially viable, corporate-controlled landscapes that are continuously packaged and repackaged for us.[14] Lacking any real ability to forge "folk" landscapes in which design results from long-term tradition, interaction, and "real" everyday activities, we spend as much time as possible in transient fantasy worlds that are dependent on our discretionary income for nonessential purchases. As the sign along San Francisco's renovated waterfront—"Best Way to see Pier 39"—suggests, we may even need to be told how to use these new "pop" landscapes. As such, festival marketplaces may be simply the current offering in a series of "Six Flags over Downtown" landscapes that will be provided for our perusal and then discarded. Shoppers will continue to swarm like locusts in search of new "places" which, although delightful, have no deeper connections with reality. Unless carefully tied to the architectural, physical, and historical setting of the city in some of the manners discussed above, festival centers could become as clichéd and predictable as the forms of retailing that preceded them.[15]

A Postscript: Leave Something for the Industrial Support System

In the hierarchy of downtown land uses, industry and associated warehousing have fallen to the bottom, pushed out by offices, retailing, and even high-density housing. In cities like San Francisco and Boston, red-brick industrial buildings have been recycled for a number of other uses and continue to be in great demand. Over the past few decades the assumption has been that industry is both declining and decentralizing and that the downtown of the future will be happily free of it. This is not a wise assumption.

San Francisco has recently taken a stand in favor of preserving at least one close-in industrial area as an industrial area and not as something else. As the northern waterfront has been recycled for Ghirardelli Square and the Cannery, and the central waterfront redeveloped for the Golden Gateway Center, space for city-serving industry is getting scarce. In a viable central city, there must be space for furnace and air-conditioning repair shops, printing operations, furniture refinishing, office supplies, food distribution, bus and trolley storage, and other support services. These things cannot simply move to the suburbs without causing great inconvenience to those who need service quickly. Even cappuccinos do not appear out of thin air. San Francisco has delimited a "South-of-Market" district that is now and has been full of city-serving functions as an industrial area that should remain just that. Many warehouses are being rehabilitated and refurbished, but for continuing operation, not for adaptive reuse. Retailing should be closer to the core of the city.

Conclusions: Urban Architecture and the Adventure of Shopping

There are a great many factors associated with the prospect of successful downtown retailing—the number of people in the CBD work force, the number of tourists, the amount and quality of inner-city housing, the level of affluence and degree of gentrification, the quality of the transit system. Nevertheless, to a very real degree the success of downtown retailing is not simply a matter of numbers. Even in the days of medieval markets and exotic bazaars, people sought out the excitement and human contact of lively shopping districts. Designers of early arcades, department stores, and shopping centers recognized the need for novelty and adventure. Successful downtown retailing depends upon the creation of a *place* with physical, psychological, and emotional ties with the life of the city. The past is prologue.

4 The American Single-Family House

The most important land use by far in the modern American city is housing. Between two-thirds and three-fourths of the total area of a typical city is given over to exclusively residential neighborhoods. Indeed, in most American cities, the freestanding, single-family home dominates the urban landscape. There are many ways to approach an examination of how and why this came to be. The topic of housing is a very complex one involving economic, political, social, cultural, demographic, and technical variables. Nevertheless, in this chapter and the one that follows, I will attempt to shed some light upon the evolution of the American residential scene. In this chapter I focus upon the single-family house, while in the following chapter I will examine the increasing variety of multiunit housing.

Houses versus Housing: Social Science and the Landscape

Most of the literature dealing with American residential landscapes falls into one of two categories—studies of housing and studies of houses. The literature of urban social geography (and related disciplines) is no exception. Studies of housing, such as John Adams's *Housing in America in the 1980s* or Larry Bourne's *The Geography of Housing*, typically feature macro, aggregate approaches, with emphases on the economic and demographic aspects of housing.[1] Such studies aim to give us the big picture with regard to changes in housing quality, size, cost, occupancy, and location. Because data sources such as the U.S. Census of Population and Census of Housing provide information by tract (at least for recent decades), many housing characteristics can easily be mapped. Indeed, maps of housing value and size have formed the basis for many models of urban social structure. For example, sectors of high-value and low-value housing can be identified, as well as areas of high ownership versus rental percentages.

Although such information is invaluable from a spatial standpoint, it tells us little about the aesthetics of the urban landscape and the ideologies and cultural values involved in its creation. For this, we must turn to studies of houses.

Studies of houses, such as Gwendolyn Wright's *Building the Dream* or Clifford Clark's *The American Family Home*, provide us with a more intimate picture of changing house forms.[2] These works emphasize the changing social, aesthetic, and technical character of houses in the context of changing American values and tastes. Other works in this category range from architectural histories emphasizing changes in design and aesthetics to social histories emphasizing such things as the changing roles of family or women in the organization of the household. These studies emphasize the two-way relationship between house form and culture—the idea that houses both reflect and shape basic culture traits. Both types of studies build upon a very important and basic assumption in modern America, that house and home are the cornerstones of a good and stable society.

Very rarely have studies of houses and housing been adequately merged. I hope that this chapter will provide at least one small step in that direction. While we can map housing costs and structural characteristics from census data, our maps of city structure may lack an important aesthetic and cultural dimension. On the other hand, studies emphasizing the changing architectural and design features of housing rarely include any spatial dimension at all other than perhaps a reference to a suburban versus an urban location. We rarely know what role changing house form is playing in the emerging social geography of the city. Although architectural histories abound for individual cities, maps of distributions of house types for cities are nonexistent.

The dominance of the freestanding single-family house in major urban settings is a relatively recent phenomenon. The evolution of this particular building type involved a great deal of experimentation over a long period of time; in the process, the urban house as a place for "a family" to live was gradually differentiated from the great variety of mixed quarters which preceded it. Indeed, the past thousand years of European and North American urban history may be seen as a search for the ideal urban house form—a search that is still going on today as the costs of the "American Dream" rise beyond the grasp of an increasing number of urbanites.

In this chapter I will briefly trace the evolution of the single-family home in becoming the norm (or at least the aspiration) for most of those living in American cities. In addition, I will attempt to merge the traditions of space and place in geography by illustrating how studies of house form and style may be integrated with maps of urban spatial structure. In other words, I will try to shed some light on the relationship between changing building technologies and landscape tastes on the one hand and the development of various types of social areas (such as rings and sectors) on the other. In perhaps no other national context has the constant search for architectural novelty and urban design innovation played such an important role in sorting out people according to class and ethnicity. As we have "progressed" from row houses on a grid through Victorians, bungalows, period revival cottages, and ranches on cul-de-sacs, American cities have become socially differentiated in patterns unknown in Europe and Asia.

The Evolution of the House: European Precedents

The urban house as we know it today—a dwelling separated from the workaday world and sheltering, at least ideally, one nuclear family—evolved in England. Its predecessor, the medieval burgher house, had existed for centuries before and to a very real degree had been the basic component of the cityscape. Only with increasing architectural specialization and the separation of economic activities into purpose-built structures did the "house" begin to take shape. The medieval burgher house in central and northern Europe was not a house in the modern sense of the word. Rather, it was an all-purpose, mixed-use building that served as an important economic unit of production and distribution in the late medieval city. The merchant owner and his family occupied only a small portion of the total space—usually the second floor—and had very few personal belongings and furnishings. While the third and perhaps fourth floors housed apprentices and journeymen, the cellar was used for storage of goods and the first floor for sales. In some cases, upper floors were used for productive activities such as weaving. Such "houses" were typically four to six stories tall and occupied small lots with narrow street frontages. They were built to last and were often used by the same family for decades, if not centuries. According to James Vance, the urban burgher house evolved by about the thirteenth century in prosperous European cities which had outgrown earlier primitive forms.[3]

The burgher house is still an important feature in middle-sized and smaller cities of central Europe. In many such cities, the *belle étage* (second floor) of a tall house in the central city remains a highly desirable place to live, especially where a combination of rent control and architectural conservation have been government policy. In such cities, social segregation by floor—that is, vertical segregation—is more important than areal segregation. Urban mixed-use buildings

The evolution of the urban house:
seventeenth-century burgher houses in Paris

are typically kept in good repair, since elites share them with the workers and students occupying the upper floor garrets. Such landscapes are extremely flexible, for spaces can be easily converted to or from residential, office, or retail uses without changing the look of the street.

The burgher house as an ideal first began to change in Renaissance England. For a variety of reasons, the exclusively residential suburban house and neighborhood were invented in London in the late seventeenth century. The sheer size of London (nearly 500,000 inhabitants by the mid-1600s) and the scale of its economic activity put great pressure on the traditional burgher house landscape. As early as the 1630s, a residential development modeled after the Place des Vosges in Paris was constructed in the then remote Covent Garden. The idea was slow to catch on, and the complex was gradually converted to a vegetable market, but the seed was planted. The human and environmental devastation brought about by the plague and the Great Fire of 1665–66 disrupted the old order of London and sent those who could afford it searching for a better, safer place to live.

The West End residential suburb began to evolve in the late 1600s and early 1700s as Bloomsbury, Mayfair, Belgravia, and Kensington came to be regarded as safe residential havens from the hustle and bustle of the city. While the Great Fire brought things to a head, there were other factors that made London ripe for the development of the suburban house. The relative security of "Fortress Britain" made city walls superfluous to a degree unimaginable in Italy or France. The economic prosperity of the London financial establishment, with its banks, insurance companies, and exchange halls, made capital available for a wide variety of investments and speculations still unheard of in Spain or Austria. In addition, the dual-centered character of London created when the court and the government were located at Westminster, well to the west of the city, gave suburbanites something to head for—a social and geographic goal far outside the confines of the traditonal city. Finally, the leasehold system that developed in London meant that owners of the great estates surrounding the city (large-ly acquired when Henry VIII took over church lands and redis-tributed them to those who could provide him support) could keep title to the land but could make it available to builders through the 99-year lease. This meant that the right to build on huge tracts of land could be obtained with a minimal capital investment.[4] "Builders" leased tracts of land, built a group of houses, and then sold the lease-holds to the upper- and upper-middle-class merchants and other pro-fessionals who had appeared in increasing numbers during the peace and prosperity of the eighteenth century.

The Emergence of a Housing Industry: Areal Expansion and Social Segregation in the English City

By the middle of the eighteenth century, a variety of political, economic, and social factors made it possible for a vast speculative house-building industry to evolve, but these same factors did not ensure that there would be a demand for all of the dwellings created by such an industry. The idea of living in a house set apart from the city was untested. Elsewhere in Europe, there were essentially three scenarios taking place. In many cities, particularly in Spain and southern Europe, there was no growth at all, and so no new proce-dures for providing houses were necessary. In other cities, slow growth, especially within the walls, allowed the perpetuation of tradi-tional procedures such as gradual, on-site expansion and enlargement of existing dwellings and the filling in of gardens. In fast-growing Continental cities such as Paris, the urban apartment building was developed and used to increase population densities in the central city and to embellish new boulevards. None of these options was suitable in London. As London approached one million inhabitants in the early 1800s, some way of providing a great deal of housing was needed. Self-built "squatter settlements" were never as viable an op-tion in England as elsewhere due to the control of many suburban areas by great estates and a variety of building regulations and taxes.

In order to attract a wealthy clientele and so ensure the financial success of early speculative house-building, the best developments focused upon residential squares. Unlike the plazas and piazzas of central and southern Europe, the squares of London were filled with greenery and were off-limits to all but residents of the estate. They were garden space rather than ceremonial centers. It is significant, perhaps, that while the best plazas were built in the very hearts of Spanish and Italian cities, the best London squares were built in the suburbs, leaving the city untouched by the innovation. The attraction of newer, greener suburbs was well under way by 1700. The attrac-

Georgian London: Bedford Square, an early example of a strictly residential, upper-class neighborhood

tion of parks and greenery was a particularly English phenomenon, perhaps derived from the image of the "country gentleman" as the epitome of the elite (in contrast to the situation in Paris, Madrid, or Vienna).

The type of house built in these new residential suburbs was a tall, thin row house not markedly different in shape and appearance from the burgher house. While the building codes and urban design regulations ushered in as a result of the fire led to rather austere and uniform brick facades, the symmetry and tasteful embellishments (such as fan windows) of these "Georgian" houses helped to establish a style that continues to be popular today on both sides of the Atlantic. The big change from the burgher house tradition was in the building's internal organization and usage. While the houses may have been shared with servants, they were completely residential and carefully separated from the commerce and industry of the city.

Not only was functional segregation important, but social segregation was important as well. No longer did the merchants live in the same dwellings (or even in the same neighborhoods) as apprentices and workers. Increasingly, working-class people were left to fend for themselves in a rental market. Since building large numbers of houses even for the well-off was a new and somewhat risky endeavor, very little "working-class" housing was put up during this period. The lot of the working class deteriorated as they were caught between a rock and a hard place—the expanding commercial core and the restricted residential suburbs. Typically, whole families lived in one room or in cellars or sheds. The idea that everyone should live in a house had not come to London by the time Hogarth's *Gin Alley* was painted in the mid-1700s. Indeed, London may have been the first city in the world to develop an extensive filter-down housing market in which the elites moved to exclusive new areas, leaving older housing to be subdivided into tenements for the poor.

James Vance has referred to this as the "failure of English urbanism," in that the unprecedented geographic separation of elites and workers led to extreme deterioration in those areas not lived in or visited by elites—out of sight, out of mind.[5] Marx and Engels were struck by the inequities visible in the urban landscapes of England. The situation did not improve greatly with the advent of purpose-built working class housing toward the end of the eighteenth century. This is not to say that the poor in the rest of Europe lived any better than the poor in England, but only that they tended to live in nicer areas because the elites were still there making sure the streets were clean. In fact, real wages increased very markedly for the English working and middle classes, and by the mid-1800s housing standards reflected this.

The Anglo-American House: The Beginnings of a Housing Industry

Until the early 1800s, London builders were nearly always small entrepreneurs operating with building technologies and organizational frameworks almost unchanged since the Late Middle Ages. Credit was always scarce, and bankruptcy was very common. It is little wonder that most cities in the world remained compact. The process of urban expansion on any scale was in its infancy.

While the building trades did not experience an "industrial revolution" anywhere near the magnitude of textile and iron industries, some progress was made. Major builders such as Alexander Copland and Thomas Cubitt revolutionized and enlarged the process of housing provision around the turn of the nineteenth century. It became possible to build not only hundreds of new houses at one time but to create "places" as well, new neighborhoods focused on residential squares. Many of the improvements involved methods of organizing subcontractors and specialists, while others had to do with the manipulation of credit. Gradually, improved technologies, as in brickmaking and plumbing, also became important. Government expenditures for such such major projects as barracks, hospitals, palaces, and museums around this time helped to create and support a building industry as well; this was particularly the case for the projects of the Regency period like Trafalgar Square.

By 1800, it was clear that large numbers of working-class houses were needed in the burgeoning industrial cities of England. As the cottage industries and segmented labor systems (such as female labor living in "dormitories") gave way to an open and competitive market for rental housing for working-class families, the means to build such housing had to be found. When builders shied away from the task, factory owners built vast tracts of row houses within walking distance of their establishments. Although large tenements were sometimes constructed, individual terraced "homes" were far more common in England as well as in the newly industrializing towns of New England. In England, as in America, "a man's home was his castle."

Since residence was now separate from workplace and houses no longer played a role in production, and since everyone (even children) worked long hours away from home, the working-class house evolved as a very minimal structure. Even so, as rent levels became separate from wage levels (usually rising faster), workers could afford little more. At best, the row houses were solidly built, scaled-down versions of the Georgian terraced mansion, with small backyards for storage and toilet. At worst, they were flimsy, narrow back-to-backs with light and air coming only from a front door and window. Typically, a common privy at the street served the entire block. Still, even at their worst, row houses facilitated and perpetuated the ideal of the "family house"—the Anglo-American notion of the proper way to live. It was the English row house in all its various manifestations that became the norm in urbanizing America. From the mansions of Beacon Hill to the working-class waterfront of Baltimore, the cityscapes of America were dominated by row houses.

The Cult of Domesticity and the Victorian House

Existing data make it very difficult to determine just what percentage of city dwellers lived in a proper house during the nineteenth century. Even in England, where housing records for the 1800s are relatively good, it is difficult to determine just what proportion of the population participated in what type of housing market. It is very likely that percentages varied greatly from city to city and over time. While Liverpool was infamous for its cellar dwellings and lodging houses at mid-century, Sheffield was known for the quality of its working-class housing. Still, perhaps one-third of the total population of typical English cities lived in some form of rookery or cellar at mid-century. For American cities, it is even more difficult to tell how ordinary people were housed in the early nineteenth century. Rapid architectural change and high rates of mobility were the norm.

During the nineteenth century in both England and North America, the middle-class house, separate and sacred from the workaday world and the world of lower-class rookeries, became the dream of the ordinary urban family. Along with this dream came the possibility of actually owning a house in the city, an idea which emerged only very gradually in the nineteenth century and became common only in the mid-twentieth century.

The emergence of the American ideal of a freestanding house with garden involved far more than just the search for more space and a little greenery. America was a new country in need of a "culture," and a wide variety of writers, planners, builders, preachers, reformers, and salesmen combined to create a culture around the single-family home. While city dwellers elsewhere in the world were content to live in a wide variety of settings, to be an American was to live in a house. This American ideal was shaped largely during the Victorian era.

The cult of the single-family home that emerged in both England and America during the Victorian era was a reaction to the chaos of the rapidly growing cities of these countries and to the importance of defining and institutionalizing the emerging urban middle class. By about the 1840s, the process was well under way as housing reformers, religious leaders, and others began to bemoan the unhealthfulness and immorality of urban housing. Filth, disease, sexual promiscuity and other immoralities, and general incivility were all thought to emanate from conditions in which a family or even several families shared one room. If people were to be "improved" (the dream of the Victorians), then housing had to be improved. This meant devising and selling an image of a "proper" house, even though, at first, relatively few families could afford to participate in this dream.

The image was a new one. Urban housing had traditionally fallen into one of three categories. For the rich, there were houses of display—houses with large halls and stately rooms in which much of the commercial and political life of the city took place. In such houses residential space took a secondary role. Burgher houses, for the middle class, were basically centers of production with little in the way of specialized residential space. Finally, the poor simply lived in rooms or cellars, lucky to have even a blanket. In none of these houses was there much in the way of specialized residential space complete with appropriate furnishings and codes of family behavior. The idea of a substantial house given over entirely to the task of proper family living took some developing.

The Victorians advocated a family-conscious, home-centered lifestyle which required careful attention to the importance of a proper house. It was in the house that the family was nurtured. Women did not work, but rather they married, raised children, and ran the "household." The home became the center of social life as women became increasingly isolated from the city. A system of "social calls," entertaining at home, and social improvement meant that a variety of spaces were necessary. Dining rooms, parlors, libraries, music rooms, nurseries, and bedrooms were also institutionalized, with proper furniture and prescribed behaviors. Christian values, moral goodness, cleanliness, politeness, and, above all, respectability were to be reflected in the home. Living in a proper house became a status symbol, a sign that the family had achieved a standing in the emerging, yet still fragile proper middle class. While only a tiny minority (perhaps 5–10 percent of urban households in the mid-nineteenth century) could participate in this dream, it had a powerful impact on American culture.

The association of middle-class individualism with life in a particular type of house contributed to a trend toward increasingly rapid architectural change and diversity in both England and North America. While Georgian terraces were still embedded in a tradition of civic urban design in which uniform housing graced important urban features such as squares and monuments (a tradition which continued in much of Continental Europe, especially Paris), Anglo-American housing sought to be different. A proper house was to be differentiated from the city architecturally as well as physically rather than serving as an integral part of it. A series of architectural fads emerged roughly after 1800, including the Greek Revival, the Romantic movement, Gothic Revival, and others which culminated in Victorian Eclecticism. Trade and commerce, colonial empires, and printing and publishing made the entire world increasingly available for imitation. By the late-1800s, a proper house could be a Swiss chalet or an Indian bungalow.

Partly due to these new ideas concerning the house as a special, even sacred, kind of place—an individualized status symbol and a place to segregate the family from the evils of the city—a new kind of urban form was emerging in England and America by the middle of the nineteenth century. As early as 1844, Engels described what was later to become known as the concentric zone model of city structure later postulated by Burgess.[6] He noted a specialized, nonresidential commercial center surrounded by areas of filtered-down, tenementized working-class housing, with "villas" for the well-to-do furthest out. This new kind of house for the upper classes had to be located well away from anything that would threaten the moral virtue of the home. The class-segregated city with housing types as a key dimension of this segregation was the result. Today, American cities epitomize this form of urban organization.

The Search for an American Urban House Form

North America is characterized by a tremendous variety of house types. This is due partly to its initial variety of cultures and associated styles and building technologies, from the Native American and Hispanic pueblos and ranches of the Southwest, to the African- and French-inspired houses of Louisiana, to the English and Dutch traditions of New York. Since then, wood, stone, brick, adobe, shingles, concrete, and aluminum siding have all been used in the search for an appropriate American look. The diversity is also due to the newness and lack of tradition in the American residential landscape. From the beginning, architectural fads and follies have led to continuous experimentation with housing form. Compared to Europe (and most other places) our architectural eras have been compressed, with an 1850s house looking very different from an 1820s house. Finally, diversity has come from our reluctance to give up rural house types even in the midst of some of the largest urban areas in the world. We delight in houses resembling Tudor cottages or western ranches (complete with a wagon wheel in the front yard) and complain about houses that all look alike. Our vision of rustic individualism, coupled with relative affluence and mobility, have enabled us to create and perpetuate a wildly varying residential scene. The complex and segregated social mosaic of the American city reflects this diversity.

Individualism and search for novelty has been very hard on place. As new styles appeared, old houses were often viewed as old-fashioned or even obsolete. Houses in America often became old before their time, and there were few who loved old (often portrayed as haunted) houses. This had not always been the case.

Until well into the 1800s, things were simpler. Cities like Boston and Baltimore were characterized by urban houses—usually red-brick row houses derived from England—while small towns and the countryside had a variety of folk housing types related to the backgrounds and occupations of those who lived in them. Over time, this distinction became fuzzy as the urban fabric loosened and many rural housetypes were constructed on the edges of expanding cities. Gradually, the city of uniform terraced houses gave way to a melange of novel and unrelated styles.

The Row House Cities of the East: Continuing English Traditions

With regard to original housing stock, American cities can be divided into two very distinctive types: those that were large and "urban" by 1850, and those that were not. The former tended to have

The row house in urban America: Baltimore

The row house as a corner store: Baltimore

English-style urban house types. After sometimes extended periods of ragged experimentation during the colonial period, as different ethnic and occupational groups tried everything from log cabins to the House of Seven Gables, a variety of "rural" houses and shacks were constructed. New York, Boston, Philadelphia, Baltimore, Cincinnati, and St. Louis all developed "proper" urban landscapes of red-brick row houses. There were big three- and four-story mansions complete with classical embellishments for the elite, and there were one- and two-story plain models for the less well-off, but red-brick row houses predominated. New Orleans and San Francisco had stucco and wooden variations on the theme. Lots were narrow (typically 12 feet for small houses and perhaps 25 feet for the biggest), often with small houses on alleys behind the bigger ones. Rates of home ownership varied markedly from city to city in the nineteenth century, but the vast majority of families were renters. Most individuals simply took rooms or "lodgings" in a house. As in Europe, row houses could also easily be converted to a mixture of residential and commercial uses or to tenements.

The uniform terrace of red-brick row houses was perfectly suited to American ideology in the late 1700s and early 1800s. Americans were generally opposed to the ostentation and flamboyance of European cities and preferred a "democratic" landscape that minimized class differences and maximized a sense of civic purpose. Good taste called for understatement and few unnecessary frills. The Protestant work ethic was to be writ large in the cityscape. Terraces of uniform houses were built upon a practical grid of streets. By about 1800, most large American cities, from Troy, New York, to Richmond, Virginia, were beginning to look properly "urban." While fire codes as well as civic ideology tended to call for brick construction, not all cities complied. New York and Philadelphia had abundant supplies of clay for the production of inexpensive brick, but Washington, D.C., did not, and many houses that were built hurriedly of wood deteriorated quickly and became some of the city's worst slums.

Building regulations in America were generally not as strict as those in England, and rarely were there requirements that, for example, building height be related to the width of the street. Therefore, American cities were often characterized by a mixture of two-story and three- or four-story row houses on the same street, giving them a jagged look. Still, the architectural uniformity that did exist tended to mask social differences rather than accentuate them. Although terraced housing looked homogeneous from the front, middle-class houses had private gardens and private toilets, while in other types of neighborhoods houses were subdivided for many families, and in some cases, gardens were filled in for a variety of jerry-built shanties and courts. Alley houses often evolved in the small service lanes behind the proper terraces. Class differences existed, but they were not displayed. From the street, the American city looked serene until the mid-nineteenth century.

By the 1820s, overcrowding was a major problem in large American cities, and a decreasing percentage of artisans and laborers could afford a proper house. The middle and upper classes had not yet

Wood-frame houses in Chicago: fire codes and the Greek Revival led to freestanding houses with the gable facing the street.

abandoned the central city, for pedestrian access to work was still necessary. Still, there was a reluctance to build anything other than the types of houses that had originated in the suburbs of London. There were many complaints that the large, solid "London-style" row house was inappropriate for cities such as New York and Philadelphia in the early 1800s, since very few people could afford such houses and many became multifamily structures as soon as they were completed. Yet builders continued to put them up because this was the style they knew and because land values and building costs required substantial structures.

While the tradition of building flat-fronted, brick row houses continued well into the twentieth century in some cities, most notably Baltimore and Philadelphia, the look was becoming passé in many cities by the 1840s, thus initiating a constant search for novelty and "improvement" that has characterized American housing ever since.

The urban red-brick row house never became the norm in most smaller American towns and villages, especially outside of the Northeast.[7] Even in New England, a variety of freestanding wooden dwellings such as the "saltbox" house dominated the landscapes of all but the largest cities at mid-century. In the Midwest and the South, a variety of freestanding "folk" houses such as the shotgun and I-house could be found in most towns.

Widespread dissatisfaction with the row house, however, began to appear even in big cities with the Greek Revival of the 1820s. The Greek Revival called for as many buildings as possible to look like Greek temples, and that meant having the gable face the street. While false gables were added to row houses in Philadelphia (and London), a proper Greek temple had to be freestanding. In cities such as Cincinnati and Columbus, a sort of semi–row house landscape evolved, as closely packed but freestanding brick houses appeared, some with gable to the street. By the time Chicago began to boom at mid-century, nearly all houses were built gable to the street, and although they were tightly packed on narrow lots, they were freestanding. They were also often made of wood, a material which allowed cheaper, faster construction, especially after the introduction of balloon-framing. Fire codes often required that wooden houses be freestanding and so helped to give cities a more rural look. Mid-century housing in Chicago was transitional in appearance. It still looked vaguely urban but changes were afoot.

American Individualism, Diversity of House Type, and the Bucolic Suburb: So Much for "Democratic" Terraces

By the 1860s and 1870s, the urban fabric began to loosen. Innovations in transportation such as the omnibus, the horsecar, and (by the 1890s) the electric streetcar enabled cities to spread out. Although urban lots were still typically quite narrow (usually about 25 feet), there was room for a freestanding house. In addition, the invention of the lawn mower in the 1850s and the increasing amount of free time that resulted from shorter working hours made it possible for people to have well-tended front and back gardens instead of, or in addition to, backyards given over to privies and storage. In the Georgian terraced house of the 1700s, attention was lavished on the front facade but the backs of houses were often ignored, since outhouses, garbage piles, stables, and storage "yards" were located there. Indeed, the word *yard* originally implied the workaday world, as in *boatyard* or *lumberyard*. Especially in working-class terraces, such yards were best kept out of sight. By the mid-1800s, things were changing.

A freestanding house set on a larger lot required, in the Anglo-American tradition, a bit of greenery. Planting a lawn of grass (as though to be used by sheep or perhaps for a fox hunt) became de rigueur for larger houses which were set back from the street. Rural imagery had come to the city. Similarly, in the backyard (most Americans still refer to it as a yard), lawns, gardens, and fountains were put in. This increasingly rustic setting seemed to require increasingly rustic houses, and so, from the mid-nineteenth century onwards, big cities were filled with rural house types. Indeed, middle-class urban Americans no longer lived in houses at all; they lived in cottages and bungalows. Many of the first freestanding houses, however, were simply former row houses set in a looser pattern.

As row housing evolved toward freestanding housing, several new house types emerged. Large gable-to-the-side houses became "colonial," as they were set in large lots and embellished with classical ornamentation. Smaller one- or one-and-a-half-story end-gable houses became "Cape Cod cottages." Usually, however, rooflines were "rotated" so the gables fronted the streets. In this way, a variety of embellishments could be used to differentiate and embellish the structures. Greek columns could be added flush to the house along with a Greek temple roofline and cornice, or Gothic points and arches could be used to turn the dwelling into a romantic "gingerbread" cottage.

As the Greek portico met the Caribbean veranda, the idea of the front "porch" evolved. The porch looked best on front-gable houses, and so this configuration became the most popular. The front porch became as "American as apple pie" and was a very important social setting for meeting neighbors and passers-by, courting, and chatting after dinner in the evenings, and, in general, it served as a transition zone between the private house and the public street. By the late 1800s, a proper middle-class lifestyle meant sipping lemonade on the front porch swing.

Interiors changed more slowly than exteriors. While the new "cult of the house" ideology that was emerging emphasized the importance of having certain types of spaces within the home, room arrangements were slow to change. The rather formal arrangement of rooms that had become normal by about 1750 in both England and America was to last at least until 1900. As the size of the typical house increased, parlors were kept in the front and service areas such as kitchens continued to occupy the rear of the house. Bedrooms were always upstairs (if there was an upstairs). Even after new styles such as Greek Revival and Italianate were introduced, the square box prevailed. The rectangular house had become the norm during the many decades of row house construction, and this form shaped interiors for decades after its relative demise. As the urban fabric loosened, and houses became freestanding, new embellishments, including wings and porches, were added, but the box was still the easiest form to construct.

As houses began to be set apart by lawns, however, the total look of the structure became increasingly important. While row houses had only fronts, freestanding houses had sides and even backs. Window and roof configuration from other perspectives had to be considered. New styles, especially the romantic Gothic Revival cottage; new building technologies, such as balloon-frame construction; abundant and relatively inexpensive wood; and the larger size of typical urban lots—all combined to increase house form complexity. The basic box became the box and wing by the 1840s, and multiple wings and gables became common by the 1870s. There was no longer a typical urban house in America.

Now that machine tools allowed mass production of intricately carved embellishments of all kinds, Victorian houses were bedecked with flamboyant detail. Wrought iron became abundant and was added to roof lines and front fences, while innovations in glassmaking made beveled and stained glass detailing popular. A wider variety of paints meant that houses could feature complex patterns of contrasting trim. The house as an expression of individualism had fully arrived by the 1870s. Turrets and towers abounded.

Still, there was some confusion over just what an American house should look like. While most rejected the homogeneity of Georgian terraced housing, there was little consensus beyond that. As a result, a bewildering variety of house styles evolved over space and time. New styles came and went in less than a decade, and some cities accepted one or another while other places did not. While some of the regional variation that emerged in the nineteenth century was clearly based on the new popularity of local vernacular traditions (adobes in the Southwest), much of it simply resulted from the whims and tastes of different local builders. Houses in Buffalo were different from those built at the same time in Cincinnati. We need to know a great deal more about the differing character and extent of various types of houses in American cities before we can attribute all of the variation in costs simply to current growth rates. Are houses in some cities (and some neighborhoods) simply better than the houses in similar neighborhoods in other cities? Do they have more staying power aesthetically and technologically?

Since innovations in both housing design and technology evolved largely during the nineteenth century, the differential adoption of such innovations is crucial to our understanding of the differing intra-urban spatial patterns that remain even today. Why has it been possible (and desirable) to preserve and renovate the housing stock in some large American cities, while in others, older houses have been far more difficult to renovate? Both initial construction and subsequent social history must be considered in order to tell the whole story. I will explore this issue in greater detail later on.

Inventing and Selling the Idea of the American House

The evolution of the American single-family house has been inextricably intertwined with both supply and demand forces. While there likely has always been a latent demand for such housing in America due to Anglo-American preferences for rustic greenery and the importance of Protestant values and the nuclear family, much of the story involves the supply side. The provision of housing in America very early became a big business as well as a social crusade. The making of the housing stock mirrors the making of America.

Which came first, demand or supply? Did the residents of Boston in 1820 yearn for the invention of the first suburbs (with housing set apart from the bustle of the city), or was the idea of the relatively isolated, freestanding house created, packaged and sold to a skeptical public? It was probably a bit of both. While religious leaders and social reformers argued for the single-family house on moral grounds, carpenters, builders, landowners, transportation magnates (from streetcar builders to, later, automobile dealers), appliance salesmen, gardeners, suburban political leaders, banks and savings and loan establishments, and a wide variety of other American institutions all had a hand in designing and selling the American Dream.

An important part of the house as a symbol of the American Dream was home (and land) ownership. As the image of the typical urban house became increasingly rustic, the connection with the ownership of a plot of land grew. While the idea was sold initially, as now, as a good investment in the future, there was also a strong connection with the rural mythology of America. Since the mid-1800s, American urbanites have been attracted to a variety of cottages, ranches, and farmhouse revivals.

Increasing home ownership was dependent upon the availability of capital. In the early years of the nineteenth century, banks had little interest in financing speculative house building. Banks wanted surer investments with quicker returns. In the 1830s, savings and loan institutions were pioneered to provide long-term, low-interest mortgages to home buyers. These institutions began to boom after the Civil War, but even so, large down payments were required, and often several mortgages were needed in order to finance a house. Still, the number and percentage of urban homeowners grew in the late 1800s. We know, for example, that the national rate of nonfarm home ownership in 1890 was 38 percent (at a time when most people lived in small towns or in rural places) and that the rate for big cities was generally much lower.[8] Although Chicago was known as the "Garden City" because of its many freestanding houses with gardens, only 23 percent of its households were homeowners in 1890. This figure no doubt fluctuated wildly during the peak immigration years of 1890–1910. Of course, many families rented freestanding houses and so lived a lifestyle that was close to the ideal, while others shared or rented space in freestanding houses with gardens.

Housing Cycles and Technology

American cities were not built at a steady pace but, rather, were subject to tremendous "boom and bust" periods. During certain years, large numbers of houses were built and loans were readily available, while in other years housing shortages and overcrowding reappeared. In attempting to uncover just what role the freestanding house played in the social organization of the city, we must not only ask what city but also what year. Our models of city structure and our generalizations about life in different types of neighborhoods, even if accurate, fluctuate around a mean.

The periodic nature of house production means that changes in housing style and technology tend to result in readily identifiable housing eras rather than a slow continuum of change in house types. Cities are therefore often made up of "era hunks"—that is, neighborhoods with particular house types resulting from a particular era—even holding constant socioeconomic variables such as size and cost. As people move about, they change landscapes as well as house size. By understanding how these landscapes came to be—the values, tastes, and ideologies associated with them—as well as the "staying power" of particular styles, we can add thickness to our generalizations about how cities are put together.

Every era has been, to some degree, a reaction to the era that preceded it. Reactions may involve aesthetics, interior arrangements, housing technologies and infrastructure, location, family roles, and a nebulous category which can be summarized under the term *lifestyle*. As we have seen, mid-century Victorian houses were a reaction to the aesthetic uniformity and perceived crowding of row or terraced housing, to the lack of separation of family life from city life, to the lack of interior space for special "self-improvement" activities such as music, and to the lack of rustic greenery. While these reactions are era-specific, a nearly universal reaction to housing from earlier eras has been dissatisfaction with outmoded domestic technology. This has been true for a very long time.

From the standpoint of cleanliness, ventilation, and plumbing, late medieval houses left much to be desired. While innovations in glass and chimney construction were important, ordinary houses in the eighteenth century were likely to be damp, drafty, smoky, dark, un-

Victorian houses, such as this one in San Diego, were difficult to maintain and aesthetically obsolete through much of the twentieth century.

plumbed, and generally unhealthful. When overcrowding was common, disease was rampant. Tuberculosis was the common killer until well into the nineteenth century. It is little wonder that reformers emphasized health as a major factor underlying the need for new housing types, and that even small improvements were hailed as great achievements that made earlier houses obsolete by comparison. For example, English "back-to-backs" with no garden and a public privy down the street were seen as far inferior to row houses with private outhouses in the backyard. Such housing was much healthier. Houses with gas hookups for light and heat were far better than those without. As improvements in water pressure and plumbing allowed water to be delivered to upper floors in some areas after about 1840, houses without water became obsolete. Indeed, much of the appeal of early Victorian freestanding houses (especially before the germ theory was developed in the 1880s) was that space itself separated residents from a general "miasma" of disease and corruption. An outhouse in a large yard was better than one in a congested court.

Each technological, aesthetic, and ideological breakthrough meant that certain types of houses were perceived as obsolete for a certain period of time. Even if older, "obsolete" housing could be improved and upgraded, there was still a period of time when such houses were less desirable. Given nearly perpetual housing shortages and the existence of an ever-stronger "filter-down" housing market as cities expanded, obsolete housing was quickly occupied by lower-income people. Compared to those parts of the world (such as China, Egypt, or Latin America) where housing styles and technologies changed little if at all during the nineteenth or even early twentieth centuries, American cities came to be socially and economically segregated on the basis of house type. Still, the process was a choppy one because technology, aesthetics, ideology, and wages did not always advance together. In addition, "progress" is sometimes circular. What seems out-of-date at one point in time might come back in fashion later. While this is especially the case with aesthetic tastes, even once-passé technologies such as the fireplace can return. If a house type contains enough valued features from past eras, it is usually worth renovating and renewing outmoded traits.

Domestic Science and the Bungalow

While the eclectic Victorian middle-class house was a reaction to the houses that preceded it, its success was not to last. Booming after the Civil War and peaking in popularity in the 1880s, Victorian domesticity began to lose favor after the recession of 1893. The old order was damaged by the severity of the recession, just as the Chicago World's Fair called for a cleaner, smoother, Classical "White City." Although industrial output boomed and wages increased during the recovery of the late 1890s, the cost of land, labor, and building materials advanced rapidly as well, escalating the cost of elaborate Victorian houses. The size of a typical middle-class house decreased from the 1880s to the early 1900s. More important, the image of an ideal house changed dramatically.

The Victorian house had been almost literally a castle. Its Gothic, vertical shape, defensive gates and steps, and highly formal interior spaces were designed to separate and protect the family from the unwholesome world that lurked beyond. It was an escape from the city, but it was also a defense against the all-too-recently tamed forces of nature. It was enclosed and cloistered. It was also a treasure house. The massive increase in the availability of factory products and in levels of affluence enabled people to spend a considerable amount of time shopping (in the newly created department stores). This emerging culture of consumerism, as well as an infatuation with paraphernalia from around the world, meant that Victorian houses tended to be cluttered. The more "stuff," the better. After all, only the middle class (and the upper class) could afford to shop. "Stuff" was a status symbol: it demonstrated that the residents knew about art and furniture, rugs, birds, wallpaper, and curtains, and so on, and that they could afford to shop accordingly. If the brick row house epitomized democracy, civic pride, and egalitarian social values, the Victorian Eclectic represented ostentatious display, class distinctions, social segregation, and a new consumerism made possible by mass production.

The turn of the century brought a reaction to the treasure castle. A new option was being built and pushed by those who would reform society and create a good and proper American home. It was the bungalow. No one is exactly sure just what a bungalow is, but my favorite definition is that it is "a house that costs a great deal more than it appears to." Simplicity was the order of the day by the early 1900s.[9]

The term *bungalow* is derived from Bengal, India, and relates to British efforts to design an informal tropical house during the colonial era. Bungalows were introduced into the American South during the mid-1800s as low-slung, pyramidal-roofed dwellings which facilitated ventilation and connection with the outdoors. In the North and Midwest, bungalows were initially associated with church camps and resorts—they were small vacation houses that served as antidotes to city life. They were not considered proper urban houses. The southern bungalow gradually diffused across the South to Texas, Arizona, and finally California.

In California, the bungalow became extremely popular in the early years of the twentieth century as the perfect informal, garden-oriented house to symbolize life in the Golden State. The California bungalow gradually evolved from its southern predecessor and became a more varied and picturesque house type. It was still low-slung (usually one-story) and informal, but it was embellished with a variety of stylistic treatments, including Japanese rooflines, Egyptian porch supports, and Tudor half-timbering. In spite of such designs, however, the bungalow avoided the clutter of the Victorian Eclectic. The bungalow emphasized connection with the outdoors and the use of natural materials such as wood shingles and stone. The arts and crafts movement was in full swing, and California bungalows were often known as "craftsman bungalows" as they diffused across the nation in the years before World War I.

Stylistically and ideologically, the bungalow represented a reaction to the formal, ostentatious, vertical, and enclosed Victorian Eclectic. Bungalows were seen as representing the triumph of modern, rational scientific thinking over the chaos and clutter of the old order. They were sunny, horizontal, modern, natural houses filled with the latest conveniences, while Victorians were increasingly seen as stuffy, formal, vertical, unhealthful, gaudy, and inconvenient. Victorian houses

This Victorian neighborhood in San Diego evolved without zoning or other types of protection.

were inappropriate for a modern American lifestyle that was based on merging a healthy outdoor orientation with modern scientific design and technology.

Once again, it is difficult to say which came first, supply or demand. On the supply side, it was increasingly costly to build, staff (with the usual servants), and maintain Victorian houses by the late 1890s. In order to include all the latest technologies—modern plumbing and bathrooms, hot water heaters, washing machines, modern kitchen appliances, electricity, and central heating (in colder climates), as well as built-in cabinets, fireplaces, and other desired features—houses had to become smaller. In addition, the one-story, horizontal design of the bungalow often required a larger, more expensive roof area. The new technology alone could add 25–40 percent to the cost of building a house. Americans had to be convinced that they wanted smaller houses. Between 1880 and 1905, a new, $3,000 middle-class house decreased in size from between 2,000 and 2,500 square feet to between 1,000 and 1,500 square feet.[10]

Several themes were developed in order to demonstrate the desirability of compact bungalow living to the American public. Foremost among them was the theme of domestic science. This theme appealed to Americans for different reasons. It emphasized (once more) the notions of health, sanitation, and "science," but it also emphasized greater equality and freedom for women and greater convenience for everyone. Two other themes, the back-to-nature and arts and crafts movements, deemphasized consumerism and display. In line with this, the bungalow was sold as a more "natural" way to live. Even the theme of social egalitarianism was revived: electricity became the servant of everyone as large houses with separate servants' quarters became passé. Indeed, servants were not only unnecessary in the new houses; they were also increasingly unaffordable. In 1870, one in seven families had servants, and being a domestic was by far the most common job for women working outside the home. By 1910, only the wealthiest households had live-in servants. Working women now had more options because department stores and offices required clerical and sales help by the early 1900s. (Until the late 1800s, most department stores and offices had hired only men.)

In retrospect, the Progressive Era of the early 1900s which spawned the bungalow seems to have been a time of excessive preoccupation with cleanliness and sanitation. (Indeed, many reformers referred to themselves as "sanitarians.") Victorian houses, with excessive detailing, heavy furniture and drapes, complex and irregular designs, and general clutter, were seen to be unhealthful. Dust and germs could hide everywhere. Heavy fabrics absorbed smoke and grime. Interiors were dank and dingy. Housewives risked their health spending long hours "chasing germs" from the home. When the presence of an archaic kitchen and toilet was added, the dangers multiplied. Domestic "science" was clearly needed.

During the early 1900s, "home economics" became a widely taught discipline in American colleges and universities. Thirty universities had departments of home economics by 1916, while nearly 18,000 students had studied some form of "household management" or "domestic engineering" in a variety of institutions by that date.[11] Some have argued that this was a ploy to elevate the position and status of women while keeping them satisfied with their role as housewives. Women were no longer spiritual nurturers dawdling away the hours with music lessons and poetry while the servants did the work; they were scientific household managers and users of the latest technologies.

A modern house required more than the installation of modern gadgetry; it required the reorganization of interior space. The bungalow was advertised as a rational, compact instrument for living. The kitchen was said to be modeled after a yacht galley so as to have the most space-conserving, efficient form possible. Other rooms in the house were designed to be multipurpose and informal as opposed to the overspecialized and rigid quarters associated with Victorians. Built-in cabinets replaced heavy furniture. The labyrinth of hallways associated with older housing gave way to informal and open connections between rooms, and even doors were minimized.

As families became smaller in the early 1900s, with children leaving home earlier and fewer extended-family living arrangements, houses could provide privacy with less space. In addition, many of the production activities formerly associated with houses, such as canning and sewing, diminished because more items could be easily purchased in stores. Recreational activities also became less associated with life at home as children went off to the Boy or Girl Scouts, and women as well as men went to social clubs. Above all, the bungalow was easy to maintain. Everything was smooth, white, and easy to clean. Enamel and porcelain fixtures and linoleum floors became popular as housewives were given "germ culture kits" to make sure the home was bacteria-free.

The horizontal character of the low-slung bungalow emphasized both convenient living and the connection with nature and the neighborhood. The vertical character of Victorian housing was as inconvenient as it was moral (i.e., compartmentalized). With a basement and two or three stories above, climbing stairways (with water, laundry, food, etc.) provided a constant form of exercise. Before indoor plumbing, hot water heaters, and modern bathrooms, the chores were monumental. The bungalow represented perhaps the first truly revolutionary change in interior spatial arrangements since the Anglo-American terraced house had evolved in the early 1700s. Not only were the spaces smaller, better-connected, and informal, but new types of spaces, such as the breakfast nook, evolved in order to facilitate efficient, informal eating. As usual, reformers argued that better houses would make for better lives. The cleaner, smoother, less-cluttered bungalow would no doubt help to lower the divorce rate and cement family relations.

The formal, highly structured Victorian house was designed to create and shape the new middle class; the informal bungalow was a sign that the middle class had arrived and that its existence was no longer fragile and threatened. Single-purpose rooms were largely replaced by multipurpose spaces as people now knew how to behave properly in a house. The exception to this was the bedroom, but even here times had changed, since bedrooms no longer had to be hidden away upstairs. The middle classes no longer needed so much "spiritual uplifting"; they could now behave rationally and "scientifically."

The middle class was also now much larger, and the percentage of people living in and owning houses increased dramatically in most cities during the prosperity of the early 1900s. Between 1900 and 1917, real income doubled, and even members of the lower middle class could afford small bungalows in most cities. While incomes were increasing, so was the production of modest houses. The years before World War I saw peaks in home production, and for the first time, large numbers of new, small, affordable houses were constructed as electric streetcars opened up peripheral areas for development. Many "suburbs" featured tiny bungalows (about 600 to 800 square feet) on small (25- by 50-foot) lots. The ready availability of inexpensive housing in such cities as Omaha, Los Angeles, and Salt Lake City enabled the rate of home ownership to double between 1880 and 1920. In Omaha, for example, home ownership increased from 28 percent of households in 1900 (which was pretty close to the national urban average) to 47 percent in 1920 in spite of an 87 percent increase in the city's total population.[12] In most larger metropolitan areas the percentages were lower, especially in the South and Northeast, where poverty was greater and building traditions different. For example, only 18 percent of the residents of Atlanta owned houses in 1920, and only 12 percent in New York City did (just after the period of peak foreign immigration). Still, not only was the production of houses strong before World War I, but the increasing availability of mortgage money from savings and loans made purchasing them easier.

The Diffusion and Modification of the Bungalow

It can be argued that the regional diversity of American urban house types began to decrease significantly around the turn of the century. Uniformity had been the rule in the early 1800s (at least for the East), but diversity had increased as the century wore on and as local climatic conditions and building traditions led to dissimilar architecture. Charleston, Atlanta, and Milwaukee, for example, each developed local vernacular styles. While pattern books and architectural journals increased in number and importance throughout the 1800s, in practice many ideas were modified. By the 1880s, a new diffusion technique had been devised: mail-order housing.

Factory-built, prefabricated houses which could be assembled by carpenters on-site in as few as ten days were available in the late 1800s, but they did not become really popular until around 1910. By that year, Sears Roebuck, Montgomery Ward, and a variety of lumber companies had promoted them widely. This was a logical extension of the infatuation with science, technology, and efficiency that was sweeping the nation at the time.[13] By the 1920s, although significant regional variation persisted, a California bungalow in Louisville could be exactly the same house as one in Atlanta or Los Angeles.

The classic bungalow has had tremendous staying power. The combination of solid construction, pleasing looks, easy maintenance,

A craftsman bungalow in San Diego

and twentieth-century conveniences kept demand for the better bungalows strong for a long time. Some have argued that the houses built just before World War I were the best-built ever because they used "real" dimension lumber and the highest-quality materials and were designed and constructed by the last of the true craftsmen.

It should be emphasized that not all of the houses built during this period were classic bungalows or even bungalows at all. For those still demanding large two-story houses, a streamlined but boxy style emerged which has been dubbed "cubic." While such houses eliminated the fussy detail and expense of the Victorian Eclectic in favor of a more modern look, they kept a degree of formality compared to the bungalow. In addition, a very common house form throughout at least the eastern half of the nation was a style which merged some characteristics of the bungalow with those of traditional farmhouses and Victorians. For want of a better term, we may refer to this house as the American Basic. It was most often two stories tall, gable to the street, with a small front porch with matching gable. Usually, there was little, if any, design embellishment. It was a basic house. For the elite, period revival houses, especially Colonial and Tudor models, became increasingly popular after 1900, while for lower-income families, tiny bungalow cottages were constructed with minimal detail. Intraurban house-form diversity rapidly increased, and so too did the number and types of social areas or neighborhoods.

Houses of the bungalow era were built in relatively remote and protected locations compared to the houses of earlier decades. In fact, most Victorian "suburbs" were not really suburbs for long. Built along horsecar routes within two or three miles of the CBD, they were often subject to the invasion of other land uses in the decades before zoning. Since display was important, many were built on major streets, which, although quiet at the time, later filled with traffic. The rapid expansion of electric streetcar lines after 1890 (in 1890, 51 cities had electric streetcar lines, but by 1895, there were over 850 systems) meant that houses could be built much further out.

The Housing Boom of the 1920s: Period Revivals

The prosperous years of the 1920s ushered in a housing boom of unprecedented proportions. Over eight million houses were built in America during that decade. It was also the period during which the "modern" American middle-class house finally came close to being the norm. Innovations in architecture, neighborhood design, and technology were widespread. Whereas only 16 percent of the population lived in dwellings with electric lights in 1912, over 63 percent had them in 1927. The value of electrical appliances made in America increased from $23 million in 1915 to $180 million in 1929. Primitive houses were becoming a thing of the past.[14]

The typical setting and location of the middle-class house also changed significantly during the 1920s. Until the 1920s, most cities were very much star-shaped because growth occurred only along a few mass transit lines. Victorian houses had been built on the lines, while bungalows were built farther out and, as there were more of them, extended for several blocks on either side. By the 1920s, increasing automobile ownership (and in some places, the motorized bus) enabled development to occur in more isolated and protected areas and in places of greater topographic relief. More important, building codes and zoning were pioneered during this period, with the Supreme Court ruling in 1926 that single-family residential areas could be protected from all other land uses. In addition to municipal zoning, home owners' associations and developers created a number of exclusionary techniques such as minimum lot and house sizes and building costs in order to protect middle-class residential areas from change. Planned residential neighborhoods with curvilinear streets, curbside street trees, and pleasing infrastructural elements such as fancy light posts and parks, while pioneered as early as the 1860s, became common during the 1920s.

Protected residential neighborhoods were thought to be a very desirable thing by the 1920s, since automobiles, gas stations, neon signs, skyscrapers, and apartment buildings were emerging as a new genre

The staying power of the 1920s: top, *Spanish bungalows in San Diego;* bottom, *period revival houses in Columbus, Ohio*

of threats to residential serenity. In addition, massive waves of foreign immigration (though stopped in 1924) had led to large and threatening exotic slums in many cities. It was thought better not to have such places nearby. Blacks too were beginning to move to cities.

During the boom of the 1920s, regional differences in house design began to diminish and intraurban variations reached unprecedented levels as books, magazines, trade journals and mail-order companies promoted period revival housing styles nationwide. The American Institute of Architects became involved by establishing the Architects' Small House Service Bureau with the intention of making good design universal by selling plans throughout the country.

People are generally quite conservative when it comes to changes in house form. During the Classical Revival of the 1830s and 1840s, the break with the uniform row house tradition was ameliorated by the wholehearted acceptance of "civic" Greek embellishments. In England as well, freestanding houses required ties to the past. During the bungalow craze, growing scientific rationality was held in check by enthusiasm for natural and even "woodsy" materials and a back-to-nature emphasis on craftsmanship. Similarly, as houses and residential neighborhoods became increasingly "modern" during the 1920s, the popularity of a variety of tried-and-true styles from the past became dominant, including Colonial, Dutch Colonial, English Tudor, and Spanish-Italian. While these revival styles had become popular for the large estates of the wealthy as early as the turn of the century, it was during the 1920s that literally thousands of small Tudor cottages and Spanish villas appeared in middle-class communities. Modern plumbing and fake half-timbering boomed together.

While the new houses looked very traditional, most of them had to be constructed according to modern building codes and regulations. Advancements in electricity and plumbing technologies required increasing numbers of experts to install and check construction so as to minimize fire and other hazards. In addition, new materials, such as concrete and cinder blocks for foundations and stucco as a durable siding, had been developed. Houses could not only be castles, they could be built like castles.

The early years of the twentieth century represent a leap in housing form, style, technology, and location in that a 1925 house was a very different thing from an 1888 house. While in Europe and elsewhere people had lived in houses for decades or even centuries with little need for significant modification, older houses in America had suddenly become obsolete after only a very short life. Indeed, one historian of housing was moved to say: "A house twenty years old is antiquated. . . . It is likely to be of a type not easily adapted to present-day conditions of living, nor to the installment and economical use of modern equipment."[15]

One of the more important aspects of a modern house (at least by the late 1920s) was the presence of a garage. The automobile was becoming increasingly common in middle-class life, and having a place to store, work on, and, in general, care for this source of family pride was necessary. At first, garages were generally built on alleys, as far from the house as possible. In most middle-income neighborhoods, alleys, which were initially developed as the "service area"—a place for trash to be picked up and the like—were no longer essential. Metal trash cans and frequent municipal service meant that the front sidewalk could serve, especially since freestanding houses allowed for the easy outside movement of things from back to front. Backyards, which were used simply for vegetable gardens and storage, were ideal spots for the new innovation. Garages could be purchased as kits (mail-order garages) and constructed "out back." Since automobiles and the various things that were used to repair them meant storing smelly oil, gasoline, and tools, and since such materials were a very real health and fire hazard, it was thought to be a good idea to build the garage well away from the house. Still, garages were necessary, and neighborhoods with either no alleys or alleys already lined with other uses such as housing were at a distinct disadvantage in the struggle to be modern.

By the late 1920s and into the 1930s, garages were moved closer to the house, and driveways were added for access to the street in front. Garages were built with the house and in the same style. They were a source of pride rather than a back shed. This, of course, required wider lots, but it provided off-street parking for more than one car. Still, garages were separate buildings. It was not until the 1950s that they were regularly integrated into the design of the house. Garages became an important differentiating leap in housing modernity.

Not all of the houses built during the boom years of the 1920s were technologically modern, stylistically cozy, and locationally idyllic. With increasing numbers of people moving to the growing cities and increasing speculation in housing, it is no surprise that there were many jerry-built developments as well as some solid, but downsized and simple, versions of what was being built for the middle class. Many such developments occurred in relatively inaccessible locations farther from the trolley lines and in areas beyond city limits where building codes and other regulations were less restrictive. In some cases, streets were only minimally paved, if at all, and services were likewise limited. Standard lots were often subdivided so that tiny houses could be built on half-lots. Still, with population and prosperity booming, there was demand.

The Pace Slackens: Housing in the Depression

The peak year for housing during the prosperous twenties was 1925. More houses (one million) were built that year than at any previous time in the history of America, and production would not match it again until the 1950s.[16] By the late 1920s, there were signs that things were slowing down. Rampant speculation and increasing numbers of foreclosures were making house production a risky business by 1928, and in 1929, everything collapsed. Housing starts decreased by 90 percent as the Great Depression deepened, and even with the advent of public housing during the thirties, fewer than half as many houses were built in that decade as in the twenties.

The Depression sent the building industry, as well as most other industries, into shock. Recessions had occurred before, but not only were they not as severe, there simply were not as many people affected. The large increase in home ownership that had built up by the 1920s meant that a vast number of people could not make mortgage payments when the economy collapsed. Even when they could afford the payments, many people walked away from houses when they realized that they owed more on them than they were worth in a deflated market. It was better to cut losses and let the bank have it. Investment in upkeep also diminished as wages declined, and the value of houses as an investment decreased by the week. Families doubled up, and boarding houses returned to popularity.

In order to prop up the failing housing industry, the Federal Housing Authority (FHA) was created in 1934 to guarantee housing loans. Although there were limits on the size of mortgage that could be guaranteed and restrictions on the type of house appropriate for such intervention, the agency did make house construction a safer endeavor. The FHA loan program and the Veterans Administration (VA) loans created after World War II have made the federal government a major source of support for the single family house. Both have continued into the 1990s.

From a stylistic and technological standpoint, middle-class housing in the 1930s represented a gradual continuation of the trends begun earlier. As construction picked up a bit in the late 1930s, those who could afford to buy a new house often found a very good value. Since so few builders were working and since the price of materials had plummeted, houses tended to be very well-built. Extra embellishments such as large garages, fences, and built-in appliances could be added at relatively little cost. In addition, the combination of declining land values and increasing use of the automobile meant that larger lots were readily available. The year 1938 may rank with 1912 as one of the best for well-built houses in America.

Although there were unprecedented boom and bust cycles during the interwar years, it was during this period that the American suburb came into its own. Americans sought to recreate a rural and rustic world on the edges of ever-larger metropolitan areas. Urban house types were rejected in favor of "country cottages" of a variety of styles.

As housing costs have soared and highways have become congested in recent years, the new challenge may well become to redesign the American Dream with a more urban look and density.

Housing Eras and Models of City Structure

By the 1920s, American cities had become areally extensive and socially differentiated to a degree unthinkable only a few decades earlier. In less than a century, the traditional walking city had exploded into a vast network of specialized districts covering many square miles. Downtowns, industrial districts, slums, and several types of residential neighborhoods and suburbs had appeared at an altogether new scale. Vast numbers of immigrants had created "ethnic" neighborhoods, and the location and expansion of such districts was beginning to attract interest and cause concern. The internal structure or geography of the city was waiting to be described and explained.

Universities boomed during the early years of the twentieth century and, with them, the relatively new social science fields—sociology, history, geography, and urban economics. Data on population characteristics were increasingly available from the census and other sources. For the largest cities, tract-level data could be mapped. Understanding the internal structure of the city was a challenge to the emerging social sciences. Scholars at the University of Chicago led the way.

In 1925, Park, Burgess, and McKenzie published *The City*, a book which introduced the concentric zone model of internal city structure.[17] The model postulated a series of concentric rings around the CBD, with population density decreasing and social status increasing from the inner to the outer rings. This pattern was described as a process of "invasion and succession," as lower-status groups invaded and gradually took over older, higher-density neighborhoods close to employment opportunities, while those who could afford modern suburban houses and a longer commute moved to the suburbs. The "filter-down" housing market was confirmed as the normal way for lower-income groups to obtain housing. This model was widely accepted and played an important role in creating the American perception of the city as consisting of an unsavory "inner city" surrounded by pleasant green suburbs. As a product of its era, the model described many American cities pretty well in the interwar years. It is inextricably based on the built environment, a product of the successive house-form eras I have so far identified and the staying power associated with the houses and neighborhoods that resulted from them.

By today's standards, the cities of the 1920s were still small in area. The innermost zones consisted largely of the transitional zone around the downtown and the very oldest houses just beyond, usually dating from before the Civil War. As we have seen, these areas were out of date from technological, social, and locational standpoints. The houses usually had no indoor plumbing, no electricity, and inadequate kitchens. They had very likely been subdivided and overcrowded for generations and, before zoning, used for a variety of economic activities as well. The row and semi-row houses in these areas did not conform at all to the growing preference for a rural ambiance. Compared to the middle-class housing norm of the 1920s, these neighborhoods were indeed slums.

The Victorian house was also aging rapidly by the 1920s. Indeed, Hollywood films from as early as the interwar era often depicted Victorian mansions as haunted houses or mysterious places inhabited by a spooky recluse. Victorian houses were not only formal, stuffy, and technologically out of date, but they were also incredibly expensive to maintain. Painting a complex Victorian house often meant spending a sum equivalent to one-fifth of the value of the house during this period. Intricate, multiple roofs often leaked, and repairing them was difficult and expensive. The large size of Victorian houses and their many special-purpose rooms made them ripe for subdivision into boarding houses, especially as typical family size decreased. They were too large to maintain without servants, and so they were often simply not maintained. Also, since such houses were often built on or near major streets, they were subject to increasing noise and pollution as automobiles, trucks, and buses began to clog the main arterials. In addition, a location on main streets made them ripe for conversion to commercial uses. Thus, in the concentric zone model, the ring of lower-middle-class residents often living at moderately high densities in boarding houses could easily be associated with Victorian house types.

Farther out, the next ring or two consisted of bungalows. Socioeconomically, these zones were described in the model as solidly working-class to middle-class. While bungalows were still considered to be modern houses by the 1920s, they were often built on small lots with no space for the automobile and located in relatively accessible (i.e., unprotected) locations.

The outermost "suburban" rings consisted of the romantic period revival styles and the rustic planned neighborhoods coming into vogue in the 1920s. In most cities, such neighborhoods were only five or so miles from the city center, and access was possible by streetcar as well as the automobile. For a variety of reasons, the outer zones constituted a very different world from the inner rings, but differences in house type alone could explain much of the model.

By 1939, when Homer Hoyt postulated the sector model of city structure, things were beginning to change.[18] A downtown building boom in the late 1920s and massive urban renewal and highway projects in the 1930s had cleared a substantial amount of the very oldest inner-ring housing. The poorest people were having to seek locations elsewhere, such as in the newly developed public housing projects. In addition, it was becoming increasingly evident that some housing, especially housing built in the twentieth century, was not filtering down but, rather, seemed to be remaining desirable indefinitely.

The sector model suggests that groups defined by socioeconomic status and/or ethnicity tend to move outward in well-defined sectors, usually along transit lines. Since people tend to seek new housing within their sector rather than by moving across town, the length of a sector is a function of the demand for new housing within it. Higher-status sectors tend to generate large numbers of households seeking to move up, and thus, new construction tends to be concentrated on the outer edges of such areas. On the other hand, working-class sectors tend to be more stable, since typical family incomes peak earlier, and households tend to remain in their communities longer. Since higher-status families move up the fastest, the largest number of vacancies available for the filter-down housing market appear in that sector, leading to an invasion of lower-income groups in the older neighborhoods. In 1939, this meant that some of the oldest row house neighborhoods in the working-class sector were remaining working-class while Victorians further out in the "good sector" were being subdivided for low-income tenements. Cities were becoming increasingly asymmetrical, bulging ever outward along some sectors while new construction lagged in others.

In some cases, relatively simple patterns resulted from a combination of very different processes. For example, a concentric ring of less desirable housing could result from the vacancy chains in one or more "good" sectors as described above, coupled with newly built marginal housing in less accessible interstitial areas between them. Thus, the inner city might contain everything from very old urban housing to very new (but poorly built) semirural housing. Maps of income and housing value sometimes mask differences in housing and neighborhood formation.

While both the concentric zone and the sector models are still being taught and each can still offer insight into the processes shaping the city, they are very much time-specific. They describe the American city as it existed in the 1920s or the 1930s but not necessarily as it exists today. To a very real degree, the ecological models postulated in the interwar years described the histories of the housing eras which had occurred up to that point. However, since the relationship between the evolution of housing during specific eras and models of city structure was rarely, if ever, made explicit, the models tended to gain a permanence and universality that may be inappropriate. For example, since World War II, houses and cities have changed.

The Postwar Housing Boom

Housing starts plummeted from an all-time high of nearly 940,000 in 1925 to only 93,000 in 1933, and production remained low in spite of a mini-boom between 1938 and 1941. As defaults and foreclosures increased, the percentage of nonfarm families owning homes decreased from a high of 47 percent in 1930 to 41 percent in 1940. With the onset of World War II, there was no chance to increase house production. While some military housing was constructed during this period, the private production of single-family homes almost stopped between 1941 and 1946. In spite of the tremendous pent-up demand caused by the Depression and continued by the war, caution prevailed in the years immediately after the cessation of hostilities.

House production in the years just after the war picked up where it had left off in 1941. In many cases, houses were built on the edges of the same neighborhoods where construction had taken place in the late 1930s, although because of the increased cost of labor and materials, these houses were sometimes smaller and less detailed. As the 1950s approached, however, the floodgates opened, and housing production reached new record levels. It was time for a new round in the "cult of domesticity." After nearly two decades of economic abnormality, America was ready for the true mass production of houses, neighborhoods, and lifestyles.

New materials and construction technologies had been developed in the 1930s and early 1940s—such as plywood, concrete slab foundations, prefabricated window units and other components, drywall and plasterboard, and aluminum sliding glass doors— but they were little used in those decades. By the 1950s, however, the need to keep costs low through the use of modern materials and mass production was important, since the cost of an average house more than doubled between 1940 and 1950. In addition, architects and developers were caught up in the Modern movement by the 1950s (although not to the degree that the designers of commercial properties were), and many felt that excessively romantic frills should be eliminated for the sake of

Post–World War II starter homes in Columbus, Ohio

streamlined beauty regardless of the cost considerations. Some architects felt that the new building materials and technologies themselves would define beauty. Less was more.

The Housing Act of 1949 was passed by the federal government in order to guarantee builders and bankers more substantial profits on large developments, and in 1950 more than one million new units were started. Whereas up until the 1930s "builders" created most new housing by purchasing a few lots at a time on the edge of the expanding city, by the 1950s housing production had become integrated as well as enlarged. This decade saw the emergence of "developers" like William Levitt & Sons, who were able to handle every aspect of housing production. They purchased vast tracts of land (aided by the capital accumulation and the low interest rates that resulted from wartime spending restrictions and forced savings), put in the streets and other elements of the infrastructure, and then built thousands of units of new, homogeneous houses. The concept was pioneered in Levittown on Long Island, as 17,000 houses were constructed in one massive development. Borrowing from the "New Town" ideas of the 1930s, these new suburban tracts were to be less dependent on existing towns and cities. They were to have their own planned commercial nodes as well as churches, schools, and recreation areas. The size and relative remoteness of such projects made the ownership of at least one automobile a prerequisite and created a certain isolation for those, such as housewives, without one.

The increased cost of materials, labor, and the new desired technologies, including modern appliances, meant that houses had to be downsized in order to be affordable. The houses of the late 1940s and early 1950s were about 12 percent smaller than those built ten years earlier. In addition, many of the frills—porches, garages, formal dining rooms, and fireplaces—were eliminated in order to cut costs. The typical house had just under 1,000 square feet, and many "economy houses" had as little as 650 square feet.

In order to make small houses liveable in the midst of an unprecedented baby boom, some aspects of the traditional house had to be redesigned. While the exteriors of postwar houses remained mostly traditional, with streamlined versions of Cape Cod colonial and the ranch being the most popular among both buyers and lending agencies, the interiors changed more dramatically. In order to make houses seem more spacious, rooms were opened up, windows were enlarged (picture windows), and sliding glass doors leading to an outside patio were added. The kitchen emerged from its relative isolation as a service adjunct to the living space of the house to become a sort of command center around which domestic life evolved. The new kitchen had visual and physical access to an informal dining area and the living room. Colorful, shiny new appliances allowed the kitchen to be more presentable than in the past. Small "utility rooms" were added next to the kitchen to house the new washing machines (and later, dryers) so that the modern housewife could cook, wash, watch television, and supervise children from one well-designed command post. Only the bedrooms were cut off from this center as (potentially) quiet places. Most houses had two bedrooms and one bathroom.

While the actual space of these new "ranches" was quite limited, the potential space was much larger. The tremendous increase in automobile use made formerly remote and inexpensive land desirable, and so, compared to lots in the city, suburban lots were large, often over 10,000 square feet. Garages, tool sheds, playrooms, covered patios, and even additions to the house could be added later. Some houses featured attics or basements that could be converted to living space when time and money allowed. The attraction of the new miniranches and vast suburban developments cannot be fully understood without a review of the social and demographic picture of the 1950s.

The "Leave It to Beaver" World of the 1950s

The suburban boom of the 1950s was a direct product of the pent-up demand generated during the 1930s and 1940s. During the Depression years, people deferred marriage in favor of simple survival, while the war years meant long periods of separation and enforced saving because many consumer products were unavailable. When ten million men and women were discharged from the military during 1945 and 1946, a huge housing shortage developed. Two and a half million families doubled up with relatives, while millions more lived in Quonset huts, trailers, converted garages, and even barns. Older boarding houses were often bursting at the seams. The tremendous demand for suburban housing was as much due to the fact that there was simply no room in the city, as it was to dissatisfaction with urban life. Most older American central cities (which have been unable to annex new territories) peaked in population and population density around the time of the 1950 census. While the subsequent plummeting of population has been described as "flight" to the suburbs, to a very real degree it represented the thinning out of quarters that had become seriously overcrowded during preceding decades. Cities, it seems, cannot win. They went from "teeming and overcrowded" to "declining and dying," as population first bulged and then thinned.

As affordable suburban housing became available, long-deferred family formation followed. The number of marriages increased dramatically, reaching a peak of 4.3 million in 1957, while the birthrate soared from 2.2 births per woman in the 1930s to 3.5 in the late 1950s. Pregnancy was referred to as "the Levittown look."[19] Twenty million women who had been employed during the labor shortages of the war years either left jobs voluntarily or were fired or demoted during the late 1940s in order to make jobs available for returning GIs. Rosie the Riveter became Harriet the Housewife. Some feminists have argued that the cult of domesticity that exploded during the immediate postwar years was one last attempt to keep women in their place. Never before had the power of the media been used so significantly in the creation of a new definition of family life.

The media portrayal of the typical American household in the 1950s was the "normal" family of mom, dad, two or three children, a station wagon, and a dog. Magazines, newspapers, advertisers, and the powerful new medium of television all offered a barrage of images in support of this norm. Advertisers emphasized the fun of being a happy housewife by showing women using cleaning products with names like "Joy" while having pleasant chats with "Mr. Clean." Television sitcoms such as "Ozzie and Harriet" entertained millions with stories based on everyday life in the suburbs. A vast array of new appliances and gadgets—televisions, stereos, power mowers, dryers, lawn furniture, and sprinkler systems—took most of the family budget. The American Dream revolved around families getting things for the house.

Much of this dream was directly supported by government policies and subsidies. The FHA mortgage guarantee program was joined in 1944 by VA programs that made it possible for veterans to buy a house with no down payment. This had the effect of propping up the emerging suburban lifestyle. Low-interest loans (often less than 5 percent) were widely available during the 1950s, and the interest could be deducted on one's income tax. Some have even argued that the federal government sought to create an America of isolated, "do-it-yourself" suburban households in order to diminish the threat of world communism during the McCarthy era of the early 1950s. Levitt himself explained that suburban homeowners would be far too busy to become communists.

One big problem with the American Dream as defined above is that not everyone could play. Minorities were largely excluded from participating in the suburban housing boom. Lenders, as well as government mortgage insurers such as the FHA and VA, required that participating houses and neighborhoods be good investments. Racially integrated neighborhoods were not viewed as good investments. Older houses were often not eligible either, since structural characteristics were often a problem. The white middle class moved to the suburbs, while blacks, Hispanics, female-headed households, and the poor stayed in the city and rented or purchased older houses using higher-cost financing. The inner city expanded as a geographically separated dual housing market became more pronounced.

To a very real degree, the poor headed for older housing. The Depression and the war years had meant deferred maintenance on most of the housing stock. The newer period revival houses of the 1920s did not yet need much refurbishing, but houses built in the nineteenth century did. Complex Victorian structures in particular suffered mightily from lack of paint, new roofing, and the addition of modern amenities. By the 1950s, Victorian housing was often seen as slum housing to be subdivided, milked, and abandoned. In many cities, the worst ghettos were carved out of the most ornate mansions.

The Star-Shaped City and the Suburb

Although the points of the star had thickened during the "recreational auto" interwar years as suburban neighborhoods were added on either side of the old streetcar lines, the city of 1950 was still basically star-shaped. This helped to make the tremendous housing explosion of the postwar years possible. The massive suburban developments of the 1950s were often located in interstitial areas between the prongs of the star. They were consequently close to the still-important shopping and office core in the CBD as well as to existing schools and recreation facilities. Since the vast housing tract was still a new idea for the middle class in the 1950s, it was comforting to be close to the family, church, shops, and jobs in the "old neighborhood." In addition, it was easier to enlarge the capacities of existing schools and recreation centers than to build new ones all at once during the immediate postwar boom.

Mobility was a problem as well. Although automobile ownership increased rapidly, highway construction did not keep pace. Before the passage of the Interstate Highway Act in 1956, expressways were rare, and commuters fought their way in and out of town on the old commercial strips. It was hard to live too far out. In all but the very largest cities, most new houses were built within eight or ten miles of the city center. When freeway construction began in the late 1950s, new routes were often located between the old "star points" and the new interstitial developments. We shall see the significance of this a bit later.

By the mid-1950s, the initial pent-up demand for middle-class housing generated during the war had begun to diminish, and a "move-up" market was starting to appear as the first wave of suburbanites sought larger, prettier houses. The filter-down housing market did not work well in the late 1940s and early 1950s because many people had doubled up or lived in temporary, makeshift housing before buying a tract home. Thus, the previous residences were not available to lower-income occupants upon the departure of their middle-class residents. By the late 1950s, however, some families were ready to move up to a new and improved version of suburbia, leaving behind relatively new houses for the next aspiring suburbanites.

Suburbia Matures: The Changing Organization of the House

By 1960, the minimal ranches and Cape Cods of the immediate postwar years had given way to larger, better-decorated houses built in a greater variety of styles. By the mid-1960s, the average house had increased to about 1,500 square feet, and some of the rooms which had been eliminated in the minimal houses of earlier years returned. Dining rooms were added to the bigger houses although informal eating areas often remained. Three bedrooms became the standard as well as two or more bathrooms (necessary as teenagers grew older). In some cases, "family rooms" or dens added recreational space to the house.

The front porch did not return, since its recreational function had been taken over by a combination of television and air-conditioned dens and since it did not fit the streamlined look of the ranch. It was viewed as an unnecessary expense. The social function of the porch, however, was not replaced, and it is probable that neighborhood inter-

The ranch house of the late 1950s: Columbus, Ohio

action has declined since the elimination of a place to sit and chat with passers-by.

The garage, however, came back with a vengeance. Many of the smaller houses of the 1950s had either no garage at all or just a "carport" to at least keep the automobile out of the sun and rain. When garages became the norm in the late 1950s, they became integrated into the total design of the house as never before. When put next to (rather than behind) the house under the same roofline, a one- or two-car garage could make a modest house seem huge. Placing the garage further up front on the lot also saved the expense of a long, paved driveway and helped to eliminate the land-consuming alley from suburbia. By the mid-1950s, the garage was placed in front of the house so that the increasingly unutilized front yard took up only half of the lot. I have dubbed this house form the GDL—the garage-dominant "L." The house facade receded in importance as the garage door became the most dominant visual element on the street. This suited the architectural minimalism of the 1950s. Longer cars and shorter driveways, however, meant that automobiles usually hung out over the sidewalk. Fortunately, few people strolled on the sidewalks anymore. Putting the garage at the front of the house made an important statement about the role of the car in American society.

Inside access to the garage via the kitchen or laundry room also became important as the garage was sanitized and dry-walled into a place for activities other than those associated with the automobile.

Often, cars were kept outside, and the garage was given over to storage or converted to a bedroom for the expanding family. The garage became an important part of the house both stylistically and functionally.

By 1960, the backyard was fully developed as a recreation zone devoid of automobiles, garages, and the disamenities associated with alleys. Swimming pools, barbecue pits, and badminton courts took over the space not used for trees and flowers. The back garden was no longer a "yard." Social life once associated with the front porch or stoop retreated to the rear of the house. People who sat out front next to the driveway in the evening were considered weird indeed.

As middle-class people moved up to larger homes, smaller postwar houses became available to "working-class" (white) families from urban neighborhoods. Americans became famous for moving constantly, and many smaller houses were advertised as "starter homes" as though they were only meant to be a first step on the road to the American Dream. Rather than expanding these houses by adding a garage or covered patio, people simply moved on. Many of these houses suffered in the process, as three or four families (usually with small children and at least one dog) passed through them in the course of a decade. While houses built during the boom years of the late 1920s were often greatly improved and otherwise cared for over the years, since there was no chance to move up for over two decades, houses built in the 1950s sometimes suffered as owners deferred maintenance in order to save money for a down payment for a new or larger house.

In the prosperous 1960s, suburban houses became bigger and more lavish. A filter-down market developed, with an ever-larger percentage of urban families moving through a variety of postwar suburban developments. As the 1960s eased into the 1970s, a serious problem developed in the central cities because of decreasing demand for space in older housing. Large developers, government insurers, lenders, highway engineers, and almost everyone else involved in creating suburbia continued to push the limits of the metropolitan areas outward. By 1970, too many houses had been constructed. Older houses in less desirable areas were simply abandoned. Many of these houses had had little or no maintenance through the Depression and war years and were in terrible condition. Housing abandonment became increasingly noticeable after the Civil Rights Act of 1968 somewhat mitigated the processes of ghetto formation that had kept blacks and other minorities locked in inner-city slums for so long. By the time middle-class blacks were ready to move to the suburbs, there was no one left to take their places (which made it harder for many families to move up).

Another factor lessening demand for older houses after about 1958 was the urban and suburban apartment boom. Large apartment complexes had been a relatively unimportant part of the total housing stock in most American cities until the end of the 1950s. Indeed, between about 1928 and 1958, private capital gravitated almost exclusively to the single-family house. By the 1960s, however, apartment construction was in full swing, especially around growing universities, hospital complexes, shopping malls, and other sources of employment. Young people were leaving home earlier, and high rates of divorce and interurban mobility meant that short-term accommodations were in demand. Instead of staying at a lodging house or renting a room in an older house, people took an apartment. The inner city continued to thin out. By the early 1970s, there were thousands of abandoned houses in cities such as New York, St. Louis, and Detroit. Middle-class America was suburban, and in some cities, the working class was becoming so as well. Only in cities with large numbers of Latino and/or Asian immigrants is widespread demand for inner-city housing still strong.

Houses as Investments: The Impact on House Form

For over three decades, from the mid-1950s to the mid-1980s, single-family houses continued to get bigger and more complex. Indeed, it seems that the house has gone through 100-year cycles since the 1780s. It gradually became larger and more complex until it peaked in size with the Victorian eclectic in the 1880s—a house type which featured special rooms for every activity and a size and appearance designed to impress all who saw it. Middle-class houses with more than 4,000 square feet were not unusual, especially if basements and attics were figured in. From the 1890s until the 1950s, houses tended to become smaller and more streamlined, with fewer special-purpose rooms. The trend toward smaller houses troughed in the early 1950s with minimal ranches of well under 1,000 square feet. Since then, special-function rooms, including everything from saunas to computer rooms, have returned, and houses have become large and impressive once more. By the 1980s, average suburban houses had about 2,000 square feet of space. Today, with outrageous home prices in many areas, there are signs that the demand for smaller, more efficient houses may once more be increasing.

In recent years, however, the trend toward ever-larger houses has been fueled as much by market value as use value. Until the 1970s, the trends in size and design were closely related to the characteristics of the occupants of typical houses. As families became affluent and "cultured" during the mid-1800s, for example, there was a need for servants' quarters and space for nurturing children away from the perceived chaos of the city; but as family size and the use of servants declined in the twentieth century, houses could become smaller with no sacrifice in liveability. When vast numbers of GIs returned after World War II and needed someplace to live, minimal houses could serve the purpose, but as the baby boom progressed, larger houses with more recreation space were desired. It all made sense from a use-value standpoint.

Since the mid-1970s, however, the role of houses in America has changed. The percentage of "married with children" households has dropped to only about 25 percent of the total, and household size is smaller than ever. More women than ever before work outside the home, and the combination of work and leisure activities means that many people are rarely at home. Even small children have lessons to take, malls to visit, and Little League. Houses, it seems, can now at last be small, compact, and "scientifically" designed for those with a busy schedule. They are not. From the mid-1970s on, houses have been designed as much for investment as use.

While houses have always been considered good investments, in reality they have not always been. Until the 1960s, houses often increased in value only very slowly, and during economic recessions they sometimes lost value. Even boom towns like Seattle saw people walk away from mortgages during the Boeing crisis of the early 1970s. From the mid-1970s until the late 1980s, however, housing values skyrocketed in nearly every urban area. There were a number of reasons for this, many of them having little or nothing to do with a real need for residential space. Much of the story has to do with inflation.

An inflationary spiral began in the late 1960s when the government attempted to pay for the war in Vietnam by printing money rather than by raising taxes. As the rate of inflation increased during the late 1960s and into the mid-1970s, the machinery set up during the 1930s and 1940s to spur housing construction (for example, FHA and VA loans and tax deductions) became increasingly unnecessary. Savings and loan institutions were required to lend money over long periods of time at low interest rates and also to pay relatively low interest rates to investors. As the rate of inflation rose above the mortgage interest rate, it made no sense to save money. People were advised to buy something, anything! Since larger, more expensive houses increased in absolute value more than smaller houses, it made sense to buy a big house. This was especially the case because mortgage interest was still

completely deductible from income tax obligations, and many affluent people simply needed someplace to shelter income. This trend
had a negative impact on the less desirable (especially minority) areas
of the city, since wealthy people moved not only to find better houses
but also to find better investments. The rich could make hundreds of
thousands of dollars just by moving around. The poor could not, and
the gap widened.

Until at least the late 1980s, houses continued to increase in size.
The popularity of the one-story ranch from the 1950s on required
ever-wider lots, since this house was typically built with the gables (or
hips) to the side. Usually, the front facade consisted of a large picture
window, an elaborate doorway, a multicar garage, and perhaps some
smaller windows. A large proportion of the front yard (in front of the
garage) was paved, and the backyard was free for recreation. More
remote suburban locations were required for such large lots. By the
1970s, the cost of land as a percentage of the total house was rapidly
increasing in many urban areas, and so the ranch had to be modified in
order to use space more efficiently. This was a difficult task because
much of the postwar housing ideology had stressed the benefits of
living in a one-story, "open" floor plan with one room conveniently
leading to the next. Life in a ranch meant not having to climb stairs
and deal with claustrophobic spaces of any kind. As the demand for
big houses was matched by the increased cost of land, however, the
two-story house made a comeback. House design became more complex; postmodern romanticism emerged as the guiding ideology. Period revival detailing (Spanish, Tudor, etc.) and colors appeared, and
the rooflines and massing became more intricate. In areas with extremely high land costs, such as California, many of the new houses
seemed wildly out of scale, bulging over the entire lot as if ready to
explode. The ostentation of the Victorian eclectic was back, although
the families in the new house type were smaller than ever (an average
household size of about 2.7 by 1980) and had much less time to be
nurtured at home as adults worked to make the house payments.

Urban Morphology and the New Suburbs

The spatial character of suburbia changed dramatically by the late
1960s and early 1970s. As the freeway system (usually including an
outer belt) was completed and as interstitial land between the star
points was filled in, new suburban houses had to be built much further out. This was especially true since much of the land near the
outer belts tended to be given over to more profitable uses than the
single-family house. Shopping centers, office parks, car dealerships,
warehouses, and high-density apartment and condominium com-

plexes followed the freeways and often formed a ring around the city and its older suburbs by the 1970s. As profitable space-extensive activities such as office and industrial parks became commonplace, land costs in relatively accessible locations soared. In order to have large lots, many developments had to be located a long way from the center city. Before 1973, this was acceptable, since both automobiles and energy were incredibly cheap and the newly constructed freeway system was seldom used to full capacity.

The provision of large single-family homes became more problematic by the late 1980s as housing prices leveled off and as fuel costs and the costs of expanding urban services to remote locations suggested that the trend could not go on forever. In some of the largest cities, a trend toward building smaller houses on the edge of the metropolitan area developed while at least some capital migrated toward renovating and rebuilding houses in more central locations. Older houses, especially those with aesthetic and technological "staying power" located in accessible, protected neighborhoods, stopped filtering down (if they ever had) and began to skyrocket in value. Thus, the deteriorated inner city has come to be at least partially encircled by a zone of permanently elite areas. While it is an extreme example, this phenomenon can be dubbed the "Beverly Hills Syndrome." In Washington, D.C., for example, nice neighborhoods inside the beltway are in great demand as commuting long distances becomes unbearable.

Historic Preservation and "Bulkification": Recent Trends in Gentrification and House Form Change

The tremendous suburban expansion of the 1950s and 1960s and the resulting overbuilding of houses led to a lot of undervalued real estate. Since the prices of even new houses tended to be stable during this period (as supply kept up with demand), older houses that had been poorly maintained and were not up to code lost value dramatically. In many cities, older houses could not be sold for an amount equal to the taxes owed on them, and so owners simply walked away. Financial institutions redlined many older areas, refusing to lend money for mortgages on houses that did not meet current standards. In effect, such houses could not be sold except for cash. Houses built in the nineteenth century before the technological leap of the early 1900s were most affected. The costs of adding modern plumbing and electricity exceeded the value of the houses.

By the mid-1960s, there were signs that the demand for at least a small segment of this older housing was beginning to increase. The combination of inexpensive city housing and increasing community awareness of historic architecture led to the tentative beginnings of

Society Hill, Philadelphia

what has been dubbed "gentrification," or the filtering *up* of houses and neighborhoods as increasingly affluent people move into under-valued real estate. Early attempts at residential restoration were prob-ably more romantic than economic, since there was no assurance that such efforts would later be deemed a good investment. By the 1970s, however, restoration had become a nationwide phenomenon.[20]

The revitalization of urban housing can be divided into two stages: historic preservation and bulkification. While both processes involve the movement of affluent people and capital into undervalued hous-ing, the ideologies and the urban design guidelines associated with them can be very different. Historic preservation efforts began in the early 1960s when cities were expanding wildly but much central city housing was being ignored. In order to attract people and investment to older neighborhoods, ideologies were developed that had little di-rect relationship to real estate speculation. During the earliest stages, the two major themes were architectural and social.

The "architectural" pioneers emphasized the need to preserve the architectural treasures that gave a city its past and its sense of place. Historic districts were created which, though usually quite small, displayed some of the earliest and quaintest houses in the city. Often, special festivals and entertainment districts were developed to attract skeptical visitors to the area and get them enthused. Home tours were used to demonstrate what could be done with older houses. In some cases, city funds were used to upgrade the neighborhood infrastruc-

German Village, Columbus, Ohio: revitalization through historic preservation

ture and to help display "history." Architectural guidelines were often introduced in order to ensure that restorations, if not historically authentic, were at least in keeping with the "official past" that was on display.

The early revitalization efforts associated with historic preservation required a lot of publicity because the housing involved was often in very poor shape and almost valueless. In the German Village Historic District of Columbus, Ohio, for example, a house without indoor plumbing or electricity sold for about $600 in the early 1960s. Today, there is little available in the neighborhood for less than $100,000. From Charleston, South Carolina, to Santa Fe, New Mexico, historic preservation and architectural conservation played major roles in the initial stages of housing revitalization during the 1960s and early 1970s. People needed to be convinced that living in a house built before the turn-of-the-century "leap" in technology meant living a historic lifestyle that was interesting and perhaps even good for the city. By the late 1970s, housing in most cities had become so expensive that the hoopla associated with historic preservation was rarely needed to attract investment.

The second theme associated with early preservation efforts was social. The restoration of older inner-city housing was seen as an emblem of counterculture ideals, a rejection of suburban homogeneity. Artists, gays, hippies, perpetual students, and political activists

CITIES AND BUILDINGS

"Bulkification" in San Diego: new, giant houses built on small lots in old neighborhoods

all found "affordable digs" and a place to be creative in older houses which could be modified and upgraded gradually. As preservation efforts succeeded, rents went up and yuppies replaced hippies.

By the mid-1980s a new phenomenon was under way in many central cities: the building (or rebuilding) of huge new houses on small but desirable urban lots ("bulkification"). While preservation efforts tended to focus on very cheap, unmodernized housing built during the nineteenth century, bulkification is associated more with the relatively stable bungalow and period revival house of the early to middle twentieth century. While it has long been common for relatively affluent people to purchase and gradually expand and upgrade such houses, the increased difficulties of long-distance commuting to remote suburbs have caused many to look for lots in older but still quite desirable neighborhoods in order to build truly monumental new houses. Such lots usually contain an existing small house. After purchase, the small house is removed and a larger one is built in its place. (Sometimes a small piece of the old house, such as a fireplace or one existing wall is left in order for the owner to be assessed for a remodel rather than a new house.)

This is a new phenomenon and one associated mainly with high-cost areas such as California and with a few older, but very desirable residential neighborhoods elsewhere. In the past, single-family houses were often enlarged with added rooms here and there, but if they were torn down, they were usually replaced by "higher and better" uses such as apartments or offices. Rarely were houses torn down and replaced by houses. Today, strict zoning and property tax policies, combined with neighborhood political power, often protect older neighborhoods from nonconforming uses. In such protected and desirable neighborhoods, massive houses—often with more than 10,000 square feet of space and covering as much of the lot as the law will allow—are replacing more modest ones from earlier eras. Since such mansions usually replace existing nice houses, the stock of houses is not increased, and social segregation becomes more extreme as the better neighborhoods get the investment. From an urban process standpoint, such rebuilding represents a complete reversal of the filter-down idea, as what is nice stays nice. Many accessible older neighborhoods are now rapidly filtering up.

House Improvement and Conflict: Personal Statements in the Residential Landscape

Much has been written about the social conflicts and displacement that can result from excessive and/or overly concentrated gentrification efforts. While most North American central cities remain predominantly low-income in comparison with suburbs, some very interesting aesthetic conflicts have arisen when poorer old and wealthier new residents in a neighborhood exhibit different landscape (house form) tastes.

In cities such as Philadelphia and Toronto, for example, young, relatively affluent gentrifiers have attempted to create codes that would encourage if not require residents to remove nonconforming accretions such as aluminum awnings and siding from older houses in "historic" neighborhoods. While the gentrifiers prefer a landscape of exposed brick, subdued colors, neat lawns without fences, and tasteful lamps, the older (often ethnic) residents may prefer such modern embellishments as sliding glass doors, bright colors, elaborate fences enclosing vegetable gardens, and perhaps a statue or two of the Virgin Mary by the front steps. When a wide variety of people all wishing to make statements with their housescapes begin competing for the same neighborhoods, some interesting aesthetic issues can arise. Rarely is a house simply a functional shelter.

Conflict can also occur in areas with extreme upgrading and bulkification. Not only do residents of long-stable neighborhoods often view massive change of any kind with a great deal of alarm, but in these cases, views and privacy are sometimes diminished and the genteel pace of life is threatened by high ostentation. The literature is full of studies of neighborhood and housing decline, but the future may call for more balance.

Regional House Prices and the Urban Landscape

By the 1980s, regional variations in urban house prices became pronounced. Although the cost of houses had increased everywhere during the inflationary 1970s, prices stabilized in many urban areas after 1980 while in others they continued to soar. Part of this reflected the greater demand for houses in certain cities, especially in the Sunbelt, but much of it reflected different investment strategies as international and intranational capital increasingly flowed to "hot markets." Los Angeles attracts such capital while Detroit does not. In addition, much of the variation in prices reflects the fact that different cities have different housing stocks and that those housing stocks have been differentially maintained in recent decades.

Most attempts to analyze the differences in house prices from one urban area to another have emphasized macro variables such as the strength of the regional economy, differential population growth and migration (Sunbelt/Snowbelt), and the employment mix in particular cities (Boston vs. Detroit); however, much of the variation has to do with the differing character of the housing stocks themselves and with micro variables such as physical site and urban morphology. Cities do not all look alike, and neither are they organized in exactly the same way. To illustrate this more fully, let us examine and compare the trends in several central city areas.

Boston, St. Louis, and San Diego are cities with very different housing stocks as well as very different housing prices. A problem that often emerges in trying to sort out the interurban variations in housing characteristics is the tremendous variation in the areal extent of cities and metropolitan areas. It is difficult to compare the average house in, say, Newark (with 24 square miles) to that in Oklahoma City (with over 600 square miles), since the former city consists of little more than the downtown and a few older residential and industrial districts, while the latter contains vast suburban and even rural areas. In order to examine the relationship between housing stock and socio-economic factors more consistently from city to city, I have identified core areas for each of the urban areas to be examined consisting of roughly 12 square miles around the CBD. This will allow us to separate, to some degree, the character of the housing stock from location, since only inner-city housing is examined. Still, some startling differences emerge in the 1980 census (Table 3).[21]

Additional insight into the meaning of these figures emerges if we

Table 3. Housing characteristics in selected core areas (1980 census)

City core	Population	No. of housing units	Average value
Boston	192,000	92,000	$55,000
St. Louis	84,000	41,000	$20,000
San Diego	104,000	55,000	$80,000

examine change over time. While the figures for the core areas of both Boston and San Diego were very similar in 1960 and in 1980 (except that the housing values in 1960 were much lower—$11,000 and $13,000, respectively), the core of St. Louis has changed dramatically. In 1960, there were over 200,000 people living there, in 72,000 housing units with an average value of $8,000. Obviously, many of the differences between these three cities have to do with such things as relative growth rates over time, employment opportunities, and differing governmental policies such as those involving clearance versus preservation. Still, the differing character of the housing stocks did play some role.

The core area of Boston was largely built before the Civil War and includes many "London style" townhouses in Beacon Hill, Bunker Hill, and Back Bay (as well as some very early houses in neighborhoods such as the North End that were originally multipurpose structures). In addition, there has been much gradual in-fill. The large, elegant townhouses of Boston have been largely converted to flats. The combination of the large size and solid construction of the buildings, as well as the preservation policies of residents and government over time (which has meant that buildings have generally been well-maintained), has enabled much of the early housing to remain valuable. The houses are big enough and pretty enough to pay their way, making a preservation ethic possible. The leadership of Boston remained in the center of the city to a degree unusual in American cities.

St. Louis was put together in a very different manner. While central St. Louis consisted of vast tracts of small working-class row houses modeled after those of northern England, the growth of the city and its transportation system after the Civil War enabled the elite to move outward toward Victorian districts near Forest Park. The industrial-looking inner city went into decline even before World War II, as the small row houses were seen as inflexible, obsolete space. Many were cleared. By 1980, the low value of the houses ($20,000) and the fact that they were too small to convert to multifamily use made renovation difficult. In addition, lenders had long redlined central St. Louis, making mortgages nearly impossible to obtain. Both population and numbers of housing units therefore plummeted.

San Diego is a different kind of city. The very oldest houses in central San Diego date from the boom of the 1880s. While these Victorians have had a bumpy road, with many falling into decay only to be renovated later for offices or bed and breakfast inns, the vast majority of houses in the core area are bungalows from the early decades of the century. Most of them have spacious gardens and room for the automobile. Although many original houses have been destroyed for apartment and condominium complexes, gradual expansion and upgrading of houses has been the norm. Second-story additions, multilevel decks, patios with pools and spas, and even total redesign have all been commonplace. Since housing is so valuable, renovation is worth the money. Houses in central San Diego are only slightly less valuable than the metropolitan average. They are seen as modern, flexible, and salvageable. In contrast, houses in central St. Louis are worth only about one-quarter of the metropolitan average. Clearly, not all of the differences in housing value from city to city are due to regional economic trends.

In San Diego, housing is valuable because it is valued. That is, because it is seen as a good investment, people have spent immense sums of money upgrading it. In many nicer, older neighborhoods, it is rare to find a house that has not been greatly enlarged and modified, and so the value goes up. We need to know a great deal more about interurban variations in the urban housing stock as well as the types of changes that have occurred over time before we can compare cities in a meaningful way. There are a number of ways to begin.

Merging House Type and Census Information

While the population and housing census provide much useful information on socioeconomic characteristics of urban areas, they give little insight into what houses and neighborhoods actually look like. In order to merge socioeconomic variables and aesthetic and technological variables, we must look at other sources of data. A major problem in doing this is the lack of comparable data for different cities. Some excellent sets of air photos from various points in time exist for some cities, and these can be invaluable in showing the degree of improvement in houses and lots (additions, pools, decks, etc.) as well as the variations in lot size and vegetation. For other cities, however, no such air photos exist (or those that do may be at the wrong scale).

Sanborn Maps, usually dating from the early years of the twentieth century and updated through the 1940s or 1950s, can provide excellent information on house size, lot size, land use, and other neighborhood characteristics as well as providing information on change over time. Originally designed to help fire departments know the territory by showing land uses and routes between buildings, these maps provide detailed footprints of the built environment. Sometimes neighborhoods with very similar census characteristics at any one point in time have very different Sanborn footprints. In addition, many differences in neighborhood character can be explained by careful examination of such maps. Maps kept by city and county assessors are similarly useful.

Neither air photos nor Sanborn Maps provide much information on the aesthetic and technological details of houses. For these characteristics, one of the best sources is the *Multiple Listing Service Guide*, published monthly for the real estate industry. While current copies of these guides are valuable and difficult to come by, old ones are useless for sales agents but still provide valuable historical information. Since these guides include pictures of the houses for sale as well as many details on size and amenities, house types can be classified and mapped for any given city with some precision. Assuming that houses that are for sale at any one time provide a fairly random sample of the houses in a neighborhood, we can use the guide to "look" at the houses throughout a city and to develop appropriate typologies. This has been done for Columbus and San Diego.[22]

In each of these two cities, "sectors of maximum diversity" were identified; these sectors contained the greatest variety of houses and neighborhoods according to census data, historical maps, and personal knowledge of the cities. All of the houses located in those sectors that were listed (and pictured) in the guide during one randomly selected month were mapped and classified into an "age and style" typology. Neighborhoods were then given names based on dominant house types ("minimal ranch," "Cape Cod," "Victorian Eclectic"). Field checks confirmed (or complicated) the initial typologies. Once the look of a neighborhood had been identified, social changes as evidenced in census data over time could be related to house type. In this way, similar social changes in contiguous but nonconforming neighborhoods could be compared to situations in noncontiguous but stylistically conforming ones. The roles of proximity and landscape (space and place) could be examined separately. Changes in neighborhood social status could be related to house design, size, and technology as well as to its location in, say, the inner city or the northwest sector. This is where the "staying power" of certain house types (as well as the lack of it) shows up.

A growing number of information agencies have computerized data on current real estate transactions which can be purchased and down-

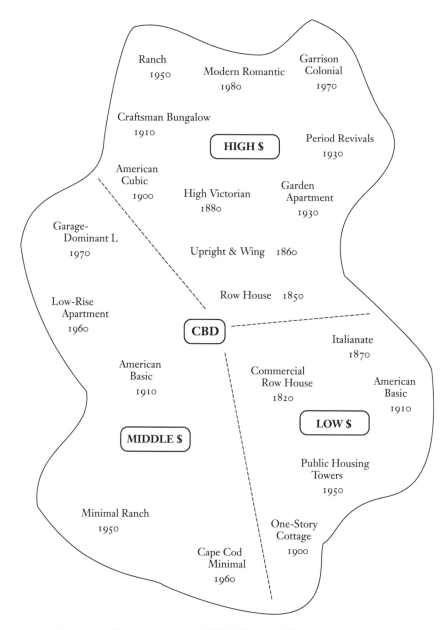

Ranch
1950

Modern Romantic
1980

Garrison
Colonial
1970

Craftsman Bungalow
1910

HIGH $

Period Revivals
1930

American
Cubic
1900

High Victorian
1880

Garden
Apartment
1930

Garage-
Dominant L
1970

Upright & Wing   1860

Low-Rise
Apartment
1960

Row House   1850

CBD

Italianate
1870

American
Basic
1910

Commercial
Row House
1820

American
Basic
1910

LOW $

MIDDLE $

Public Housing
Towers
1950

Minimal Ranch
1950

One-Story
Cottage
1900

Cape Cod
Minimal
1960

American Housing Styles and Neighborhood Character

*Most models of city structure classify housing on the basis of such factors as age,
value, size, and level of maintenance. Housing styles and aesthetics are rarely
factored in. In reality, the look of the city matters. Certain types of housing have had
more staying power than others, even when size, age, and location are held constant.
Not all housing has aged at the same rate. Creating maps of house types and styles
can help us monitor urban change.*

The semirural inner city in the minority sector of Columbus, Ohio

New suburbia in the largely minority sector of Columbus, Ohio

into tenements and allowed to deteriorate in the years before World War II. These houses became inferior as tastes changed.

During the Depression and World War II, little new housing was built, and people (black and white) rented rooms in the older houses. The central city populations of several cities which have been unable to annex new land peaked at the time of the 1950 census, and many neighborhoods were overcrowded. With the construction of massive new suburban tracts of "starter homes" beginning in the late 1940s, whites gradually abandoned the overcrowded and obsolete Victorians. Blacks spread out and seemed to occupy an ever larger portion of the inner ring of the concentric zone model. The "inner city" idea took hold, as blacks were barred from the new housing tracts.

By the late 1960s, the pattern began to change. Middle-sized cities were running out of available Victorian houses. Many had been destroyed for downtown expansion, while others (on better streets) became newly fashionable for law offices and other commercial uses. The next ring of older houses tended to be resistant to ghetto-making techniques such as racial steering and blockbusting (illegal after 1968 but still practiced). The nicer neighborhoods of bungalows and period revival cottages built during the late 1920s had great staying power. They had been well-maintained by long-term owners during the years when it was impossible to move up to new houses. The Spanish cottages of southern California, for example, never lost their appeal, and since they came equipped with electricity, plumbing, garages, and the like and were easy to paint and maintain, they did not filter down. Many black home-seekers returned to the sector where the initial settlement had been.

Since the original black slum had always been viewed by builders as a disamenity to be avoided, construction in the sector was spotty. New tract houses were built further out as the points of the star-shaped city widened and vacant land or cemeteries provided a buffer. By the 1960s, many of the "starter homes" here were becoming available as whites moved up to bigger suburban ranches in better parts of town. Many of these houses had suffered as a result of several families, all with kids and dogs, moving through them over a few years' time. Blacks moved rapidly outward along a corridor of little resistance, and the area of the ghetto seemed to increase markedly as vacant land was skipped. As black populations thinned in the Victorian houses and as their sector expanded through lightly developed territory, the ghetto became anything but high-density inner city. Indeed, as apartments and condominiums sprang up in the more desirable neighborhoods (but not in the black sector), the ghetto emerged as one of the lower-density sections of the central city.

In the last ten years, the areal expansion of black communities has slowed, in part because of less in-migration from the South. Other factors have been important as well. With the enforcement of civil rights laws, many blacks have moved into new houses and large apartment complexes around the outer belt and in other locations. In addition, new and better-built houses have been constructed on vacant land in the black sector to meet the needs of an emerging black middle class. Since the houses are of high quality and since many whites still avoid the sector, the houses offer a good bargain for middle-class blacks who wish to remain in the community yet enjoy a high-quality suburban lifestyle. This diversity of housing options has served to create very different types of neighborhoods all within what many whites still view as the ghetto or the "inner city." House-form typologies help to illustrate the story.

Conclusions

The major land use in cities is housing, and in most North American cities, this means the detached, single-family house. While architectural historians have traced housing styles and social historians have examined the meanings and uses attached to various types of houses, little of this information has found its way into attempts to analyze city structure. Geographers and others interested in mapping the social organization of cities would do well to flesh out general studies of housing with spatial studies of actual houses and neighborhoods, including aesthetic and technological qualities. In this chapter, I have attempted to briefly describe possible linkages between the staying power of particular house types and the continuing desirability of certain zones of the city. Different house types have experienced such social processes as filtering down and revitalization differently. As housing eras progress, city structure changes. Models of city structure based on housing obsolescence as of the 1920s must be modified to reflect this.

The provision of housing in America is a dynamic and constantly changing exercise, with each "housing era" having a different impact on the morphology and social organization of the city. Generalizations developed in one era may not be suitable for another. There have been clues that present trends cannot go on indefinitely. The crisis in the savings and loan industry has led to several adjustments aimed at decreasing housing speculation and channeling capital into more productive enterprises. A limit has been placed on the amount of interest that can be deducted from income taxes, and only a primary residence and a second home qualify. As a smaller and smaller percentage of the population can afford a single-family home in most large urban areas, it may well be that we shall see new trends in house form before too long. If so, new trends in the social geographies of cities are sure to follow.

5 Multiunit Housing and City Structure

Until the early years of the nineteenth century, the residential landscape of the typical American city was dominated by the single-family house. While cities such as Venice and Paris had pioneered a full range of housing options over the preceding 300 years, the densities, preferences, and investment strategies that prevailed in America precluded such options. Americans went about the business of building houses. The past 150 years can be characterized as a long and somewhat difficult struggle to introduce other types of dwellings into the American urban landscape.

Even in the year 1800, not everyone wanted or could afford a proper house. Since the multipurpose and multiclass "burgher house" was never common in America, the tradition of having a variety of apprentices and boarders living on various levels never caught on. As the house became increasingly separate from the working city, both spatially and functionally, it was seen as a refuge from such indiscriminate mixing, and other options gradually evolved for those who did not own a house. Many of the options were gender- and class-specific: the options for immigrant women, for example, were quite different from those of professional men.

Residential Options in the Early 1800s

One of the options considered especially suitable for a young lower-class woman was to live as a servant in the home of an upper-class or even middle-class family. Large nineteenth-century homes had built-in servants' quarters, servants' entries, and servants' stairways. Large numbers of cooks, maids, and nannies were needed to staff the houses of the emerging middle class. Another option especially suited for women, particularly in the emerging industrial centers of the Northeast, was the dormitory. In cities such as Lowell, Massachusetts, or

Manchester, New Hampshire, the female industrial labor force brought in from the farms of New England to work in the textile mills resided largely in a variety of purpose-built dormitory-like boarding houses. Women shared rooms, took their meals in-house, and were subject to very strict hours and rules of conduct. While such dormitories also existed for men and even families, they were absolutely essential for young, unmarried women. In big cities, a variety of YWCA-type dormitories evolved to serve the same purpose.

For men, it was permissible to take up lodgings in a wider variety of places, but by the 1820s the residential hotel had evolved as the ideal bachelor accommodation (see Chapter 2).[1] In hotels, men could have full access to the employment opportunities of the city, take their meals in a dining room, and have a full range of hotel services from laundry to housekeeping. Even men with good incomes and prospects might wish to avoid the encumbrances associated with setting up housekeeping. Hotels provided an option for a price.

Men, especially, found it easier to live in a variety of nonresidential structures at, over, or behind a place of employment. Night watchmen, construction workers, tavern keepers, and laborers often simply lived in a room or a shed at work. Such accommodations were often necessary for those who worked at different locations, such as road builders, and for whom a journey to work in the days before mass transportation was an impossibility. Women, with the exception of domestics (and perhaps prostitutes), were much less likely to live at work.

In many cities, shantytowns (the word *shanty* coming from the Irish *shan tig*, meaning "old house") emerged on the outskirts of urbanized areas with the sudden arrival of large numbers of poor immigrants after the 1840s. Such squatter settlements appeared periodically, when times got tough, right through the Great Depression of the 1930s, but they became less and less of an option as transit lines expanded and property speculation and development spread the city edges far beyond walking distance of centers of employment and as zoning and building regulations made such structures increasingly nonconforming and illegal. Nevertheless, they were an important part of the American urban scene well into the nineteenth century, and vestiges remain today embedded in the inner cities of many American metropolitan areas. Like the options mentioned above, however, this one too has diminished, if not disappeared, in the twentieth century.

Perhaps the most common type of accommodation for all lower-income urban residents, but especially for families, was the subdivided or "tenementized" house. The three- and four-story row houses that had been originally constructed for the affluent in cities such as

New York or Boston could easily be subdivided by floor (including the basement) for use by several families. Each family got a room or two, although the spaces were sometimes awkward as stairways passed through supposedly private space. In the early decades of the nineteenth century, privies were outside, and public water pumps were sometimes a block or more away. Living at close quarters made for some interesting health problems. The situation was made worse when backyards were filled in with additional tenements, thus cutting off light and air circulation from interior units. Many early subdivided tenements consisted of little more than one all-purpose living-working-cooking-eating room and one sleeping room per family. As land costs rose, the space and amenities (such as air) per family decreased. While the red-brick facades of the terraced housing often remained unchanged, they increasingly masked unkempt and disorderly interiors. Dark and damp cellars designed only for cooking and canning were rented out as separate living quarters and quickly became associated with tuberculosis and high infant mortality. Designing adequate spaces for multifamily living had not yet been accomplished as the mid-century mark approached.[2]

It is difficult to say just when the first American versions of the purpose-built tenement evolved, but it was most likely during the mid-1800s in lower Manhattan. As more and more row houses were subdivided and converted to multiunit housing, the inadequacies of this procedure became evident. Until about the 1850s, new housing in New York City was built only for the affluent. As elite residential areas moved northward, first to Gramercy Park and then to Central Park, older housing was filtered down and converted to multitenant use. Elite housing, however, often covered only a fraction of the lot, since a rear garden was thought to be desirable. In addition, there were often "wasted" interior spaces for hallways and grand entryways. When conversion occurred, therefore, much jerry-rigging was necessary in order to maximize return and pack in the greatest number of people per lot. The result was often a "rookery" or ad hoc, makeshift structure; interior and exterior accretions were added with little thought given to the circulation of either air or people. It was perhaps a combination of greed and social conscience that led to the development of the purpose-built tenement in New York City during the third and fourth decades of the nineteenth century.

The Tenement and the New York City Grid

Since most of the innovations leading to the development of high-density residential building types occurred in New York, it is useful to examine the morphological context of these developments. In the year 1811, all of Manhattan above 14th Street was divided into a north-south grid with 200- by 800-foot blocks. Twelve major north-south avenues would form the short ends of the blocks, while smaller east-west streets constituted the long sides. There were to be no service alleys, and lots would typically be 25 by 100 feet. Three aspects of this grid were detrimental to air and light (and solar) requirements for housing on Manhattan. First, the residential east-west blocks provided sunshine for those facing south but none for those facing north. Second, since there were no alleys and lots could be completely filled in (at least during the early years), there was often no "open space" to the rear of dwellings. Third, the narrow 25- by 100-foot lots presented nearly insurmountable problems to those attempting to design interior spaces in multiunit buildings. The lots were considered to be narrow but adequate for single-family houses but all but impossible for tenement design. Nevertheless, the lots existed and the piecemeal redevelopment of lower Manhattan during the nineteenth century meant that lot assembly was very difficult.

The first purpose-built tenements were simply speculative boxes full of people. They sometimes covered up to 90 percent of the lot, with as many as 18 rooms per floor and only the front and back two having any access to air or light. They were called "railroad tenements" because they featured a string of rooms along a narrow corridor like a train car. Since the typical tenement had a height of five stories plus a cellar, it was possible to squeeze hundreds of people into a tenement on a 25- by 100-foot lot. (Interestingly, medieval Edinburgh and several cities in Spain had managed to pack people into 10- and even 12-story pre-elevator buildings. It seems that without the threat of the English or the Moors at the gate, it was difficult to get Americans to climb that high.)

While tenements were not tall, they were dark. As late as 1865, even small interior air shafts were considered to be a significant improvement over standard practice in tenement housing. In the 1840s, as piped water and water closets became common in new construction, wash basins and toilets were placed in the cellars for communal use. The quality of the tenement was sometimes measured by the ratio of toilets per family. The emerging middle class was of course aghast at the prospect of communal bathing and toilets for families. As the Lower East Side filled with tenements, the middle and upper classes headed northward where the single-family row house was still the accepted standard. By the 1850s, the "tenement house problem" had emerged as an urban reality. The perception of an evil inner city was on its way.

In 1865 there were over 15,000 tenements in New York City, and

Mid-nineteenth-century tenements, New York City

there was increasing political pressure for some sort of reform and regulation, if only to stop the spread of filth and disease. The Tenement House Act of 1867 at last legally defined the tenement (as a residence with three or more unrelated families living independently of each other) and mandated certain requirements, such as fire escapes and a maximum of 20 people per water closet. Such regulations proved very difficult to enforce, however. In 1879, a subsequent act added requirements for air circulation and set standards for maximum lot coverage. The result of this act was the "Old Law" or "Dumbbell" tenement, so named because of the air shafts running lengthwise between buildings where light and air from the front or rear could not otherwise reach. The buildings thus looked like dumbbells from above. During the boom of the 1880s, as massive waves of immigrants arrived, thousands of dumbbells appeared in New York City. By 1900, greater New York City had over 80,000 tenements housing a population of 2.3 million people (about three-fourths of the city's total population). By this time, New York City had the highest population density in the world, surpassing even Paris and Bombay. The 25-foot frontage lot, however, remained the norm, and tenements remained dark, stuffy, and crowded. As America became urban and industrial, variations on the dumbbell theme appeared from Boston to Chicago.

CITIES AND BUILDINGS

Tenements in the North End of Boston

The Diffusion of the Tenement

The term *tenement* and perhaps the concept of the tenement as a form of housing distinct from other types was common from about the mid-1800s until the early decades of the twentieth century. By the 1920s, it was no longer necessary to differentiate a "tenement" and an "apartment," as the latter term had expanded to include just about any form of rental housing. The diffusion of the tenement per se, therefore, was a nineteenth-century phenomenon. Since the tenement was difficult to define legally and architecturally (i.e., it could be a subdivided house of any style with just a few households or a monumental, purpose-built structure housing hundreds of people), its diffusion is nearly impossible to trace. Unlike office buildings and apartments, tenements were rarely designed by architects, or, if they were, the architects rarely publicized their involvement. Similarly, cities seldom took pride in tenement buildings or pictured them on postcards or brochures. They could be anything and they could be anywhere; they could even be converted warehouses or factories. Nevertheless, it is possible to make some generalizations concerning the impact of the tenement on various types of American cities.

Purpose-built, speculative tenements were built wherever a combination of high land costs and low-paid (usually immigrant) labor made them profitable. The North End of Boston and even the northern slope of fashionable Beacon Hill were filled with three- to five-story brick tenements during the mid-1800s. As in New York, the Boston tenements tended to be built in a continuous row house configuration. Further west, in cities such as Cleveland and Chicago, while such structures existed, large wooden houselike tenements dominated many neighborhoods. Tiny side yards were thought to be solutions to the problem of inadequate light and ventilation. In most of the industrial cities of the Northeast and Midwest, however, the most common form of tenement continued to be the converted house. These were often large but inadequately designed for multifamily use. It is no wonder that they presented a negative image of the central city and that they wore out quickly.

In southern and western cities, the tenement as a specialized type of building was not common. In the South, most cities were stagnant and slow-growing during the latter years of the nineteenth century, and they did not attract large numbers of immigrants. Low-wage labor was supplied by blacks, who tended to live on the outskirts of town or on "the other side of the tracks" but still within (long) walking distance of employment. In the South, and to a lesser degree in the West, low-income housing could be provided by tiny houses on very small (often subdivided) lots. Narrow, cheaply constructed "shotgun" houses on 12- by 25-foot lots were common in the South, and high densities could be achieved by having large, extended families living in small two-room cottages. Allowing large numbers of unrelated blacks to live in a tenement in the center of the city was thought to be a very bad idea in the South. It was also thought to be a bad idea in the North during the nineteenth century, but there, the prospect was less likely, since there were very few blacks. Border cities such as Baltimore and Washington had some tough decisions to make.[3]

While tenements were certainly built in some western cities such as San Francisco and Seattle, other cities hoped to avoid "urban densities" by looking to local traditions. In Los Angeles, for example, tiny cottages were built around a courtyard, often on a single urban lot. In the case of these "Cholo courts" (so-named since the residents tended to be Hispanic), it was assumed that much living would go on outside the dwelling in the surrounding dust.

While the poor had long been required to live in something other than proper free-standing houses, the middle class and even the upper classes began to search for housing options during the latter decades of the nineteenth century. Since tenements were out of the question, both functionally and semantically, something new was required.

The Luxury Apartment Building: A Different Tradition

The word *apartment*, like the word *tenement*, was for decades very difficult to define. Until the mid-nineteenth century, an apartment could be just about anything from a set of rooms in a hotel to rental rooms in a boarding house. The purpose-built apartment building came much later to the American city than to the European city and also much later than the tenement. While specialized structures containing apartments had been pioneered in Venice as early as the fifteenth century and had become quite common from Vienna to Paris by the eighteenth century, there was still no such thing as an apartment building per se in mid-nineteenth-century America. The idea had to be borrowed and sold to a skeptical public.[4]

Unlike the tenement, the apartment conjured up images of luxury living with a full range of services and servants. The apartment was intended to house, not the unwashed masses, but rather, affluent urban residents who wished to live in the midst of the cultural and economic life of the city without sacrificing either space or quality of life. Like the tenement, the American version of the apartment was pioneered in New York City.

The delayed arrival of the apartment building in America had to do with both urban form and urban cultural values. While major European cities such as Paris and Vienna remained compact well into the nineteenth century and beyond, American cities tended to sprawl almost immediately. For a wide variety of cultural reasons—including attachment to the royal court, cathedral, and monumental center, coupled with a perception of the countryside as the realm of peasantry—the elites in Europe tended to remain in and around the city center, at first in mansions and palaces and later in apartment buildings made to look like mansions and palaces. Also, for a variety of economic and political reasons, English-style suburban housing was normally not an option in Europe. Nineteenth-century redevelopment schemes such as the construction of the Ringstrasse in Vienna or Haussmann's boulevards in Paris often utilized the construction of large apartment buildings along the new streets to help defray the costs of road building. In this way, the elites maintained residences in the center of the monumental city. European apartment buildings came to be a sort of civic architecture. The largest and grandest structures on the main boulevards housed people rather than, as in America, offices or stores.

With only a few exceptions, as in Beacon Hill in Boston, American elites saw no particular reason to remain in the city center. In New York, the affluent quickly moved out of the core of the city toward

English-style residential squares such as Gramercy Park and Washington Square. By the mid-nineteenth century, mansions were under construction in midtown Manhattan, well away from the major concentration of tenements. Transportation innovations such as the omnibus and the horsecar made commuting several miles into the CBD possible. By the 1860s, however, as the population of New York City surpassed one million, it was clear that such expansion could not go on forever.

By the 1860s, the high cost of land had made even small houses too expensive for many New Yorkers who considered themselves to be middle class and who shared the middle-class ideology of a family-centered lifestyle. At the same time, in an attempt to perpetuate the single-family house, the city was subdividing lots into ever narrower dimensions (as narrow as 13 feet) and houses were built deeper on the lot, making light and air more problematic. Houses were thus getting more expensive and less liveable, although advances in lighting, heating, and plumbing helped to ease the transition. Many families lived in two-family homes—not yet a tenement but less than ideal. As white-collar jobs expanded enormously in the late nineteenth century, more and more people felt priced out of an appropriate place to live. By 1860, two-thirds of all New York families lived in some kind of shared quarters, and so the "family home" was already more of an ideal than a reality. By 1900, single-family houses of any size were no longer built in Manhattan and for decades before that they were an endangered species. Yet, the twentieth-century transportation system—the subway and most of the bridges and tunnels—did not yet exist, and so commuting into Manhattan was not all that easy in the mid-1800s.

The residential hotel was an option for some families, but it never fully escaped its image as a *hotel*—a place for mobile people who were not really interested in building a "home." Tenement living, of course, was simply not an option for the proper middle class.

French Flats: The European Way to Live

Not only was land becoming too expensive in Manhattan for the construction of single-family houses, but there was beginning to be, by the 1860s, increasing reluctance on the part of some to leave the growing attractions and amenities of the central city. New York City was maturing and becoming at least a little bit more like Paris. Ladies Mile had developed along Broadway as a center for glamorous department stores, shops, and theaters, and Central Park was being developed as a major green promenade for the elite. Architects and builders were looking to Europe for answers to the housing dilemma. To retain a middle-class population, the city needed apartment buildings.

Middle-class Parisians had been living in apartment buildings for at least 300 years, and by the eighteenth century, such accommodations were considered to be the norm. The ethnic homogeneity of Paris (compared to New York City) and the tradition of social heterogeneity in the burgher house meant that apartments were simply not controversial in France. In America, the whole idea was thought to be a bit socially dangerous and risqué. Consequently, the apartment was introduced to New York as not only a European (i.e., sophisticated) way to live but also as very luxurious so that there would be no mistake that the residents would all be of the upper crust. The first American apartment buildings (called "French flats") tended to have very large quarters, since the idea sold to the elite was that they could live in the city without sacrificing space. Rooms were large, and there were lots of them. Of course, there were servants' quarters as well.

It is perhaps ironic that the reorganization of the social geography of Paris accomplished by Haussmann's boulevards helped to make the apartment building attractive to Americans. While Paris had long been characterized by a degree of social mixing unheard of in America (or England), the grand boulevards lined with luxurious apartment buildings that were created during the 1850s and 1860s demonstrated how social segregation could be accomplished in the midst of a teeming city. The large apartment building seemed to provide a way to stay in the city and yet be separate from it. The full range of services included in an apartment building could help to internalize life and make unwanted contact with the masses less necessary.

At first, the European apartment building was a difficult structure to fit into the New York City grid. Long, narrow, uniform lots made interesting courtyard arrangements difficult to construct. In addition, most European apartment buildings were designed to look like palaces, a tradition that did not merge easily with the English row house look of mid-century New York. Both of these problems were soon solved as the truly monumental New York apartment evolved.

Things started slowly at first. The Stuyvesant, generally regarded as the first purpose-built, middle-class apartment building in New York, was completed in 1869–70 on East 18th Street near the Ladies Mile shopping district. Constructed in the French "Second Empire" style on a double lot, its aspirations were obvious. It is difficult to say with certainty that the Stuyvesant was the first apartment building in New York because a great many trends were coming together about the same time: houses were being remodeled into apartment-like dwellings, residential hotels were increasingly serving a stable population in an apartment-like setting, and so on. Nevertheless, it was a very early example of the genre, and it helped to get the ball rolling.

During the 1870s, the term *apartment* gradually caught on and displaced *French flat*. By 1876, *luxury apartment* had become a common semantic linkage, as buildings evolved from small, houselike structures intended for only a few families, to full-blown, monumental New York apartments.

Technology, Lifestyle, and Location: The Apartment Comes of Age

It was during the boom of the 1880s that the apartment building evolved into something really new and distinctively American. A wide variety of technological innovations during this period made it possible for the large, capital-intensive apartment building to demonstrate to potential residents the wonders that could come with apartment life. Steel-frame construction and the invention of the comfortable electric passenger elevator meant that apartment buildings could be taller than ever, thus providing views and greater separation from the street. Electric lights, telephone switchboards, central heating, and even early versions of air cooling could be found in luxury apartments long before they were possible in comparably priced houses. Beauty salons, shops, cafes, and restaurants could all be contained within the building; and amenities even included prepared food delivered to private suites. Modern laundry facilities in the basement (along with the appropriate operatives) and shops on the ground floor meant that household maintenance was easy with a minimum of servants. To live in a modern apartment building was to be on the cutting edge of technology.

Modern technology coupled with many traditional European services such as a concierge to ensure security and propriety and a full range of domestics meant that life could be easy in such a place. Such amenities did not come cheaply. Large apartments in modern buildings could rent for as high as $7,000 annually in the 1880s, but since comparable space, services, and convenience were impossible to achieve in a house, the demand was there. By the late 1880s, truly mansionlike apartments in palacelike apartment buildings were becoming common. In newly developing areas around Central Park, lot assembly was easier, especially given the return expected on such buildings, and so apartment buildings which took up all or most of a city block rather than just a few lots could be constructed. With greater heights (and rents), grand interior courtyards were possible. Such buildings were a far cry from dumbbell tenements. In fact, although both tenement and apartment buildings were types of multi-unit housing, they were considered by the legal system to be two

Luxury apartment buildings, Upper East Side, New York City

entirely different things, for apartments but not tenements were allowable in certain districts.

Location was very important. The creation of Central Park meant that New York finally had a permanent amenity comparable to the grand boulevards and gardens of European cities—someplace that was worth holding onto. Of course, initially the streets around Central Park were not considered to be central at all. In fact, when the giant Brewery Gothic "Dakota" apartment building was constructed at Central Park West and 72nd Street, it was so-named for its remoteness from the city: "It might as well be out in the Dakotas." Still, the anchoring amenity of Central Park coupled with the development of the large luxury apartment building stopped the northward march of affluent neighborhoods. The elite now had someplace worth regarding as a permanent home, and the large apartment enabled housing to compete successfully with other land uses for a desirable, accessible spot in Manhattan.

Monumental apartment buildings were pioneered on Central Park West and on Fifth and Park Avenues in the Upper East Side. Over the past 100 years, these elite residential areas have expanded, but they have not moved. Even the south side of Central Park, embedded in the Midtown office core, remains partly residential. Over the years, large apartment buildings have been constructed in a number of Manhattan amenity locations, including Riverside Drive and parts of Greenwich Village.

During the latter part of the nineteenth century and the early years of the twentieth century, the contrast between the living conditions of the rich and of the poor was perhaps greater than ever before or since. The rich could live in spacious 20-room apartments overlooking Central Park that included the best of the new technologies while still maintaining a full staff of household servants. The rich could have electric lights, central heat, modern plumbing and stoves, and telephones, as well as maids, cooks, and a concierge. The poor, on the other hand, were still likely to live in dark, damp cellars, rookeries, and early tenements without running water, toilets, electricity, or anything even approaching adequate heat. In addition, they were likely to be located in or near industrial areas with intense noise and pollution. Donald Trump notwithstanding, things have tended to even out a little bit for most people over the past decades. A variety of exposés around the turn of the century such as Jacob Riis's *How the Other Half Lives* brought some of these contrasts into the open.[5]

The Diffusion of the Apartment Building

During the 1880s and 1890s, the large apartment building appeared in only a few of the largest American cities. The tremendous capital investment that was required limited the innovation to only those cities with a sizable threshold population of affluent central-city residents. The exotic, foreign, and controversial nature of the apartment building also limited its acceptance to those cities with some tradition of high-density living, as in hotels or subdivided row houses. Nevertheless, by 1900, large apartment buildings were found in such cities as Washington, Boston, and Chicago.

Both Washington and Boston had traditions of middle-class hotel dwellers. From such structures, it was only a small step to the introduction of luxury apartment buildings. In Washington, old row houses had been converted to "flat buildings" as early as 1870, but it was not until the 1880s that the purpose-built apartment house was successfully introduced. Portland Flats, constructed on Thomas Circle in 1880, is regarded as the first such building.[6] The introduction of the apartment building was much needed in Washington, since row houses and hotels had been the only multiple-occupancy options up to that time. With no tradition of tenements, everyone in the rapidly growing city had to seek space in some kind of house, and those seeking space in convenient central areas were said to be most unhappy with the available accommodations.

Developers from New York City were responsible for the first apartment buildings in Washington, and so the route of diffusion is easy to trace. Victorian apartment buildings in Washington tended to

Top, *apartment buildings in San Francisco;* bottom, *an apartment building in Washington, D.C.*

be U-shaped, 6-story buildings with an average of about 40 apartments, although in 1894, the 12-story, 160-foot-tall Cairo Apartments became the tallest private building in the city and led directly to the city's height limits. The influence of hotel living was pronounced in early Washington apartments, since few had kitchens. Apartments caught on for many who had homes elsewhere and were in Washington for only part of the year. In the early decades, most apartments were located in an emerging amenity sector near Connecticut Avenue. A plentiful supply of low-paid black servants made food delivery from central kitchens an attractive option. Large apartment buildings quickly became popular in Washington, and that city has been one of the top five "apartment cities" in America throughout the twentieth century.

In Chicago, the apartment building was introduced after the infamous fire of 1871, as architects and developers converged on the city to participate in its reconstruction. Even though there were few natural barriers impeding the areal expansion of Chicago and no real tradition of hotel or tenement living, the apartment building was accepted in the city because of the need to provide housing quickly and because there were more affluent people who wanted to live along the shore of Lake Michigan than there were available lots. As in the case of New York's Central Park, Lakeshore Drive provided a combination of centrality and amenity that facilitated the acceptance of multiunit housing. Beyond the lakeshore, Chicago became a city of single-family bungalows and two- and three-story walk-up flats in the tradition of converted row houses.

By the early years of the twentieth century, the large apartment building had diffused in significant numbers only to a few American cities—Boston, Washington, Chicago, San Francisco (again with the aid of a disaster), and, to a lesser extent, other major cities such as Detroit and Cleveland. Elsewhere, they were still a novelty. In Columbus, Ohio, for example, a four-story granite-faced apartment building was considered to be a "folly" when it was constructed in the early 1900s, even though it is still in good shape today. In Columbus, and cities like it, houses were still the norm at the turn of the century even though only a minority of households could afford to own one.

American cities can be differentiated on the basis of their acceptance or rejection of multiunit housing. While Washington quickly became a center for apartment-building construction, nearby Baltimore largely rejected the idea, at least for a time. Although larger than Washington and with a greater working-class population, Baltimore sought to solve its housing problem through the construction of very small row houses. As a consequence, central Baltimore filled up with one- and two-story single-family row houses on lots only 12 feet wide. Land was far too expensive to build such structures in Boston or New York, but in Baltimore the perpetuation of a London-style land-lease system made it possible to provide "houses" to a low-income population, since residents did not always have to buy the land under the house.[7] Even Philadelphia, in spite of its great size,

resisted apartment construction. In 1900, while over half the population of New York City lived in buildings with over six units, only
about 1 percent of the population of Philadelphia did so. Today, the
problems encountered in revitalizing the central cities of Boston,
New York, Washington, and Baltimore are often very different because of the very different housing traditions. Throughout America,
from Atlanta to Seattle, different building traditions, land costs,
home ownership patterns, and social geographies emerged as the large
apartment complex was either accepted enthusiastically, accepted on a
very limited basis, or rejected altogether.

The Apartment Controversy: Social Concerns and Feminist Ideology

While tenement buildings may have been scandalous, the need for
some type of high-density housing for the poor, at least in New York
City, was not controversial. It was simply a fact of life. However,
apartment living for the middle and upper classes, who had a choice
and who could be expected to act as moral role models for the rest of
society, was quite controversial. The Victorian preoccupation with a
family-centered "home" as a refuge from the city did not mesh well
with apartment living, which was seen as dangerously communal.

The mid-nineteenth century was characterized by unprecedented
urban growth and social change in both America and Europe, and so it
is not surprising that there was a great deal of discussion about the
types of residences appropriate for this new urban-industrial society.
Every type of development, from socialist utopian communities to
those of isolationist religious sects, advocated some type of ideal housing arrangement. The big issue really boiled down to whether or not
some type of family-centered, house-oriented society should be encouraged and perpetuated or whether some new, more efficient communal form of housing and society should be developed. We can dub
these the traditionalist and the progressive views.[8]

Since I have already discussed the Victorian ideology of home as
refuge (the traditionalist viewpoint) in the preceding chapter, we can
examine mainly the progressive, pro-apartment view here. The
progressives—feminists and socialists among them—argued that
single-family homes were outmoded and inefficient and therefore
entirely inappropriate for the modern city. Modern technology at the
time was expensive and rare. Progressives felt that ubiquitous access
to such modern features as electricity, running water, and central
heating could best be accomplished in large buildings. One large
furnace, stove, bath house, kitchen, etc., could serve far more people

loaded into geographic information systems. While such data is typically expensive, stratified samples can be utilized to reduce the costs. Finally, fieldwork is of utmost importance. The urban literature tends to dichotomize cities into inner city and suburban realms, but anyone who has looked carefully at the cityscape knows that there are infinite variations on these themes. By developing house-form and neighborhood typologies of more complexity and detail, we can begin to understand the morphology of the city at a different level. We can factor social history and ideology into our maps of housing value and income.

House Types and Social Change in the City

Neighborhood house-form typologies can add depth to our understanding of social change in the city. For example, studies of racial change and ghetto formation have nearly all emphasized either spatial contiguity or environmental quality (including housing quality). In other words, ghettos have been formed as blacks and other minorities have been channeled into nearby and/or inferior residential locations. Rarely have scholars examined the sequence of housing types (or residential landscapes) involved in such moves over time. I suggest that in many middle-sized urban areas (though probably not in New York, Boston, or other large "tenement" cities) a four-stage model of racial change can be built around the availability of certain types of houses at different points in time. I used Columbus and San Diego as case studies for this idea but also examined several other cities in less detail.

During the early decades of the the twentieth century, the most common location for an incipient ghetto was at the edge of town but close to the CBD, that is, in one of the interstitial areas between transportation corridors. These disheveled and underserviced areas often contained a variety of industry and nonconforming, jerry-built housing not completely unlike squatter settlements. Streets were often unpaved, and water came from wells. There were sometimes downtown or waterfront locations as well, but these were subsequently destroyed in various urban renewal efforts while the peripheral, semirural neighborhoods usually continued to give character to the sector. The "houses" were often shanties, sometimes built randomly over poorly defined lots.

Beginning in the 1920s, the ghetto typically expanded inward toward the Victorian houses which were being left behind by people seeking "modern" bungalows complete with plumbing, electricity, and parking. The size of Victorian (and pre-Victorian) houses and the difficulty of maintaining them meant that they were often subdivided easier than many small ones. In addition, maids, cooks, and other servants could be used more efficiently by a group of people (at least by the middle and upper classes).

Feminists argued that in the modern city, housework and child care should be socialized and paid for, thus freeing women to participate in other types of employment as well as in the cultural life of the city. Domestic chores in the nineteenth century involved quite a lot of manual labor, especially for those without piped water and modern stoves. Hauling water and food home, cooking in a hot, poorly ventilated kitchen, and washing and drying clothes were jobs women were expected to do without compensation. Progressives argued that efficiency and equity would be better served by having families live in private apartments, but with communal kitchens and laundry facilities. In this way, a private family life could be maintained while women could either be paid to do the laundry or cooking for the building or could take turns using the most modern, efficient equipment. Day-care centers would also be provided in-house for those who wished to work elsewhere. One large furnace or laundry could do the work far more efficiently from both a human and energy standpoint than hundreds of small ones. For many progressives, the ideal was somewhere between the family hotel and the modern apartment building.

Some progressives argued that large apartment buildings could also offer valuable recreation space to the residents. Rooftop gardens, which became common in luxury buildings with the development of new clothes-drying technologies, could be places of outdoor recreation for children in the daytime and families at night. Courtyards, also increasingly common by the 1890s, could be used for educational lectures and political activities as well as for recreation. Of course, these suggestions (especially the part about political activities) were not widely appreciated by traditionalists.

In addition to being modern and efficient, apartment buildings could be centrally located so as to make possible women's participation in the civic and social life of the city. Traditionalists viewed all of this with a great deal of alarm. For them, the "indecent propinquities" of apartment life would be a constant threat to the moral family. The idea of women participating in a world outside the home was not as attractive to traditionalists as it was to feminists. Indeed, the expression "my wife doesn't work" (meaning "my wife doesn't work outside of the home") became a proud boast for the Victorian and (at least early-) twentieth-century male. Progressive arguments failed to sway those who saw the home as an isolated retreat for women. To a lesser degree, these discussions continue into the 1990s.

Arguments over morality and efficiency influenced not only the acceptance of apartment living but also the design and organization of apartment space. Collective kitchens largely died by the twentieth century, as did most of the other "socialist" ideas. It is hard to say whether these ideas failed because of the desire for privacy and independence on the part of families coupled with the difficulties of cooperative living, or whether technological innovations made such cooperation unnecessary. By the early years of the twentieth century, small, inexpensive appliances such as vacuum cleaners, refrigerators, toasters, stoves, fans, and bathroom fixtures, together with the increasing availability of canned and packaged food and other products, meant that families could live a modern life in private. Advertisements aimed at women emphasized the fact that housework (with modern products) was not only lots of fun but was soon to become even easier. Apartments, even in large buildings, gradually became more self-contained. For a variety of reasons, it was deemed important to create an idealized "homelike" ambiance within the apartment, complete with fireplaces (even nonfunctional ones), kitchens, dining rooms, parlors, and the like. Anglo-American landscape tastes and materialist attitudes could not be eliminated easily by arguments for efficiency.

Another possible impact of traditionalist arguments on apartment design was the development of the duplex, or two-story apartment. Traditionalists (moralists) objected to having bedrooms on the same floor as living quarters, even in houses. In apartments, the dangers would be increased many-fold. A visitor who chanced to glance toward an open bedroom might get ideas and begin the "French flat shuffle" to that destination. This could be avoided by designing apartments like two-story houses. Realistically, this could be accomplished only in luxury apartments, since interior stairways took up a great deal of space. In New York, some palatial apartments were even three or more stories as owners attempted to replicate in a penthouse what they had earlier owned as a free-standing mansion when land values on Fifth Avenue were lower.

Urban Design Issues and the Early Apartment Building

Since there was far more demand for housing in the Victorian city than there was for office space, it stands to reason that apartment buildings would have been among the first structures to reach great and controversial heights, especially after the advent of the elevator (and piped water and gas for cooking and heating) made the upper stories far more desirable and profitable than the lower ones. As we have seen, this was the case in Washington, D.C. This demand for residential space coupled with social outrage at the overcrowded conditions in many tenement complexes, meant that many argued for controls over the size of residential buildings. Also, since apartment buildings tended to be built in the very best of neighborhoods, issues of light and air access among lower, nearby buildings were also important.

While the various tenement laws passed in New York City from the 1850s onward attempted to set size limitations on such buildings, it was always difficult to decide just whether or not apartment buildings were subject to the same controls. To be safe, many apartment builders continued to call their projects "apartment hotels" and to emphasize a full range of collective services such as dining rooms and laundry facilities. Hotels were exempt from size limitations. Also, cooperative apartments in which tenants owned shares in the building, and so (theoretically) managed the building themselves, were exempt because these owners obviously did not live in tenements. Much of the rhetoric and ideology aimed at getting people to buy into such "home ownership" was aimed at ensuring that there would be no difficulties encountered in the construction of very tall (and profitable) buildings, since coops were not subject to controls until much later.[9]

Some of the early apartment buildings were truly monumental, especially considering their locations in residential districts. The Ansonia, built in New York at Broadway and West 73rd Street in 1903, reached 17 stories, with another 3 stories or so in turrets. It covered an entire city block and contained 340 apartments (as well as 40 miles of water pipe, 2,071 steam radiators, and 7,849 electric outlets). There seemed to be no limit to the size that apartment buildings could reach. The Ansonia was constructed at a stop on the new subway system then under construction. The subway system helped to create nodes of exceptionally high demand.

Apartment buildings, like all other types of buildings in New York City, were subject to the height and bulk guidelines written into the zoning ordinances of 1916, which stipulated that height be a function of street width. Setback requirements were also mandated. The luxury apartment buildings constructed along Park and Fifth avenues during the 1920s reflect these laws as well as economic considerations. The new requirements made lot assembly even more important, as allowable building volume was a function of the size of the lot. Tall buildings could only be built as towers covering a small precentage of the total lot. The legislation was refined by the Multiple Dwelling Law of 1929, which allowed the height of towers to exceed street width by a factor of three providing that they did not exceed one-fifth of lot coverage. As a result, the tall, narrow "twin-tower" apartment evolved as epitomized by the San Remo and Century apartment buildings. The latter was completed in 1931 just as the stock market crash brought luxury apartment construction to a temporary halt.

The End of the Tenement: The Apartment Takes Over

Throughout the latter decades of the nineteenth century, New York and other cities wrestled with legislation and other policies that would encourage if not ensure minimum housing standards. Legislation requiring cross-ventilation, fireproof materials, adequate toilet facilities, and maximum lot coverage gradually improved the nature of the tenement buildings under construction by the early years of the twentieth century. Competitions aimed at improving tenement design were held and widely publicized, especially during the 1890s. Influenced by interest in social housing in Europe, especially London, American philanthropists and city officials sought to perfect the multiunit environment.

The construction of tenements in the rigid and congested lower Manhattan grid had always presented problems. By the early 1900s, however, subway and bridge construction made more peripheral sites plausible for working-class housing. New tenement configurations were proposed and built. Buildings in the shape of an O, U, H, or T ensured better access to light and air, with as much as 50 percent of the total lot given over to communal recreation space.[10] At first, the new ideas probably had more influence on the design of luxury apartments than on tenements (the inclusion of rooftop gardens, for example), but as new areas with cheaper land became available and as philanthropical organizations increased their interest in housing, significant improvements in tenement design gradually occurred.

There was also considerable political interest in getting well-designed working-class housing constructed in relatively remote locations. Cities were seen as hotbeds of political discontent where anarchists and socialists spread dangerous ideas. Getting workers to move to cleaner, spacious "suburban" locations might be just the answer. As tenement design improved, there was less and less need to refer to tenements as something other than apartment buildings. By 1920, the term was falling out of usage, except to refer to older buildings constructed during the nineteenth century.

Meanwhile, many new apartment buildings featured downsized, less luxurious units and fewer collective services. Just as single-family houses tended to get smaller during the Progressive era of the early twentieth century, as the "efficient" bungalow replaced the "fussy" Victorian, so too were apartments streamlined, and for many of the same reasons. As the use of servants declined, it was no longer necessary to have servants' quarters built into any but the most luxurious apartment buildings. As small electric appliances proliferated, the spaces given over to cooking and washing diminished. Electric lighting and cooling meant that all rooms did not need an outside exposure, and building regulations increasingly allowed for double-loaded corridors with light entering on only one side of an apartment. The development of automatic self-service elevators meant that the number of people needed to run even a tall building diminished. In Victorian times, an elevator required not only operators but a full-time engineer to keep the apparatus working. Smaller families and greater numbers of single clerical workers in cities meant that design innovations such as the "studio" apartment could be introduced without the slum connotation that single-room living once had. Modern gadgetry could make even tiny spaces pleasant.

During the 1920s, housing became less gender- and race-specific. While Victorian cities usually included "homes for working women" based on the earlier industrial dormitory, by the third decade of the twentieth century, it was no longer thought to be scandalous for single women to take a flat. Similarly, the "bachelor apartments" built in the 1800s (usually without kitchens and other "feminine" work spaces) were off-limits to women and families. By the 1920s, some men had evolved to the point of being able to live on their own in real apartments. Conversely, working women began to occupy "bachelorette" pads.

In the nineteenth century, most tenements and apartments had been built specifically for one race. Special tenements intended for blacks were constructed, usually in very different locations from those built for whites. By the early years of the twentieth century, the development of block busting and steering techniques increased the "racial change" dimension of urban housing. While discrimination persisted during the 1920s, it was less likely to be built-in and permanent. As the urban office and department store boom in the twenties led to a demand for more young workers of all races, apartment buildings evolved to provide a variety of housing for a variety of people.

The Garden Apartment: The Second Wave of Diffusion

As the model tenement and the middle-class apartment building began to merge in the 1920s, a new type of apartment environment evolved. Mass transit in the form of subway and commuter railroad lines in big cities, and streetcar systems in smaller ones, opened up new, relatively bucolic areas beyond the confines of the Victorian city.

At least some of these became apartment districts. In New York City, new neighborhoods in Brooklyn and Queens, such as Jackson Heights, were developed as apartment districts. In Washington and Chicago, the older apartment corridors along Rock Creek Park and Lakeshore Drive, respectively, boomed and expanded. More significantly, cities that had resisted the Victorian apartment now developed apartment districts as well. The Country Club District of Kansas City, the West End of St. Louis, the Hollywood-Wilshire area of Los Angeles, Capitol Hill in Seattle, and the Near South Side in Minneapolis are but a few examples. These areas were only a short streetcar ride from the center of the business district, but they were relatively green and spacious. Many of these districts were instrumental in the creation of a relatively permanent high-status "sector" emanating from the CBD. While lower-density residential areas close to downtown could be invaded by nonconforming uses, large apartment districts could hold their own. Such apartment corridors played an important part in the development of the "sector model" of city structure.[11]

In many cities, purpose-built apartments, as opposed to apartments in converted houses, became a significant part of the total housing stock for the first time during the 1920s. In Los Angeles, for example, only 8 percent of the building permits issued in 1920 were for apartments, but in 1928, the proportion had risen to 53 percent. In Chicago, a majority of the permits for the entire decade of the twenties was for apartments.[12] Even "row house cities" such as Baltimore and Philadelphia began to develop apartment districts. The apartment building, however, had changed. While open land around large apartment buildings was nonexistent before World War I, by 1930 it was almost expected.

To a very real degree, the boom of the 1920s was focused upon "garden apartments"—large rambling complexes that often looked more like rustic resorts than urban housing. While traditional urban apartment buildings had to be squeezed into the existing urban fabric, "suburban" garden apartments could be built at a truly massive scale on several acres of land. For example, the Broadmoor, a nine-story, crescent-shaped complex completed on Washington's Connecticut Avenue in 1929, occupied only 15 percent of its 5-acre site. The Broadmoor contained 179 apartments and a dozen hotel suites. Because of its distance from downtown as well as its self-consciously resort-like ambiance, it provided a wide range of services in-house, such as a large public dining room. Significantly, there was a basement parking garage for 118 cars.[13]

Not all garden apartments across the nation conformed so closely to

Garden apartment, San Diego

Le Corbusier's "skyscraper in a park" image as the Broadmoor. Nevertheless, the emphasis on green space was increasing. Well-manicured gardens and fountains filled the courtyards of apartments from Boston to Los Angeles. The large complex especially continued to play the role of an internally oriented refuge from the chaos of the city yet one that was convenient to it.

Many of the apartments built during the 1920s were not garden apartments by any means. As the term *tenement* was dropped and as the apartment gained wider acceptance, small, minimal apartment complexes could be built in cities more easily. In large and middle-sized cities throughout America, four- to eight-unit "walk-ups" were constructed with few of the amenities or services once associated with the term *apartment building*. Although many were disguised to look like houses, in the sense that they shared as much domestic imagery as they could carry—stucco and red tile roofs in California, Tudor trim and fake gables in Ohio, etc.—they were technically more like tenements than apartments. These "one-lot boxes" have come to play a very important role in the housing stocks of many American cities.

Just as Baltimore and Philadelphia resisted the diffusion of the Victorian apartment, some of the cities lacking a multiunit living tradition resisted the apartment during the 1920s. In San Diego and in several other new cities of the Southwest, a compromise was sought. Borrowing equally from the traditions of the Cholo court and the California bungalow (as well as perhaps from some church camps and resorts in the East), the bungalow court appeared in the first decade of the twentieth century. The bungalow court consisted of several small, free-standing bungalows arranged around a courtyard. Three 25-foot urban lots could provide enough room for six to eight bungalows as well as a two-story apartment enclosing the rear of the lot and a spacious courtyard. Each unit was to be a separate house which could be decorated (within reason) to the tenant's taste. Around each house, there was room for a small private garden in addition to the communal one and for various embellishments such as hanging plants and lawn chairs. People could thus live at fairly high densities along mass transit lines but still enjoy the outdoor good life of California.[14]

During the 1910s and 1920s, bungalow courts were built by the hundreds in cities the size of San Diego and by the thousands in the Los Angeles basin. They were sold not only as pleasant and convenient places to live for those not ready for the burdens of a house but also as ideal "trainer homes" for women. Here, single women holding jobs downtown could learn to be homemakers on a small scale. Everything was there—kitchen, parlor, garden, etc.—to provide valuable training for the eventual housewife, yet the burden was small enough not to interfere with the outside job. In addition, the indecent propinquities of apartment life could be avoided and security was high, since all of the neighbors could see the doors of other residents. The innovation was (and is still) quite popular, but it lasted only until the Depression brought an end to construction in 1929. Bungalow courts were not revived in the postwar boom although many small "courtyard apartment buildings" featuring connected units could be seen as a variation on the theme.

The Boom of the Twenties and City Structure

While much has been written about the emptying of central cities that occurred as people sought the American Dream of a suburban home, to some degree the phenomenon of the garden apartment played an important role in this redistribution of population as well. The fact that large apartment complexes were often constructed by unions and other organizations meant that entire assemblages of people could be induced to move more or less together. Also, the existence of large amounts of relatively affordable rental housing in desirable, relatively rustic locations meant that, for the first time on any scale, large numbers of people who were unable to afford a house could move out of tenements and makeshift quarters downtown.

In New York City, for example, the construction of large apartment buildings in the Bronx helped to facilitate a massive Jewish exodus from the Lower East Side during the 1920s. The community could be

Apartments in a converted house, San Diego

recreated in the high-density but newer landscape, and so moving out did not mean dispersal or social disruption. The Jewish population of the Lower East Side fell from 706,000 in 1923 to 297,000 in 1930, while that of the Bronx rose from 382,000 to 585,000 during the same period.[15]

The 1920s was a time of great optimism in general, but especially with regard to the creation of desirable housing. Records were set nationally for the most houses constructed in a given year, and more housing was created in New York City during the 1920s than at any time before or since. Two-thirds of the new units in New York were apartments. The overbuilding that occurred during the twenties allowed for the removal of much of the old, substandard housing stock. Between 1920 and 1929, 43,000 Old Law tenements were torn down in New York City. In other parts of the nation, the garden apartment allowed for the depopulation of areas in and around downtowns where people had been living in subdivided houses and other makeshift quarters over stores and offices. The unprecedented demand for office and commercial space in the American downtown during this period, coupled with new apartment options, led to the specialized "office tower and department store" downtown. The lives of the relative few who were left downtown in deteriorating hotels, houses, and older tenements were viewed as increasingly abnormal as most people settled in homogeneously residential neighborhoods. The "zone in transition" of the concentric zone model began to take shape. On the

Public housing in New York City

other hand, the garden apartment districts of the 1920s have held up well from Brookline in Boston to Hollywood, California. Many have played important roles in the revival of urban culture in the post-1970 period.

The Great Depression and the End of the Boom

With the stock market crash of 1929, the construction boom came to an end for all types of building, but especially for capital-intensive projects like skyscraper office towers and large apartment complexes. In Chicago, for example, 37,000 apartments were constructed in 1927, but the number plummeted to 1,500 in 1930. While the construction of single-family homes picked up a little in the late 1930s as small developers took advantage of low land and labor costs, apartment buildings did not share in the recovery. The major exceptions to this were apartments built as public housing and apartments built in conjunction with the war effort during the early 1940s. In general, the next apartment boom did not begin until the 1960s.

During the 1930s, state, local, and federal government agencies began to take over the role played by housing philanthropists during the 1920s. With millions of people out of work, especially in the construction industry, governments attempted to prime the pump by sponsoring new residential communities. At first, government projects perpetuated the philanthropists' interest in suburban garden apartments and planned suburban communities such as Greenhills,

Ohio, and Greenbelt, Maryland. Most of these projects were aimed at the "deserving poor," people whose lives had been temporarily disrupted by the Depression. Government-sponsored highway programs and other projects geared toward expanding urban infrastructures facilitated this orientation. Later, however, public housing became intertwined with the goals of urban renewal and slum clearance.

The new highways, bridges, and civic centers built by government agencies during the 1930s often required the demolition of existing "slums." There were certainly slums still in existence in 1930, as a great many substandard houses lacking indoor plumbing, electricity, and central heat had survived the boom of the 1920s. These were seen as an embarrassment by civic officials, who worried about fire hazards, public health, and possible immorality. Grand projects in the image of those being increasingly publicized by modernists such as Le Corbusier could remake the landscape of the inner city. By 1932, the nation's first super clearance project was under way as 50 acres of the Lower East Side were prepared for new development. By 1941, most of the area was covered with high-rise public housing towers, thus institutionalizing a low-income ring around the CBD.

By the late 1940s, the high-rise "tower-in-a-park" had become the model for public housing in New York City and was soon to spread to big cities throughout America. By the mid-1950s, tower projects had been constructed in Philadelphia, St. Louis, Baltimore, Cleveland, Chicago, San Francisco, and nearly every other metropolitan area with a population of one million or more. Designers sought to break with existing urban morphology as much as possible by not only substituting massive open spaces and superblocks for "congested" streets but also by setting the buildings at angles so as to completely change the rhythm of the existing grids.

Public Housing Towers and the Making of the Inner City

While many generalizations about the inner cities of America attribute the social problems found there to life in the aging, filtered-down housing stock, some of the worst areas are actually relatively new. They are dominated by public housing towers built largely during the 1950s. High-rise public housing towers have not been an unmitigated success as a type of apartment building. Some critics lay the blame on the scale and design of the buildings, arguing that the spaces just do not work for human beings. Others have suggested that the major fault lies with the administration and maintenance of the structures, especially policies relating to the selection of residents.

In his book *Defensible Space*, Oscar Newman argued that towers in a park are devoid of a sense of territory or neighborhood.[16] That is, they provide no defensible, "claimable" territories for residents to watch over and feel responsible for. Neither the vast open spaces around the buildings nor the dark, double-loaded corridors within them provide social space for casual interaction and surveillance. The reliance on elevators and enclosed "fire stairs" also diminishes interaction space. While traditional neighborhoods provided a gradation of territories from major street to residential street to stoop to house, towers in a park did not. All was public space right up to the apartment door; there were no appropriate niches for socializing beyond the door. Residents do not sit in double-loaded corridors and watch the people go by as they might on a stoop or a well-placed bench.

Using crime figures by building from the New York City Police Department, Newman attempted to demonstrate that density per se has little to do with antisocial behavior. Comparing complexes of equal density—one containing low-rise buildings with open stairs and differentiated outside space, the other containing towers with fire stairs and no claimed outside space—he found the crime rate to be much higher in the latter even though the two complexes were located across the street from each other and housed the same type of tenant. In the towers, elevators quickly ceased to work (partly as a result of vandalism and partly as a result of maintenance budgets), making the upper floors of a 12- to 20-story building nearly uninhabitable.

Many "tower slabs," such as those in the infamous Pruitt-Igoe Complex in St. Louis, have been torn down as a bad idea. Others have been converted to housing for the elderly under the assumption that it was only unruly teenagers who made life in the towers unbearable. They are no longer built for low-income families. The problems remain, however: Chicago police records show that the Robert Taylor Homes, consisting of 28 high-rise apartment buildings, alone account for 11 percent of the city's murders.

Others argue that design was less of a problem than policies of admission and retention. Beginning with the industrial dorms of the late eighteenth century, multiunit housing in America had always been characterized by strict rules and regulations. Philanthropic housing throughout the nineteenth century and well into the twentieth was considered to be sort of a reward for good and proper behavior. Prospective tenants were interviewed carefully, and only those with some means of support and a good family life were admitted. In the postwar era, most of this changed, and by the 1960s anyone could be admitted to public housing and no one could be thrown out. Any restrictions based on proper behavior or income were subject to cries of racism and sexism, since single black mothers with teenagers were most likely to be affected by them. Still, high-rise public housing and unruly teenagers tended to be a bad mix. Security and propriety played second fiddle to tenants' rights and freedoms. In recent years, some projects have tightened up (often under the iron-handed administration of a black woman), and design has been less of a problem. Clearly, our negative impressions of "teeming, aging, decaying" inner cities could use some revision. Many older neighborhoods have had remarkable staying power, while newer ones nearby have declined precipitously. It is important to examine the residential landscape of the city with great care.

This is not to say that all public housing has been a disaster. Many smaller, well-managed complexes have done exactly what they set out to do—provide decent, low-cost housing for the working poor and the truly needy. Indeed, Newman himself points out that many seemingly hopeless projects were turned into desirable and successful residences through careful reorganization and redesign. Still, it is wise to differentiate between housing design problems and neighborhood problems in describing the social geography of the city.

The Apartment Building and Urban Ecology

By the end of the 1950s, two distinctive types of inner-city residential zones had emerged in many of the larger American cities: a luxury and garden apartment district and a low-income public housing district. Because very large and specialized buildings are associated with each of these two of areas, change over the past several decades has often been minimal. For example, while the elite residential area in Manhattan moved perceptibly northward almost by the decade from the 1820s until the end of the nineteenth century, the Upper East Side has remained a desirable residential area for nearly 100 years. While there has been some commercial intrusion from the Midtown office core to the south, large luxury apartment buildings are valuable enough to pay their way even on expensive land, especially when their existence is reinforced by residential zoning. Park Avenue has been *the* place to live since before World War I. Similarly, monumental apartment buildings such as the Dakota, the San Remo, and the Century have graced Central Park West for decades, and no changes are in sight. Such large apartment buildings resist the forces of "invasion and succession" built into ecological models of city structure. Similar neighborhoods can be found in the Gold Coast of Chicago, on Russian Hill in San Francisco, and on Connecticut Avenue in Washington.

Public housing towers have also helped to create unchanging, institutionalized social districts. East Harlem, once an Italian neighborhood but now known as "Spanish Harlem," was rebuilt in the early 1950s. Two-thirds of Spanish Harlem now consists of public housing projects. The boundary between the Upper East Side and Spanish Harlem was originally located at 96th Street, since the rail lines went underground (under a magnificent Park Avenue) south of that point but emerged as a smoky, disamenity north of it. Now the boundary has been made permanent by distinct architectural traditions because that is where the luxury apartment and the public housing project meet. The boundary is not likely to change. The gentrification of the Upper West Side in recent decades has been at least partly due to the impossibility of expanding the Upper East Side into the area of public housing. The pattern has been repeated in other large cities, as in the case of the infamous Cabrini-Green public housing projects in Chicago, located just inland from the luxurious Gold Coast.

Ecological models that emphasize such variables as density and distance (access) serve poorly when we are faced with such dissimilar types of neighborhoods located in such close proximity. Only a close-up examination of the architectural spaces and microlevel social conditions can provide insight into what is really going on in the city. In large American central cities, the very best and the very worst areas are often only a few blocks apart but miles away in terms of architectural traditions. Both ghettos and gold coasts are often given a certain permanence through design.

The Apartment Building Becomes Ubiquitous: The 1960s to the 1980s

Because of the hiatus in apartment building construction between 1930 and 1960 and the concentration of public housing towers in only a few of the nation's largest cities, the national distribution of multiunit housing in 1960 was very similar to the pattern in 1930. While there are no comprehensive figures for numbers of apartment units by city, the census does provide information on "units in structure" (which includes units in converted houses, barracks, dorms, and other buildings not really built to be apartments). The figures for structures with ten or more units, can be used as a pretty good surrogate for apartments, especially since few converted buildings would be likely to have so many residences. To compare the number of apartment units in 1960 with the number in 1980, we can use structures with ten or more units as an arbitrary cutoff point to identify "large" apartment buildings (as opposed to converted houses, walk-up flats, and other makeshift housing).[17] The arbitrary cutoff point of ten greatly underestimates the importance of apartments in American cities, but it does allow us to focus on areas with large apartment buildings as unique landscape features giving character to place.

In 1960, New York City was by far the predominant location for multiunit dwellings. The New York SMSA had as many dwellings in structures with ten or more units (hereafter referred to as "10+ buildings") as the next 23 largest metropolitan areas combined. Manhattan alone contained more dwellings in 10+ buildings (over 600,000) than the Chicago and Los Angeles metropolitan areas put together. In 1960, the apartment was a New York way of life. While metropolitan New York had over 1.5 million units (43 percent of its housing stock) in 10+ buildings, only Chicago, Los Angeles, and Washington had as many as 100,000; and only Washington, Chicago, and Miami exceeded 15 percent of total housing units in large structures. Most American metropolitan areas were characterized by single-family homes and very small apartment buildings. On the average, only about 5 percent of the total housing stock of the rest of the top 30 metropolitan areas was in 10+ structures, even in very large cities such as Philadelphia.

In 1960, most large apartment buildings were still located in the central cities of metropolitan areas. Many politically independent suburbs disallowed all multiunit housing during the first half of the twentieth century for fear that immigrants and other "undesirables" might be attracted. Although such policies continued into the 1960s in some communities, especially in regard to low-income housing, exclusionary zoning based simply on the number of units diminished. Apartment buildings tended to cluster even more with the widespread acceptance of zoning during the late 1920s and into the 1930s, since single-family areas, even within cities, came to be viewed as areas to be protected in the face of rising land costs and speculative ventures. Since the vast majority of employment opportunities remained centrally located until after midcentury, such multiunit concentrations made sense, especially where there was continued reliance on mass transit. In most large metropolitan areas, 80 to 90 percent of the 10+ structures were located in the central city in 1960.

For a wide variety of reasons, both the interurban and intraurban location of large apartment complexes began to change dramatically after about 1960. Since 1962, more apartments have been built in the (political) suburbs than in central cities, and the biggest booms have been in the newer metropolitan areas of the South and West rather than in the industrial cities of the Northeast. For example, while only 12,000 units in 10+ structures were added in the Buffalo area between 1960 and 1980, greater Houston gained 298,000 (Table 4). With the

Table 4. Change in number of dwellings in 10+ buildings, 1960–80, and percentage of total housing units in 10+ buildings, 1980: selected SMSAs

	Number	Percentage		Number	Percentage
South/West			*North/East*		
Los Angeles	+444,000	24	Detroit	+83,000	11
Houston	+298,000	27	St. Louis	+55,000	9
San Francisco	+136,000	21	Pittsburgh	+53,000	9
San Diego	+121,000	20	Buffalo	+12,000	6

exception of the traditional apartment centers of New York, Chicago, and Washington, metropolitan areas in the Sunbelt had become the centers of apartment construction by the 1970s and 1980s.

The regional shift in apartment construction after 1960 has largely been simply a matter of differential growth. Many of the older cities and metropolitan areas of the Northeast lost population, so housing construction of all kinds was in the doldrums. While some apartment buildings were built in such cities for the elderly or as part of new suburban nodes or urban renewal schemes, there was likely to be less motivation for choosing an apartment than in areas like southern California because low rates of population growth were usually associated with low prices for single-family homes.

The shift of apartment construction to the Sunbelt has also been partly a function of the greatly increased importance of retirement there. From Florida and South Carolina to Arizona and California, apartment-centered retirement communities have burgeoned. The 1970s' trend toward second homes and time-share condominiums also fueled the apartment boom. Table 4 shows the percentage of total housing stock in 10+ buildings in selected SMSAs. Obviously many of our generalizations about the "crowded" older cities of the Northeast and the "sprawling" cities of the Sunbelt may need to be revised. Some of the highest percentages are in the South and West. People are far more likely to live in a large apartment building in Houston than in Buffalo.

In addition to the regional shift, there was a shift of apartment buildings to the suburbs around cities in all regions, leaving fewer than half of the units in 10+ structures located in central cities by 1980 (Table 5). Vast complexes of middle-class garden apartments came to be seen as appropriate ways to develop expanding suburban nodes along outer belts and other major highways. In some locales, apartment buildings were constructed in conjunction with new shopping malls, university campuses, hospitals, office parks, and other centers of employment. Adequate parking became more important

Table 5. Percentage units in 10+ structures in central cities, 1960 and 1980

City	1960	1980
Chicago	91	58
Atlanta	91	37
St. Louis	89	41
San Diego	85	50
Boston	65	40

than access to public transit. As apartment living became more popular and accepted among the middle class, political resistance in suburban communities broke down.

It is possible that many of our ideas about density gradients and inner city–suburban contrasts may also need revision, since some of the highest residential densities are now found along the outer belts of major cities. Clearly, a look at the local building traditions of specific cities is in order as we attempt to generalize about urban form. A city with a long-standing central city "apartment tradition" like San Francisco is likely to be structured quite differently from one like Atlanta where apartment buildings are a recent phenomenon.

Demographics and the Demand for Apartments

The changing intraurban location of apartment buildings has resulted from a variety of somewhat more complex trends and forces. Apartment construction tended to take a back seat to single-family housing during the 1950s due to a combination of demand by those who had deferred family formation until after the war and the incredibly low cost of land (about 11 percent of the total cost of a house in 1949) resulting from opening up vast tracts for automobile-oriented suburban developments. Other than public housing and a few upscale garden apartments, few multiunit dwellings were added to the housing stock for a decade and a half after the war. By the late 1950s, it was time for apartment construction once again.

The boom in apartment construction after 1960 was fueled by a combination of rapid household formation and unprecedented affluence. Even in cities where total population was not increasing, a combination of children leaving home earlier for university educations or jobs, divorces, retirement, and interurban mobility meant that space was needed for new, often smaller households. Higher levels of affluence and expectations meant that most people were no longer content to share space with families or to take a room in boarding houses. People wanted their own place.

In most cities, apartment construction was at first rather tentative, with a concentration on small, in-fill projects in older neighborhoods, usually along transit lines. These apartments were often boxy complexes with a minimum of design or amenities that were a throwback to the walk-up flats of the 1920s. Many were built on a lot-by-lot basis in neighborhoods which could not mount an effective resistance. The combination of a barrage of single-family house-centered ideology (reinforced now by television sitcoms and ads) and the bleak character of many pre-1965 postwar apartment complexes tended to heighten the image of a classic landscape contrast. Apartments were seen as a place to get started and perhaps as a place to retire. They were places for the "newlywed and nearly dead." Real living took place in houses.

By about 1965, however, another change was on the horizon. The large, well-located luxury apartment returned. A new image for multiunit housing was created with the construction of such "role-model" projects as the Marina Towers in downtown Chicago and the United Nations Plaza in Manhattan. Luxury apartments reappeared on the West Coast as well with towers constructed along the Wilshire corridor and at Marina Del Rey in Los Angeles and atop Russian Hill in San Francisco. Throughout the nation, swimming pools and other amenities were built into new apartment complexes as an attractive "apartment lifestyle" began to develop.

The advent and widespread acceptance of condominium ownership after 1968 greatly facilitated the production of middle-class and luxury multiunit housing. With the development and legalization of the condominium, it was possible to buy an individual apartment (rather than purchasing a share in a cooperative venture, a possibility that had existed in New York and some other cities since the 1880s). Apartment ownership meant that residents in multiunit structures could now deduct mortgage payments from income taxes and experience "wealth creation" through the inflation of housing prices just as house buyers could do. Moving out of an apartment and into a house to obtain these financial advantages was no longer necessary by the 1970s. The term *luxury condo* came to be a semantic linkage comparable to what *luxury apartment* had been in the 1870s and 1880s.

The apartment building has come full circle over the past century. Just as in the 1880s, many apartment buildings today (as well as condos) are intended for the relatively well-off, built in the very best locations, and equipped with the latest amenities and technologies. Large residential towers are currently being built in the very best locations in terms of both amenities and accessibility. Multiuse towers such as the John Hancock in Chicago or Trump Tower in New York City occupy sites in the heart of major financial districts. Throughout

The luxury apartment building returns: Marina Towers, Chicago

the nation, from the Boston waterfront to the San Diego waterfront, a variety of apartment and condominium complexes have been built. While the construction of many of these projects has been facilitated by political decisions, such as zoning certain areas for "return-to-the-city" residences, others have resulted from economic and social trends, such as the saturation of some downtowns with office, retail, restaurant, and hotel space and the development of an affluent, pro-urban subculture. Signs in midtown Manhattan suggesting that "if you lived in this complex you would be home now" are meant to appeal to weary commuters. The signs also suggest the luxury possible in such buildings—spas, balconies, gyms, cafes, and so on.

Luxury apartments and condominiums have also captured amenity locations well beyond the central city. From Miami Beach to Coronado, California, residential towers overlook a variety of oceans, bays, lakes, golf courses, and parks.

Permanent Buildings and Permanent Residents: New Generalizations about Life in America

Large downtown luxury apartment buildings, sprawling garden apartment complexes, and public housing towers all have a built-in permanence that did not characterize the more flexible, smaller-scale landscapes of earlier cities. The very size of these buildings creates the neighborhood around them. They do not experience land-use changes in the same way that the houses of the nineteenth century did. They do not become industrial or commercial as land rent increases. To a degree, the same permanence may be increasingly true for the residents of such environments.

While the classic American pattern of residential moves associated with life cycle changes has been from family home to an apartment to a "starter home" to a bigger home and then possibly back to an apartment in retirement, there is reason to believe that this pattern is increasingly atypical. No longer can multiunit housing be thought of

CITIES AND BUILDINGS

Apartment buildings in an amenity location: Marina Del Rey, Los Angeles

as simply a temporary residence, a place to get started. For many of the poorest Americans, public housing of some sort has become a permanent home because they have little prospect of moving up to a house. This is especially true as the tiny houses that were once grouped together on subdivided lots or on the edge of town in many cities become rare relics of an earlier era of building. In some cities, gentrification of older housing and the general inflation of housing values have also diminished the prospect of moving out of public housing.

While the poorest segments of the population have always had a certain percentage of their number permanently residing in multiunit housing, especially in larger cities, the real change in recent decades has more to do with the middle and upper classes. At least since the late nineteenth century, a minority of middle-income people in large American cities have chosen to live in apartment buildings for their entire lives. While such a choice would be considered the norm in cities such as Paris, Vienna, or Madrid, in the United States permanent residents of multiunit housing have often been viewed as being slightly different, except perhaps in New York City. Such residents are thought to have skipped the "normal" life-cycle progression. Today, however, with the high costs of housing in many areas and the increasing congestion of freeways and other modes of transportation, there may be an increasing number of people in an increasing variety of cities choosing multiunit options. This is especially the case with condominiums, since ownership allows the tax and investment advantages associated with the single-family home. It may be time to revise our notions of a "normal" American way of life. We could use more studies of families and individuals who have spent lifetimes in pleasant, desirable, middle-income multiunit environments. "City living" is becoming a viable, permanent option in many American metropolitan areas, just as it has been for centuries in many of the cities of Europe.

Apartment Types and Distribution: The New Urban Landscape

After nearly a century and a half of experimentation, American cities at last have a wide variety of multiunit options. The percentage of total housing stock in buildings with ten or more units has increased dramatically in most metropolitan areas over the past decades, especially in the Sunbelt. For example, while 10+ structures increased from comprising 9 percent to 18 percent of the housing stock of greater Boston between 1960 and 1980, the comparable percentages for Houston and Phoenix were 4 percent to 27 percent and 2 percent to 16 percent, respectively. Even "sprawling" Los Angeles had 24 percent of its dwelling units in 10+ structures in 1980 (see Table 4).

The Sunbelt city of San Diego provides a good example of both the increasing numbers and changing variety and locations of multiunit housing in a moderately large but fast-growing American city. In 1960 the San Diego metropolitan area had very few large apartment buildings, and only 6 percent of its total housing stock was in 10+ buildings. Of the few large apartment complexes that existed, 55 percent were located in and around the downtown area. Most of these could be classified as low- and moderate-income rentals. As a generalization, in 1960 the classic high-density, low-income core surrounded by low-density, high-income suburbs still existed. By 1980, things had changed.

In 1980, the San Diego area had 141,000 units in 10+ buildings, or 20 percent of the total housing stock. Nearly 50,000 units were in buildings with more than 50 dwellings. Half of the 10+ buildings were located outside of the city of San Diego, and only 13 percent were located in or around the downtown area. Both the variety of building types and the variety of locations were unprecedented in the area. High-rise luxury condos overlooked the water in La Jolla and Coronado, while modest low-rise complexes were common in suburban El Cajon. Apartments and condos came in almost all sizes,

Condos in a converted warehouse on the Boston waterfront

shapes, prices, and locations by 1980, and the variety has continued to increase.

In an era of rapidly escalating land prices, it is clear that some American cities are underbuilt. The former reliance on construction of single-family houses, especially in very accessible and/or attractive locations, has led to some conflicts and controversies as pressures to tear down houses in favor of multiunit complexes (often involving rezoning) increase. In San Diego, in-fill projects have greatly changed the character of many neighborhoods, and battles over everything from access to natural light to parking spaces have led to building moratoriums in several areas. The juxtaposition of ranch houses and towers often makes for some difficult aesthetic problems.

Most models of city structure postulate a density gradient outward from the CBD. Many suggest that decisions about where to live are based upon a trade-off between access (center) and space (periphery), with affluent populations generally opting for more space and so a location in the outer zones of the city. With a much larger percentage of the populations of most metropolitan areas living in multiunit housing than ever before, such trade-offs become less relevant. Today, spacious apartments and condominiums may exist in any part of the urban area, and so amenities both inside and nearby the building are the key variables. Trade-offs may occur, but they are likely to have more to do with architecture, spas, views, and other amenities than with space. In addition, since the apartment boom has taken place very largely in the suburbs over the past two decades, peripheral locations are often the highest-density ones for those seeking multi-unit housing. Similarly, the highest amenity areas, such as beaches and lakeshores, are likely to be very high-density environments. Conversely, central city apartment buildings are often located amidst single-family homes in preexisting, low-density neighborhoods. In many American cities, the density gradient has become extremely bumpy, with peaks and valleys everywhere. As urban architectural options have become more varied and complex, so too must be our generalizations about the way cities are put together.

6 Drive-in Dreams

Decades of Design on the American Commercial Strip

The commercial strip—defined as a major street of considerable length lined with commercial activities—is not an American invention. The Champs Elysées in Paris, the Diagonal in Barcelona, the Paseo de la Reforma in Mexico City, and the many High Streets in English towns and cities are but a few examples of commercial strips outside of North America. However, the evolution of the commercial strip as an incubator for a set of new and unique building types, as opposed to simply being an extension of downtown, both functionally and architecturally, is a distinctly North American phenomenon. The commercial strip has become a dominant element in the landscapes of North American cities and has been the focus of both critics and admirers of the American scene. America has shaped the strip, and the strip has shaped America.

Over the decades, commercial strips have become the "dirty old men" of the American scene. They are often criticized and much maligned, yet few writers have actually attempted to describe in detail how they have come to look and function the way they do.[1] Much of the criticism has been contradictory, with some arguing that the strip is too chaotic and messy while others maintain that it is too dull. While some have said that the strip is too futuristic, others have suggested that it is behind the times. Two things are certain: one is that the buildings along the strip have generally not appealed to architects, planners, and other students of the urban scene; and the other is that criticism of the strip tends to be more emotional than for most other types of urban settings. For example, a recent newspaper article described a major commercial strip in San Diego as

> that gaudy, linear six-mile strip of signs and undefined architecture. . . . a thoroughfare of visual blight. Development pro-

ceeded piecemeal over the decades, resulting in a hodgepodge of store fronts, signs and shopping centers that create confusion for motorists. . . . vacant store fronts attested to the street's gloomy commercial appeal; signs were abominable; second-hand stereo and automobile dealerships were vying for attention next to new, L-shaped shopping centers that were becoming more prolific; zoning seemed haphazard; street lighting was inconsistent.[2]

It is difficult to determine just why so many people have found the strip distasteful. Some of the criticism may be class-based in that strip-haters never fail to mention the abundance of used car dealers and secondhand stores. Some criticism reflects a bias toward a European/Renaissance architectural ideal that emphasizes unity and harmony over diversity. Some of the criticism is just plain wrong. For example, while the article quoted above mentions "vacant store fronts" and "gloomy commercial appeal," such storefronts are rare, and the number of businesses along the strip has consistently increased. Clearly, we need to examine both the evolution of American commercial strips and the evolution of our attitudes toward them.

While critics of the strip have greatly outnumbered its admirers, there have been a few fully credentialed defenders of the built environment along American highways. In *Learning from Las Vegas*, Venturi, Brown, and Izenour maintain that "it is the highway signs, through their sculptural forms or pictoral silhouettes, their particular positions in space, their inflected shapes, and their graphic meanings, that identify and unify the megatexture. They make verbal and symbolic connections through space, communicating a complexity of meanings through hundreds of associations in a few seconds from far away. Symbol dominates space . . . if you take the signs away, there is no place."[3] Others have argued that strips, quite apart from the way they may look, are valuable additions to the urban scene because, quite simply, they work. Grady Clay contends that

> as long as the North American economy continues to grow, the highway strip is likely to continue serving a vital function as a linear disposal area for surplus urban energies. As surpluses change, the strip will react. . . . The efficient strip is the path of least resistance. On the strip, one can set up shop in a hurry, dispose of a cargo to dozens of buyers, move in or move out quickly, and deal in short haggles. It is a place of easy transactions. If you do not like it, try down the road.[4]

It is hard to deal with the strip objectively. It has come to stand simultaneously for all that is right and all that is wrong with American cities. It represents chaos and flexibility, poor taste and economic opportunity, unwise planning and efficiency, and congestion and mobility. Like the skyscraper and the single-family house, it tells us a great deal about American cultural values.

Changing Values and the Flexible Strip

Compared to most architectural landscapes, the commercial strip has been characterized by frequent, rapid, and massive changes. While major downtown buildings and typical residential neighborhoods have provided relatively stable images of American architecture, commercial strips have symbolized aesthetic flexibility and transitory tastes. The stability of downtown skyscrapers and department stores, for example, is explained by the fact that they involve large amounts of capital and are built to last for several generations. While some modifications may occur over time, the original architectural statement usually remains intact. Similarly, the American house has been characterized by architectural conservatism. Traditional house types (ranches, English Tudor, Spanish, etc.) have remained the most popular ones, and neighbors often object to nonconforming additions. The look of the commercial strip, on the other hand, has changed continuously, and a design popular only last year is likely to be passé this year. Change is never uniform along the strip, however, and so a certain often mentioned "chaos" is built into the look of the strip as buildings representing a variety of eras and styles compete for attention. There is a related historical layering of economic activities along the strip, since new uses (currently yogurt shops and video rentals) are quick to appear while older uses sometimes remain long past their primes.

The architecture along the American commercial strip can be seen as an almost immediate reflection of and response to changes in American aesthetic, political, and economic values. Innovations in design, transportation, and land use quickly show up on the strip; the gas stations, drive-in theaters, motels, diners, minimalls, and automobile showrooms that typify the American "Miracle Mile" can be read like a text on American cultural history. The strip is a mirror and a temporal collage of American culture.

The architectural forms found along the strip do not represent particular building types and functions in the same way that skyscraper office towers or single-family houses do. In fact, the dominant form along the strip has sometimes been referred to as the "decorated shed"—that is, a minimalist structure capable of taking on whatever persona happens to be in vogue at the time, from "early giant arti-choke" to "boomerang modern." Nevertheless, the architecture of the strip has evolved in systematic ways over the past 100 years, and a close examination of the strip can tell us a lot about the built environment of the American city. It can also reveal much about American landscape tastes.

Urban Eras and a Typology of Commercial Strips

A linear collection of commercial activities, while quite literally a commercial strip, long predates the vernacular strip as an incubator for unique functional and aesthetic architectural forms. Even ignoring the Champs Elysées and other European precedents, we can identify early examples of a strip orientation or strip mindset in North American cities going back to at least the early 1800s, when Main Streets began to evolve. These antecedents, however, did not provide the context for development of a unique architecture and ambiance. With the advent of the automobile and a great variety of new automobile-related land uses, such as gasoline stations and motels, a unique strip architecture began to evolve. Through a variety of eras, along outer belts and frontage roads, the evolution has continued.

There have been at least eight stages, or eras, in the evolution of strip architecture, which I have termed Main Street, Main Street Extension, the Streetcar Strip, the Early Automobile Strip, the Streamlined Automobile Strip, the Classic Automobile Strip, the Environmental Strip, and the Corporate Megastrip. By examining each one, we can better understand some of the relationships between spatial context, socioeconomic context, and architectural innovation.

Main Street as the Original Strip

By the early 1800s, if not before, American cities were nearly always laid out upon a grid. With the development of special-purpose buildings in the mid-nineteenth century, commercial activity tended to concentrate on one main street, while the rest of the grid was relegated to secondary uses.[5] The medieval (and postmedieval) cities of Europe had been characterized by functional differentiation (though not commercial-residential separation)—weavers tended to live and work on one street, while goldsmiths tended to live and work on another. In the American city, every important business sought a location on Main Street, while residential and industrial activities located elsewhere. Main Street was the first exclusively commercial strip with its own look and architecture.

Main Street was meant to be imposing. Every building on it was designed to have a definitive front that conformed to the architectural

The main street, Charleston, South Carolina, was an early (i.e., eighteenth-century) commercial strip.

tastes of the time, whether it was Italianate or Romanesque. Since the backs and sides of such buildings were often simple and unadorned, it was on Main Street that the "decorated shed" tradition began. False fronts on Main Street made American cities more imposing than they actually were. It was not until the invention of the skyscraper that business buildings (other than the often monumental city hall) had to have four "designed" sides.

The fact that town grids focused on a main street rather than on a public square or plaza had a major impact on the morphology and ideology of American cities. While some American cities were designed around courthouse squares and other types of civic spaces, such plazas usually lost out to Main Street rather quickly. Main Street was *the* place to be, and when cities grew and more space was needed, Main Street was extended, and American cities typically became more elongated and less square or circular in shape.

The important point here is that the later prominence of the commercial strip was inherent in the way Americans thought about cities and how cities should be organized. Americans never thought of their cities as compact, walled, internally focused places designed to protect a sacred center from outsiders. Rather, American cities were frontier settlements—gateways to somewhere else—which were designed to facilitate movement and expansion. Commercial districts were not "set in stone" as they often were, literally, in Europe. In America, commerce took place on the move, on the road, on the *strip*.

Early extensions of a main street: Louisville, Kentucky

Architecturally, a unique contribution of Main Street was its definite, but distinctly opposite, front and back organization. With major expenditures going for the facades (including false fronts) of buildings, the backs of even the most imposing edifices often became disamenities. Behind Main Street were the service alleys, storage sheds, trash piles, stables, and tenements of the working city. Compared to European and other traditional cities, the interface between the commercial core and the predominantly residential districts beyond was a messy one. Very early on, a sort of "zone in transition" was visible behind Main Street. Meanwhile, Main Street grew longer as businesses continued to concentrate along it.

Main Street Extension and the Streetcar Strip

Most American cities were originally located on a major transportation corridor, whether a harbor, a river, or a major railroad line. Typically a frontage road (often Front Street) paralleled the waterfront or rail line and provided space for shipping facilities, lumberyards, and the like. While there are many exceptions, such as State Street in Chicago, Main Street usually ran perpendicular to this corridor and away from the disamenity of the loading docks. During the late nineteenth century, as "better" businesses sought locations on higher ground, Main Street was extended.

Broadway, in New York City, epitomizes this pattern. Broadway—and, farther north, Fifth Avenue—came to be the longest main street in America, and throughout the nineteenth century nearly everything of importance in New York was along it. Because Broadway was the central spine of activity, a location even a block or so away from it could spell doom for an entreprenuer. The gradual extension of Main Street toward a desirable zone of better residences has been discussed in the section on zones of assimilation (Chapter 2), and so I need not repeat it here. Suffice it to say that the zone of assimilation, or Main Street extension, represents the success of the linear city over the more compact square or circular center associated with many traditional cities. The extended streetcar strip represented a continuation of this way of organizing urban space.

With the advent of horsecars in the 1860s and electric streetcars in the 1890s, both of which ran on fixed rails, main streets and their extensions became even more dominant because access to them was guaranteed by predictable transportation. So far, none of this was unique to North America. London, Paris, and Mexico City were also growing enormously and space for commercial expansion was needed on Oxford Street, Champs Elysées, and Paseo de la Reforma. By the turn of the century, however, these cities begin to diverge. While main street extensions elsewhere in the world were developed relatively carefully and slowly (often using Paris as a model), with buildings that were comparable to if not larger than those in the traditional downtowns (as along the Champs Elysées), in America the process of expansion became more confused.

In the American city, two major trends began to work at cross-purposes with regard to the creation of streetcar-oriented commercial strips: the construction of bigger buildings downtown and the overextension of the strip. The extension of streetcar lines in America took place just as the tall building was being perfected. By the early decades of the twentieth century, office buildings with several hundred thousand square feet of space could be constructed in and around the PLVI. Companies seeking prestige located in them. While the business districts of London and Paris continued to expand horizontally into a number of streets and districts, those of large American cities imploded and expanded vertically. Similarly, large department stores and government buildings clustered around the PLVI, where the streetcar lines came together. Demand for office and retail space on the expanding strip was limited.

There were also too many commercial strips in the typical American city, and most of them were too long. Rather than being part of a design plan, as in Paris or Mexico City (but not London), American strips were products of speculative development alone. Private companies built the streetcar lines often in conjunction with selling land for single-family homes. As lines were extended endlessly to reach land being developed for housing, commercial property along the strips was devalued. While much of it remained vacant for years, some lots were filled with "taxpayer" buildings—small, one-story structures which were intended to generate enough income to pay the property taxes until demand for space increased and proper downtown-type buildings could be constructed. Since demand for bigger office buildings and other downtown functions rarely came to the strip, most of the temporary "taxpayers" are still in existence and have housed primarily drugstores, soda fountains, barber shops, and real estate offices.

Obviously, some early streetcar strips were more successful than others. In cities with high population densities and limited room for expansion, such as San Francisco, many streetcar strips have remained viable to this day. In most cities, however, large numbers of commercial buildings were built flimsily in the first place and have deteriorated badly over time. Boarded-up pawnshops and sleazy pool halls along the older strips play prominent roles in the negative image of the American city.

The Architecture of the Early Automobile Strip

The evolution of an architecture unique to the commercial strip really begins with the automobile. It was during the early decades of the twentieth century that the American commercial strip diverged quite remarkably from those of other nations. As is often the case, the story involves the interweaving roles of changing transportation technologies, capital accumulation, entrepreneurial opportunities, land values, city structure, and landscape tastes. Reading the commercial strip text allows us to pursue many "avenues" of research.

Much of the uniqueness of the American commercial strip came from architectural innovations aimed at servicing and making room for the automobile. In 1900 there were only 8,000 cars registered in the United States; by 1920 there were 8 million. During the 1920s, the number of registered automobiles nearly tripled, and by 1930 there were 23 million cars in America.[6] As travel by automobile became the norm, a variety of auto-related functions evolved, and new architectural forms reflected this. The architecture of the automobile strip could not be borrowed easily; it had to be invented.

The first steps were tentative. Gasoline pumps were set up outside existing stores, and automobile showrooms were located in existing multistory warehouses. Parking was made available in the alleys behind Main Street. Except for the presence of the cars themselves, the city did not look much different. Out along the strip, however, changes were afoot.

The already long streetcar strips that had evolved by the early 1900s grew much longer with the advent of the automobile. National legislation such as the Good Roads Act of 1916 and the Highway Act of 1921 allowed federal funds to be used for road construction, and the total number of miles of surfaced highways doubled during the 1920s. Not only did the strips become longer, but they became a lot more numerous, because a commercial strip could now evolve without the expensive infrastructure of a trolley line. Since many strips were already underbuilt, with much prime, highly visible commercial land still available at affordable prices, the time was right for the emerging auto-entrepreneur. A minimal capital investment could get you a big lot, a big sign, and a shed. The product could be anything from apples from a nearby orchard to rebuilt tires. The emerging strip was a place to get started, the twentieth-century equivalent of the inner-city immigrant quarters of the traditional city.

Gradually, a new architecture evolved to fit the new economic environment. Land uses geared to accommodating automobiles along the new strips had to be invented. To some degree, it was a matter of "form follows function" as new building types evolved to serve new economic activities. John Jakle and Keith Sculle, among others, have researched the origins of such strip components as gasoline stations and motels.[7] The gas station, for example, began as a shed with pumps but gradually evolved to have canopy-covered service islands, enclosed service bays, an office, and restroom facilities. At first, stations tended to be cloaked in such traditional architectural garb as Colonial or Tudor, especially when there was concern about the structure fitting into a residential neighborhood. By the 1930s, however, gasoline stations had become unabashedly modern, partly to emphasize the futuristic ideology and design of automobiles and partly to combat the gloom of the Depression with suggestions of a better "road" ahead.

Motels evolved through the merger of auto camps and resort (often church) camps. With increased travel by automobile during the 1920s, many towns and cities set up free campgrounds in order to get people to stop and shop. The traditional hotel, with its sedate lobby and fancy dining room, was not always appropriate for families having a travel adventure in a Model T. Gradually, "strip entrepreneurs" built cabins grouped around a central courtyard reminiscent of the resort camps of the eastern United States. These cabin complexes were already becoming common along the roadside by the time the

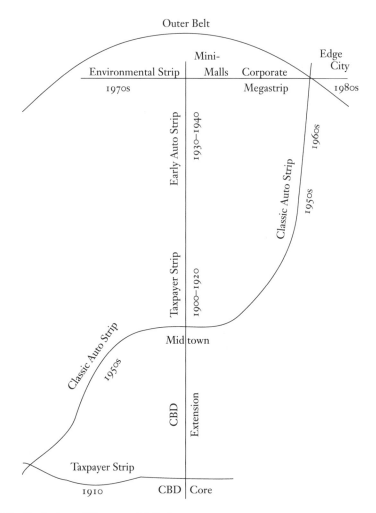

The Evolution of Commercial Strips

*The earliest commercial strips were simply extensions of downtown business streets
made possible by the expansion of streetcar systems. The strip looked and functioned
very much like downtown streets. With the arrival of the automobile, the strip took
on a variety of new space-extensive forms and functions, including camplike motels,
drive-in restaurants, and gas stations. At the same time, architecture to attract a
moving clientele featured such eye-catchers as giant milk bottles and revolving
chickens. More recently, the strip has grown up with the new outer belts and is lined
with mid-rise hotels and offices and a variety of shopping malls. In the process of
overbuilding, many older strips have been left to decay.*

term *motel* was coined in 1925 in San Luis Obispo, California. Although other terms, such as *tourist court, motor court, cottages,* and *cabins,* were used for decades, by the 1950s most complexes had settled on the word *motel.*

Restaurants and "tea rooms" sprang up along emerging strips to feed hungry motorists. As was the case with gas stations and motels, since such businesses had been nonexistent only a few years before, there was no precedent for their design. The safest look for such structures, and for motels, was thought to be domestic imagery. "Kozee Kottages" and "Dew Drop Inns" abounded, usually emphasizing the look of home. "Bungalow Tea Rooms" complete with fluffy yellow curtains and a fireplace reinforced the image of domestic serenity. While such architecture was safe, it did not really attract much attention—and most roadside entrepreneurs wanted to attract attention.

By the late 1920s, two new kinds of strip architecture had become common: signature architecture and exaggerated regional architecture. Both aimed at attracting customers. Signature architecture, or representational signage, had been around in some form at least since the Middle Ages, when tailors hung giant scissors in front of their shops and vintners displayed barrels. In a day when few could read, these images worked well. Legibility was also a problem on the twentieth-century strip. Motorists traveling at 30 miles per hour could not be expected to read detailed and often messy homemade signs. They needed to "read" the scene more quickly. The answer was signature architecture on a scale unknown before.

It has been suggested that the idea of using signature architecture along commercial strips had its origins in the San Francisco Exposition of 1915.[8] When funding for an ethnographic display was left out of the budget, private interests decided to take over and create an exotic commercial strip that would pay for itself. A commercial "Midway Plaisance" had proved very successful as an adjunct to the Columbian Exposition in Chicago in 1893, and so there was a precedent. The "ethnographic strip" of 1915 related external architecture to the products inside: a giant Golden Buddha housed a Japanese concession, while models of an Indian pueblo, Blarney Castle, and a Samoan village featured other treats and displays.

Signature architecture quickly caught on along automobile-oriented commercial strips, since it allowed small entrepreneurs to call attention to their businesses while enabling motorists to read the landscape in a hurry. For a variety of reasons, Los Angeles rather than San Francisco became the center of the innovation, although the look was almost nationwide by the 1930s. The mild climate of southern

Inventing the architecture of the strip: the gas station as cottage, in Delaware, Ohio

California facilitated experimentation with lightweight stucco forms that could be molded into any shape quickly and cheaply. The sprawling nature of the Los Angeles Basin meant that large tracts of cheap land existed on heavily traveled roadways between major nodes of activity. In more traditionally organized urban areas, such land was often either too expensive or too remote, at least during the early 1920s. As auto-oriented businesses sprang up along these arteries, "California Crazy" architecture evolved, complete with giant snow cones, artichokes, doughnuts, coffeepots, frogs, hot dogs, pianos, ships, brown derbys, and a variety of human symbols. As signature architecture diffused across the nation, it was given the name "duck architecture," after a building shaped like a large white duck on Long Island, New York (poultry was sold there). With duck architecture, small businesses could become famous (some would say infamous) overnight. While outrageous and unusual architecture was rarely, if ever, numerically dominant on any strip, there were enough landmark buildings to give character to the new highways. A building in the shape of giant duck is not soon forgotten.

Ironically, though the world fairs were originally intended to teach good taste to a crass and disbelieving American public, they ended up introducing the wild and whimsical shapes of the commercial strip. More giant doughnuts than "white cities" were built in America after the fairs were over. (Perhaps a compromise between the two architectural extremes was White Castle, a chain of hamburger restaurants that offered a predictable product in a predictable, uniform white "castle.")

The second type of architecture to appear on the American commercial strip during the 1920s was "exaggerated regional." A cousin of signature architecture in many respects, regional architecture sought to create a place fantasy instead of (or in addition to) a product fantasy. Restaurants designed to look like fishing boats in Maine or tepees in Texas appealed to passing motorists. Regional architecture was especially popular on strips in the West, where a variety of symbols from cowboys to cacti could be used to embellish a site. Aesthetic confusion sometimes arose when Cape Cod structures were built in New Mexico and pueblo restaurants appeared in Vermont. The line between regional architecture and signature architecture was sometimes blurred.

Both types of architecture were most pronounced along the strips built for the automobile on the outer edges of cities. Nevertheless, as they became more popular and as automobile use increased within cities, they gradually invaded the older streetcar strips and even Main Street. Where land was still cheap and lightly developed along streetcar strips, vacant lots provided space for parking and the occasional duck. Small "taxpayer" buildings could also be removed or modified. Diners and a variety of teapot-shaped cafes sometimes slithered between major buildings downtown. All of this, of course, was quite controversial.

The Streamlined Automobile Strip

The early automobile strip fostered several revolutionary changes in the way American cities looked and functioned, yet at the same time, most of its architecture was basically conservative and derivative. While the strip represented economic democracy in that petty entrepreneurs could make their presence felt, critics of the strip condemned its handmade, somewhat jerry-built ambiance. Similarly, while many new economic activities had evolved, their newness was usually disguised in traditional domestic or regional imagery, such as tepee gas stations. Even ducks were . . . well . . . familiar creatures. Commercial strips were easy to criticize.

Many felt that it was time to have an architecture more suitable for the new society that was being created by the automobile and other forms of new technology. By the 1930s, the strip was becoming more sophisticated. For one thing, more highways were being designed to accommodate automobiles. Ways of controlling traffic and decreasing the number of accidents were sought. During the 1920s, traffic signs and lights were invented, installed, and standardized, and highways

White Castle restaurant, Louisville, Kentucky

were given numbers. Lines were painted on the road to create lanes and divide traffic. Beginning in the mid-1930s, parking meters were used to increase parking turnover (as well as municipal revenue). The modern strip had arrived, and it cried out for modern architecture. Tepees and traffic lights seemed to clash.

Although the Depression was very hard on the building industry, it did not bring a halt to the growing use of automobiles or the growth of automobile-related enterprises. Government programs led to a doubling of miles of improved roads during the 1930s, and gas stations, motels, and the like soon lined them. The Depression did bring a certain dissatisfaction with the "ancien régime" and its clutter of pseudotraditional buildings; there was now a tendency to look forward toward a brighter future. The architecture that evolved to reflect this was called "Streamline Moderne."

Streamline Moderne reflected the design innovations which were occurring in automobiles, airplanes, appliances, and other symbols of the new machine age. After all, cars no longer looked like carriages, so why should gas stations look like carriage houses? Influenced by the emerging Bauhaus or International style from Europe as well as by the geometric look of art deco, Moderne buildings featured a sleek, rounded look and clean, white tiled or ceramic surfaces. Gas stations, cafes, diners, automobile showrooms, and furniture stores all came to look as sleek and streamlined as the automobiles that passed in front of them. Suddenly the ducks and tepees looked out-of-date as another

The Blue Diner, New York City

layer was added to the landscape and the chaos of the strip increased. Fortunately, many decorated sheds could be easily redecorated.

Advocates of the streamlined strip emphasized its honesty and its appropriateness for the machine age it served. Both exteriors and interiors featured modern materials and technologies rather than domestic or exotic imagery. Soda fountains had Formica counters and gleaming steel mixers, while gas stations were designed above all for the efficient servicing of automobiles. Varied textures and peaked roofs gave way to glass and steel, flat roofs, and visible equipment. The aesthetic contrast between the commercial strip and nearby residential neighborhoods was heightened, since Moderne was never a popular style for houses. In America, a sharp line was drawn between the machine age commercial landscape and the landscape of domestic tranquility; this did not exist to any degree in other nations. Gabled roofs and shutters remained popular on commercial buildings even in countries which had pioneered the International Style, while Moderne was used widely in apartment buildings. In America, by contrast, the strip and residential areas each had their own look.

To be successful, entrepreneurs along the strip still had to attract attention to their establishments. What was lost in advertising with the demise of ducks and tepees could be regained through lighting by the 1930s. Neon, which had been invented in the late 1920s, became almost synonymous with the American commercial strip, as colorful and decorative signs began to light the night. Neon-lit and sign-bedecked towers graced many streamlined buildings. Words like "cozy" were seen less often in ads for the new strip.

By the mid-1930s, many commercial strips were getting very crowded, even those running between cities. Jakle reports that one 47-mile stretch of U.S. 1 between Trenton and Newark, New Jersey, had "300 gas stations, 440 other businesses, and 472 billboards," while a 48-mile section of the highway west of New Haven, Connecticut, had a gas station every 895 feet.[9] Maybe the strip was becoming too much of a good thing for the small entrepreneur.

By the end of the interwar period, commercial strips had developed a sufficient variety of economic activities to have their own spatial patterns or geographies. For example, gas stations were numerous and tended to be distributed uniformly along the strip, usually clustered at corners. Motels tended to locate in groups 4 or 5 miles from the city center (in typical midsized cities) so as not to compete with downtown hotels. Grocery stores and the new supermarkets tended to locate a mile or so apart so as to serve a classic hinterland. Commercial strips may have looked chaotic, but they were beginning to have an underlying, predictable spatial organization.

The interwar period had been a time of great experimentation on the commercial strip. New styles and designs had come and gone, and a great variety of new building types had been invented, including the first drive-in restaurants and movie theaters. Some things worked and some, like the drive-through supermarket, did not. Just as everything was about to come together, however, World War II intruded, and things were put on hold as gas was rationed and train travel was revived. The Classic Automobile Strip had to wait until the postwar years.

The Classic Automobile Strip: 1948–1973

From the opening of the first McDonald's drive-in restaurant in 1948 to the gas crisis of 1973, the car culture reigned supreme on the American commercial strip. Growing levels of affluence, increased leisure time, and the emergence of a teenage subculture all contributed to the importance of the strip as a center of activity. Among the most visible trends affecting the strip during the 1950s and 1960s were the tremendous increase in the sheer number of commercial strips as interstitial suburban developments sprang up between the points of the old star-shaped city; the explosion of drive-in activities, including restaurants, theaters, and banks; the development of a true strip architectural style that suited the new activities and helped to create a sort of carnival atmosphere along the strip as "cruising" became a major form of recreation (strolling was definitely passé); the growth of franchise or chain operations, which infused the strip with larger amounts of capital than had ever been the case during the era of the small enterpreneur; and the construction of the first planned shopping centers. In many cities, the strip was replacing downtown as *the* place to see and be seen.

The basic spatial structure and organization of American cities changed markedly in the postwar years. The star-shaped city that had been the result of a reliance on trolley and bus lines gave way to a more circular urban area as interstitial areas were filled in. The plentiful supply of new land made accessible by the automobile meant that the cost of land as a percentage of total building costs decreased. It therefore became possible to use several acres of land in the middle of suburbia for such extensive land uses as drive-in theaters and miniature golf courses. Lots of new commercial space was available on the road to suburbia.

The relationship between socioeconomic structure and spatial structure was clearly elucidated on the strip. The popularity of drive-in activities was due not only to unprecedented levels of automobile ownership, but also to the demographic and residential changes that were occurring during the postwar years. Record levels of family formation and high birthrates meant that young, more affluent families were a market to be catered to. Drive-ins allowed families with several small, unruly children to eat out and go to a movie without disturbing anyone else. People could dress casually in such controversial garb as Bermuda shorts and be entertained cheaply at drive-ins (unless the cost of the car was factored in). Such family outings not only fit nicely into the "Ozzie and Harriet" domestic imagery of the 1950s, but they were increasingly necessary because the relative isolation of the new suburban neighborhoods made it difficult for mom and the kids to do much of anything until dad got home with the car.

Drive-in restaurants first appeared in the 1920s (the Pig Stand in Dallas, 1924), but it was not until the 1950s that they became something more than sheds serving snacks. Cruising to the large, octagon-shaped, brightly lit, canopied restaurants (usually with names like "Eddy's") was exciting. Although never really common, the possibility of witnessing innovations such as roller-skating waitresses was always there. By the late 1950s, young people socialized into this culture came to view the automobile and the strip as fulfillers of every basic gastronomical, recreational, and procreational need.

Along with socioeconomic and spatial changes came architectural innovations more expressive of the new age. As the strip got bigger and more affluent, most of the architectural styles traditonally associated with it seemed puny and outmoded. Taxpayer strips, cozy cot-

The Classic Automobile Strip: McDonald's, San Diego, ca. 1970

tages, stucco ducks, and white, boxy gas stations were just not making architectural statements appropriate for the new tail-finned auto culture. This was a time of unbridled optimism; America was a wonderful place which dominated the world economically and militarily. With A-bombs and Corvettes, how could we lose our position at the top of the heap? A new look was needed for the strip.

The architectural styles and building types that evolved on the Classic Automobile Strip have been given many names, most of them whimsical. As buildings along the strip became larger and were set well back from the street, unusual, futuristic roof-lines were used to attract attention. The term most often used to describe the new look was "Exaggerated Modern," but Tom Wolfe's "Boomerang Modern" is more descriptive. In his classic book, *Kandy-Kolored Tangerine-Flake Streamline Baby,* he describes a street in North Hollywood: "Endless scorched boulevards lined with one-story stores, shops, bowling alleys, skating rinks, tacos, drive-ins, all of them shaped not like rectangles but like trapezoids, from the way the roofs slant up from the back and the plateglass fronts slant out as if they're going to pitch forward on the sidewalk and throw up. The signs are great too. They all stand free on poles outside. They have horrible slick doglegged shapes that I call boomerang modern."[10]

Many features were common in the landscape of Exaggerated Modern architecture: large arrows and sparkling decorations shaped like stars or sputniks (to symbolize the space age), flashing neon signs, unexpected angles, and seemingly unrelated and mismatched sets of squares, circles, and trapezoids. Alan Hess maintains that "streamlining had glorified efficiency—doing more with less—an appealing idea in the difficult economic conditions of the thirties, but elaboration and even excess suited the abundance of the fifties."[11]

Above all, the new style symbolized movement and flight. Describing "Googie architecture," a type of Exaggerated Modern named after a coffee shop in Los Angeles, Douglas Haskell suggests that "it starts off on the level like any other building. But suddenly it breaks for the sky. The bright red roof of cellular steel decking suddenly tilts upward as if swung on a hinge, and the whole building goes up with it like a rocket ramp. But there is another building next door. So the flight stops as suddenly as it began. It seems to symbolize life today. . . . Skyward aspiration blocked by Schwab's Pharmacy."[12]

The unprecedented excesses of Exaggerated/Googie/Boomerang Modern buildings led to unprecedented levels of strip criticism. While one or two such buildings along a strip might have served as landmarks, six or seven sometimes created a scene of jumbled, disjointed chaos, since not only did the buildings fail to relate to each other, but the parts of each building seemed unrelated as well. Peter Blake called the American landscape "God's own junkyard" and described the strip as "highways lined with billboards, jazzed-up diners, used car lots, drive-in movies, beflagged gas stations, and garish motels."[13] In a series of articles, David Lowenthal attempted to show that American landscape tastes during this period favored an abundance of big, chaotic, formless, futuristic, and unrelated individual features.[14] While truly "exaggerated" buildings were always relatively rare compared to the vast numbers of intervening modest structures, they did tend to focus both criticism and admiration on the strip.

The architectural exuberance of the strip was mirrored by economic exuberance. There seemed to be no end to the number of gas stations (sometimes four at one intersection, all giving away dishes or silverware) and fast food restaurants that the strip could support. The number of motels increased from 13,000 in 1939 to 62,000 by 1961 as many downtown hotels closed or became residential. With so much money to be made, franchises quickly overwhelmed the petty entrepreneur. Pioneered during the interwar years (White Castle, 1921; Howard Johnson, 1935), chains allowed people with a minimum amount of capital to buy a franchise and run it as an individual business with the aid of an already recognizable product and architectural logo. McDonald's, with its Exaggerated Modern roofline and golden arches epitomized this trend. All along the strip, Joe's Gas and the Dew Drop Inn gave way to Shell and Holiday Inn. Although the

Boomerang Modern and other innovations: left and opposite top, *San Diego;* opposite bottom, *Phoenix*

buildings remained exaggerated, they became more predictable. The strip was soon subjected to yet another round of criticism, at least by a few, for its "placelessness."

Edward Relph, in his book *Place and Placelessness*, argues that the architecture of the strip may appear to be chaotic but that it is really too simple; it declares itself too openly.[15] While traditional landscapes were characterized by ambiguities, contradictions, complexities, and modifications that made them interesting, the American strip was filling up with buildings which were unifunctional: one building serving only one purpose. The landscape was becoming "univalent," each building having its own significance unrelated to place except through proximity. Even the old ducks and tepees, while exhibiting a bit of chaos here and there, somehow had mirrored the whims and aspirations of real places better than the golden arches of McDonald's. Still, for a while at least, the strip worked.

Cruising through the carnival atmosphere of the "Kandy-Kolored" strip was fun, especially for those not deeply concerned with architectural criticism. The colorful chaos of tail-finned cars creeping through a landscape seemingly full of neon towers, windmill-filled miniature golf courses, sombrero-shaped restaurants, and not-quite-watchable-from-the-street drive-in movie screens was an experience you just could not have in most parts of the world. Recently, a field called "commercial archeology" has evolved for those seeking to better understand, and in some cases to preserve some of the best examples of, this part of our architectural heritage.

During the 1960s, a few omens began to appear which suggested that the Classic Auto Strip might not last forever. The number of drive-in movies peaked nationally in 1961 and has been rapidly declining ever since. Smaller cars (and bucket seats) have been blamed, but changing tastes and escalating land values have been more important. By the late 1960s, nearly every type of drive-in began to diminish in number. There were three main reasons for this decline. First, self-service was taking the place of curb service, so that people had to get

out of their cars and walk inside, even to buy gas. Doing everything while sitting in your car was no longer possible. Second, the planned shopping center began to offer settings for eating, drinking, and shopping that were worth getting out of the car for. While most early centers (through the mid-1950s) were little more than indented strips with parking out front, by the early 1960s the mall had arrived. New American pastimes and subcultures began to form. Finally, land values were becoming too high to allow for space-extensive activities such as drive-in theaters and cruisable restaurant parking lots.

The bloom was already off the strip by the time the gas crisis hit in

1973, but that year marks as good a time as any to recognize the demise of the Classic Strip and the arrival of the toned-down "Environmental" version.

The Environmental Strip: 1973–1985

By the early 1970s, many Americans were beginning to doubt the wisdom of continued unbridled growth and to voice concerns about environmental deterioration. The optimistic attitudes of the postwar era gave way to more somber images of a polluted and mismanaged American landscape. In a world where people sang songs about country roads, watched television specials on the destruction of natural habitats, and recycled aluminum cans, the futuristic, often wasteful glass and steel, neon-lit boomerang modern strip seemed inappropriate, if not gross. It is no surprise that the "back-to-nature" ideology quickly appeared on the ever chameleon-like strip in both forms and materials. The gasoline crisis of 1973 only served to drive home the point.

As political measures were taken to control pollution of the air and water, some activists began to attack what they saw as visual pollution, especially along the American commercial strip. There were deeper reasons for their hostility toward the strip than criticism of its aesthetics. Chester Liebs writes: "From its very beginnings, roadside commercial architecture had generally mirrored the longings and preferences of the population at large. Most recently the Exaggerated Modern visually encoded a nation that had been hot-rodding over the landscape, polluting the environment while exhausting valuable natural resources. It is not surprising that this vocabulary of images for wayside vending would be criticized, denounced, and rejected by a society beginning to challenge the values of the postwar period."[16]

In addition to environmentalism, other ideologies were beginning to have an impact on the strip by the mid-1970s. The historic preservation movement, which gained momentum during preparations for the Bicentennial celebrations of 1976, made a considerable contribution to the look of the strip but in an ironically perverse way. Preservationist ideologies showed up not in attempts to preserve the considerable architectural heritage of the strip but rather in efforts to falsely historicize and romanticize it. The strip soon filled up with exposed brick and decoratively "timbered" structures which featured beveled and/or stained glass, fireplaces, flowered carpets, and black and white photos of top-hatted men and gingham-clad women in "granny" dresses. The quiche-and-spider-plant look of the newly renovated "Olde Townes" invaded the strip. The juxtapositioning of "Granny's

Old Place" and the "Sputnik Drive-In," however, further contributed to the surrealism of the strip.

The socioeconomic context of environmental concerns, historic preservation aesthetics, the gasoline crisis, higher land values, and the increasing popularity of mini–shopping centers all led to a new architectural look along the strip: "Woody-Goody." The Woody-Goody look was, above all, subdued. Dark-shingled mansard roofs and buildings surrounded by "natural vegetation" replaced the trapezoidal extravaganzas of earlier years. Signs also became more "natural"-looking, as the names of restaurants were branded onto rustic logs rather than twirling atop poles. Developers sought an architecture that was more compatible with the environment and less "confrontational." The Woody-Goody revolution was aided and abetted by a number of new players who had been much less in evidence or even nonexistent during previous changes in the look of the strip. Of primary importance were planners and corporations.

By the 1970s, most downtown redevelopment schemes and urban renewal projects were either completed or under way, and planners began to turn at least a little attention to the strip. Reflective of the new ideology, sign control ordinances, landscaping requirements, and parking and access regulations began to evolve. The exuberance of the strip was to be contained and directed. Again there was controversy. While some argued that good planning was long overdue on the strip, others suggested that it represented a victory for those who sought to create European-inspired, centrally planned landscapes that were inappropriate for the American strip.

Those who fought such things as sign controls tended to be the local petty entrepreneurs. Those who had corporate franchises were less concerned. Corporations were generally quick to take down their giant, revolving signs, since such high-profile organizations liked to be seen as good neighbors, which implied an environmental awareness. They also no longer needed such signs. Large corporations could achieve name and product recognition through television advertising. Once large numbers of people began to hum "You deserve a break today," McDonald's was free to tone down its golden arches to a minimalist, two-dimensional version of the real thing. For businesses without a television budget, the prospect of attracting customers was more difficult. Sign controls applied to everyone on the new kinder, gentler strip.

The new look and spatial organization of the strip also projected some very significant functional changes. The most obvious was the drastic decline in number of gas stations. For instance, on a 6-mile stretch of El Cajon Boulevard, one of San Diego's best examples of a commercial strip, the number of gas stations peaked at 52 in 1950 but plummeted to 11 by 1988, and many of these were limited-service minimarts. Fast-food outlets, on the other hand, increased in number from 2 to 61 during this period, and many of them also grew in size and in the complexity of offerings. As Americans became more sophisticated, "burger and sushi" places were no longer inconceivable. During the same period, the retail sector also expanded from 121 to 161 outlets along the boulevard, with video stores leading the way.[17]

As land values increased along El Cajon Boulevard and planning ideologies were accepted, more restaurants and retail outlets moved into planned mini-shopping centers with toned-down mansard roofs and signs that were most easily seen by those already in the parking lot. Many such centers were constructed on land once occupied by a gasoline station. As if to say "thank you" for a collective exercise of good taste by private enterprises, the city built a grassy median along part of the boulevard and undergrounded some of the overhead wires. Chaos along the strip just wasn't what it used to be. Bob (Bob's Big Boy) and Jack (Jack-in-the-Box) were replaced by bark-filled flower gardens leading to homogeneous buildings with logos that had to be known to be recognized. According to Kent MacDonald, "in the mess of the Fifties strip we sorted information, scanning the profusion of words and images, creating connections between them. Today we face a strip that is overprocessed, sifted through, and denuded of its vitality. To engage this sterile environment requires no act of imagination, merely a passive mind that can make a calculated response to stimuli."[18] For a while, nearly everyone seemed to relish criticizing and dismantling the "Fifties strip." Now that it is disappearing, some people are beginning to miss it.

The Corporate Megastrip: From the 1980s to Century 21

The beginnings of the Corporate Megastrip long predate 1985, perhaps going back as far as the development of the Wilshire Boulevard "Miracle Mile" in the 1930s, but it was during the heyday of the savings-and-loan-spawned building boom that it reached its apogee. Starting in the late 1960s, new megastrips evolved as frontage roads near freeways and outer belts. For a while, there was little other than scale and the existence of a regional shopping center to differentiate these strips from those elsewhere. Gas stations, fast food, and motels abounded. By the 1980s, however, much had changed. New malls were built and old ones were expanded until the emergence of massive "mallvilles" internalized the business of the megastrip. Multistory motor hotels appeared and replaced motels, only to be replaced them-

The restrained look of the "environmental" 1970s, San Diego

selves by towering hotels complete with convention facilities. Office parks and medical centers, each surrounded by extensive parking lots and multilevel garages, made the megastrip look more like a downtown skyline from a distance. Up close, however, it remained an automobile-oriented strip but one that reflected both the outlandish expenditures of capital and the high levels of discretionary income that characterized America during the 1980s. This strip, too, may be coming to an end. While some of these megastrips have blossomed into less striplike urban subcenters, many have kept their linear, frontage-road character.

Some have argued that the megastrip is the new downtown. If so, the strip has come full circle over the past 100 years since the days when buildings comparable to or better than those of lower Manhattan were built farther north on Broadway. Typical megastrips, however, have maintained a certain strip ambiance if not a really unique architecture. In San Diego's Mission Valley, for example, two regional shopping centers, a sports stadium, several massive hotels and convention facilities, and a variety of office buildings cluster around several exits along a 6-mile stretch of freeway. They are linked to the highway but not to each other, and so a new downtown, at least in the sense of intensive, face-to-face interaction, has not arrived.

The style most associated with the megastrip of the 1980s is postmodern. Postmodern architects have largely rejected the worship of "rational" solutions and functional "less is more" buildings in favor of a return to whimsy. At its best, postmodern architecture can mean pink and mauve turrets and towers which add a sense of playfulness and fantasy to a corporate structure. At its worst, it can mean a jumble of unrelated historical references that can make the fifties strip seem tame by comparison. While every section of the modern North American city, including the downtown, has experienced some postmodernism, the megastrip is most likely to epitomize it. With nearly all of its largest structures built during the 1980s, the megastrip can exude a powerfully colorful presence.

The return of whimsy to the strip raises some questions about the degree of objectivity that has characterized earlier criticism of strip aesthetics. It may be that rather than being "ugly, chaotic, gaudy, cluttered, and messy," the strip was simply out of step with the prevailing wisdom of the time. The "tastemakers" of society have typically worked in the corporate centers and city halls downtown, not along the strip. During the peak boomerang exuberance along the strip in the 1950s and 1960s, the architectural style that dominated the downtown was functional modernism, so that the downtown and the strip contrasted mightily in terms of design standards. Today, just as the "modernist agenda" of clean, minimalist, towerless, and signless buildings has been accepted on the strips of earlier eras, downtowns and the new megastrips have begun parading a plethora of pink protuberances.

In some cases, there has been an actual raiding of strip artifacts. For example, in 1983 a 6-acre drive-in movie theater on El Cajon Boulevard in San Diego was torn down to make way for a shopping center. The logo of the theater, the Campus Drive-In, had been a giant neon majorette complete with twirling baton that had appeared on the back of the screen structure, facing the street. The majorette was given to the "Save Our Neon Organization" for storage, and it now appears as the logo for a cinema nine-plex in a shopping mall, along with a replica deco-streamline tower. In Boston, a giant milk bottle that once housed a dairy bar on a Massachusetts strip has been restored and given a prominent position on the newly renovated waterfront as a snack bar in front of the Children's Museum.

Shopping centers have also "discovered" neon, and so have many downtown hotels and nightspots. Large, exotic neon signs may grace the downtown skyline, but there is very little left on the old strip. El Cajon Boulevard, for example, is tasteful now but out of date. Aesthetic conflicts are developing, however: although the city has forced the removal of many large decorative features as a result of sign control ordinances passed in the environmental 1970s, it has officially declared others to be historic sites. To make up for the lack of visual

The megastrip: Phoenix, Arizona

whimsy on the El Cajon Boulevard strip, the city has recently installed a large pink and turquoise neon sign which boldly proclaims "The Boulevard." The more things change, the more they remain the same.

Strip Types and Strip Geography

Individual commercial strips have always had their own regional personalities, even in the face of nearly universal trends and conditions. Over the past few decades, however, strips have experienced increasing divergence at both the interurban and intraurban levels. While some trends are visible everywhere, local conditions (such as land values and social climate) are more important than ever. It is useful to classify strips on the basis of function as well as design in order to better understand some of the increasing differences between varying types of strips.

In the pre-megastrip days, the biggest contrast in types of commercial thoroughfares was between those that had evolved as streetcar strips and those that had evolved to serve the automobile. The former were not only built up to a greater density, but they were also dominated by neighborhood-serving businesses such as hardware stores and groceries. Automobile strips tended to have sprawling land uses, such as gas stations and motels, that appealed to passing motorists. Until the 1960s, the two types of strips tended to converge in function, as gas stations, drive-ins, and motels were built everywhere.

"The Boulevard" sign was recently erected by the city of San Diego to add visual interest to an old strip previously purged of visual clutter.

Lately, however, this trend has been reversed as many older streetcar strips have become more community-oriented, while newer strips appeal to a mobile clientele.

During the 1960s geographers identified four types of economic activities which tend to be dominant along certain sections of commercial strips: (1) hierarchical, (2) highway-oriented, (3) urban arterial, and (4) specialized.[19] All of these functions may be located on parts of the same strip, or they may give prominent identities to different streets. Hierarchical activities are those serving a stable hinterland population, such as grocery, drug, furniture, and hardware stores. These tend to be spaced regularly and predictably on the basis of population density and access routes. Usually, a full range of hierarchical activities, from banks to beauty parlors, come to be grouped in commercial nodes (increasingly in planned centers), and these nodes act as minidowntowns for neighborhoods. Highway-oriented functions serve a mobile threshold population, and so have little to do with the population densities and characteristics of the immediate neighborhood. Instead, these functions (such as gas stations and motels) are related primarily to the amount of traffic flow. Some activities, such as fast-food outlets, serve both stable and mobile populations.

Urban arterial functions are space-extensive activities which are inappropriate for most other types of locations. Lumberyards, brickyards, junkyards, plant nurseries, and drive-in theaters take up too much space to be located in malls or even in other types of strips. They also may be considered aesthetically marginal. Typical urban arterial activities are not linked either to each other or to the surrounding community. They can be located in any place with enough room. Finally, specialized strips such as "a mile of cars" or "stereo strips" offer a wide selection of similar products in the hope of attracting comparison shoppers. Specialized strips are characterized by strong internal linkages rather than by links to the neighborhood or the highway.

Most strips have a mix of activities, but this may be changing. Space-extensive activities of all kinds are declining along most strips. Urban arterial functions, such as lumberyards, are moving to industrial parks, and pure auto-related functions such as drive-ins and gasoline stations have declined drastically in number. Even sprawling discount stores, with their massive parking lots, have become less ubiquitous on many urban strips.

Although the trend may have peaked, space-intensive activities have been booming along the strip. Minicenters with video rental shops, yogurt shops, dry cleaners, and pharmacies have thrived, along with a variety of eat-in and take-out food outlets.

Economic Growth and Decline on the Strip

As cities have grown and changed, strips have reflected many of the social and economic problems and conflicts that have pervaded the American urban scene. Just as strips have been a mirror of mainstream American society in terms of design and aesthetics, so too have they mirrored social inequalities in terms of economics. One of the most important ways to classify commercial strips is in terms of their overall economic health. Some strips have suffered from economic decline to the point of nearly total abandonment, while others have experienced congestion and chaos as a result of hyperdevelopment. Economic decline along the strip is one of the most visible problems facing American cities.

As we have seen, aesthetic blight is a very difficult thing to measure, especially along the commercial strip, since the tastes, whims, and wisdom which shape it change continuously. Economic blight, on the other hand, is easier to monitor. While the two may be related in that some businesses may avoid "ugly" areas, other factors are more important.

Geographers have identified four types of decline-related blight along the strip: economic, frictional, physical, and functional.[20] The first two are related to changes in the demographic and socioeconomic structure of American cities; the second two are more concerned with the built environment of the strips themselves.

Economic blight relates to the declining populations and decreasing levels of affluence found in many inner-city areas. Many early streetcar strips served relatively narrow residential corridors that were squeezed between rivers, industrial facilities, harbors, and other non-residential areas. The commercial success of such strips depended on a dense surrounding neighborhood and on streetcar ridership. Neither exists today. When the population along a strip consists primarily of elderly, low-income, and minority households, commercial success is unlikely simply because of the lack of buying power. A variety of government agencies are likely to occupy much of the space. The hinterland is too small and too thinly populated to support neighborhood commerce, and automobiles are likely to bypass the older streetcar strips. This leads to the second problem: frictional blight.

Frictional blight results from the difficulty of moving potential customers along the strip. Narrow, poorly maintained commercial thoroughfares—especially those with many twists, turns, traffic lights, potholes, and awkward spaces—do not appeal to modern shoppers, who are used to freeway speeds. Even when they are not really congested, older strips may seem relatively inaccessible and clogged compared to newer megastrips.

Physical and functional blight are related more to the nature of strip buildings themselves than to the location of the strip in the changing socioeconomic organization of the city. Physical blight refers to the deterioration often encountered on older strips. Structures initially cheaply built as "taxpayers" or as decorated sheds, were often simply not worth maintaining. Like skid row, older strips were often redlined and building-coded into oblivion.

Because of the rapid design changes that often occurred along the strip, aesthetic obsolescence sometimes reinforced physical obsolescence when buildings were out of phase. This is related to functional blight. Functional blight occurs when the structures along the strip lack the kinds of spaces needed for modern commerce and cannot be easily modified to create them. While the major problem along the older strips has usually been finding adequate space for parking, the presence of unifunctional buildings has also been a problem. Structures designed to be gasoline stations are very difficult to use for functions unrelated to automobiles, although some very interesting attempts have been made (such as a shop specializing in ten-gallon hats). The same is true for structures designed to look like giant snow cones or artichokes. Similarly, streamlined buildings can be difficult to change into "Woody-Goodies."

In the final analysis, the main reason for all types of blight and deterioration along the American strip is commercial overbuilding. For nearly fifty years now, as new fads and fashions have come along and new highways opened up, commercial ventures have been invented, financed, and built. The strip has provided the space for trial and error. What could never have been done downtown (or in a strictly controlled European city) could easily be done along the strip. The strip was an incubator. Rarely if ever was any attempt made to determine if new commercial space was actually needed. As new buildings were built, old structures were thrown away. It would be interesting to know if the economic growth generated by the construction of new commercial districts has outweighed the economic (and social) decline that has been its by-product.

Not all of the older strips have declined. Strips associated with the zone of assimilation and with the gentrification of older neighborhoods have sometimes experienced hyperdevelopment. Parts of both Wilshire Boulevard in Los Angeles and Central Avenue in Phoenix are lined with high-rise office buildings, resort hotels, restaurants, and cinemas. Along other strips, such as Union Street in San Francisco, art galleries and boutiques have taken over the spaces once occupied by hardware stores and local taverns. In Columbus, Ohio, a deteriorating section of North High Street has become an art gallery and cafe district known as the "Short North." These older strips provide either conveniently located overflow space for downtown activities (Wilshire Boulevard) or highly visible, upscale, pedestrian versions of the traditional specialized function strip (Union Street and the Short North).

Other older strips have experienced revitalization as focal points for neighborhood identity and pride. While in some cases gay or ethnic pride is involved, as in Castro Street in San Francisco, more often there is simply a felt need to improve the commercial ambiance of the neighborhood. In San Diego, where the populations of most central city neighborhoods are stable or increasing due to apartment and condominium construction, the revitalization of several older commercial strips has been spearheaded by neighborhood associations and community groups. In addition to planting street trees and installing benches, they have refurbished and re-illuminated large signs (first installed in the 1940s in order to proclaim neighborhood identity) which overhang the major intersection. In some cases, sidewalks have been decoratively repaved.

There are indications that at least some traditional commercial strips in neighborhoods with stable populations may become increasingly important as shopping destinations for nearby residents. To a very real degree, this may reflect the fact that many economic activities valued by the communities have few options but to locate along such strips. As not only downtowns but the zones of assimilation and discard have been revitalized, rebuilt, and renovated into dazzling office, hotel, and nightspot districts, many activities have been forced to relocate. Major shopping centers are not a solution, since neither the rent nor the ambiance is appropriate for, say, a shoe repair shop or a place to take music lessons. Consequently, some strips have experienced considerable growth based on such neighborhood-oriented functions as bicycle shops, family restaurants, used book stores, card shops, barber shops, and take-out food, as well as grocery stores and video rentals. As through traffic and highway-oriented functions have declined, neighborhood businesses have taken up the slack.

Ethnic Change and the Commercial Strip

Studies of ethnic, especially immigrant, business districts have usually focused on "Chinatowns" and "Little Italys" in and around downtown zones of discard. These areas often contained highly symbolic "banner streets" rich in references to the local subculture. Street markets, large signs in the native tongue, and numerous festivals gave such districts a strong sense of place. Immigrant "ghettos" were a place to learn the ropes and gradually develop skills that would facilitate success in the new land. While such districts still exist today, in most cities they have diminished in number and size as well as in importance.

Urban renewal, freeway construction, stadium and convention center projects, waterfront revitalization, and gentrification have all taken a toll on traditional near-downtown ethnic districts. From the North End of Boston to North Beach, San Francisco, ethnic commercial districts are threatened by high land values and competing land uses. With downtown space at a premium, new ethnic commercial districts have appeared on the strip. While older "taxpayer" strips are most often the destination of immigrant entrepreneurs, a surprising number have found space along automobile strips.

The relationship between ethnic businesses and commercial strips is not an entirely new one. Blacks, for example, long barred from many downtown areas, tended to have banner streets well beyond even the zone of discard. Beale Street in Memphis, 125th Street in Harlem, 14th Street in Washington, D.C., and Mount Vernon Avenue in Columbus, Ohio, are but a few examples. In the early 1960s, Allan Pred compared middle-class white, low-income white, and black commercial strips in Chicago in order to explore, among other things, relationships between black subculture and land use and de-

Ethnic identity along the strip, San Diego

sign.[21] He found that the black commercial strip contained a greater number of certain business types than expected, such as valet services, beauty parlors, record stores, and billiard halls. Facade design and signage also reflected black landscape tastes and preference. As black communities have expanded into lower-density suburban areas, black commercial strips have become common and highly visible.

The most remarkable ethnic changes along American commercial strips have come over the past two decades, as newly arriving Hispanic and Asian groups have created long and colorful banner streets there. These groups realize that to survive in America, businesses must serve a motorized clientele. Big signs (often advertising ethnic-oriented goods and services in the native language) and plenty of parking are part and parcel of the new ethnic landscapes.

In Miami, there are Cuban strips complete with billboards in Spanish urging football fans to support the Dolphins. Throughout the Los Angeles Basin, dozens of miles of duck architecture have been converted to *la arquitectura pata*. Drive-up taco stands and colorful markets line the suburban strips. Such strips appear most unusual when the signs and wall murals are hand-done in group-specific styles and colors. On the northern edge of Detroit, for example, Arabic strips with flowing Arabic script painted onto the sides of buildings have appeared.

Since the early 1980s, the fastest-growing ethnic banner streets in California have been those developed by Southeast Asians.[22] From

Sacramento in the north to Orange County and San Diego in the south, Vietnamese, Cambodian, Thai, and Chinese businesses have flourished on suburban auto strips. Because many Asian immigrants have moved into the 1960-era apartment buildings which are found near the auto strips, many businesses on the new banner streets tend to be neighborhood-oriented, with a preponderance of food markets and the professional offices of doctors, lawyers, and real estate agents. Along El Cajon Boulevard in San Diego, where nearly one mile of the 6-mile strip has become predominantly Asian, the number of food stores had decreased from 80 to 32 between 1950 and 1970 as supermarkets consolidated sales, but by 1988 the number had risen to 48 as small ethnic stores boomed. Similarly, the number of services rose from 480 to 556 between 1970 and 1988, and many such businesses have signs in Chinese characters.

Many of the restaurants along banner streets appeal to a wider public, and the building design and signage are meant to be noticed. Mini-shopping centers (rumored to have been built with Hong Kong money) catering exclusivly to Asian businesses have proliferated. An Indo-Chinese Chamber of Commerce monitors changes along the strip.

The strip has once more become an incubator. Instead of being a place where new automobile-related enterprises are invented, it has become the entry zone for newly established ethnic businesses. In America today, dragon parades at Chinese New Year festivals are likely to be located in front of fast-food outlets in suburban minimalls, and yuppies eat brie in the revitalized zone of discard.

Coming Full Circle: Housing on the Strip

Housing was quite common along early streetcar strips, since commerce tended to concentrate at trolley stops and major intersections. On most strips, housing was the predominant land use. Commercial zoning had become more common by the time automobile strips began to develop, and so housing was less often encountered there except where highways long predated commercial development. Still, it was by no means rare. As strips boomed in the 1950s and 1960s, the quantity and quality of houses along the strip declined. Some houses were converted to other uses and front yards became parking lots. Others were left to deteriorate until commercial buildings could be constructed. Housing did not fit in on the "bigger-is-better," futuristic, neon-lit boomerang modern strip. Who wanted to live next to a giant revolving chicken? Today, however, the trend toward smaller-scale, neighborhood-oriented businesses, and the de-

Housing above first-floor shops, San Diego

cline of such things as gas stations and drive-in theaters is making the strip a little cozier.

Especially in cities where land values are high and housing is expensive and in short supply, efforts are being made to get housing back on the strip. Part of this has to do with supply and demand, since the number of businesses needed to fill the booming minicenters cannot expand indefinitely without a concomitant increase in demand, and part of it is changing attitudes toward zoning and land-use segregation. Just as mixed residential-commercial buildings are being encouraged in revitalized downtowns, so too are they being experimented with along the strip. Since the mid-1980s, multistory structures with restaurants and offices on the first floor and apartments above have begun to appear on the strip—a 500-year-old "brand-new" idea. High-rise apartment and condominium towers are going up on megastrips as the perception of a need to keep people and businesses apart breaks down.

On some strips, housing is being constructed without a commercial component. Especially where space-extensive functions like discount stores and drive-in theaters have vanished, large apartment complexes seem an appropriate replacement as businesses cluster in nearby planned centers. Herein lies a controversy: There are so many trends affecting commercial strips and so many competing ideologies that planning for the future has become difficult. What should a commercial strip be like?

Many strips have become increasingly residential for another reason. Some of the older motels have been converted to "apartment motels" complete with kitchens, while others have simply been rented unchanged on a weekly or monthly basis. As the number of SRO units in the zone of discard declines, people who once might have sought shelter there have turned to the strip. With this trend, many of the vices once associated with inner-city red-light districts have appeared on the strip. Prostitution, for example, once largely confined to downtown hotels in and around the zone of discard, has become a major activity on several strips as "Johns" have become motorized. The strip provides a hospitable setting for the hooker, since she (and increasingly he) can stand at a bus stop, eat at a fast-food chain, rest on a park bench, and do business in a motel or a car. A constant stream of slow-moving traffic makes advertising easy.[23] A large percentage of the arrests for prostitution in San Diego in recent years have occurred on El Cajon Boulevard and strips like it. The strip has become an "immoral landscape" for other than aesthetic reasons, although many of the ladies contribute in both areas.

Podding versus Gridding: Spatial and Aesthetic Issues

For well over a century, a grid of streets was considered to be as American as apple pie. Long, straight streets served to tie the city together and to create regular, predictable patterns of blocks. As early as the turn of the century, some began to argue that this regularity was unnecessary and that streets were far too abundant. Perhaps borrowing from "romantic" preindustrial city scenes and even from late-nineteenth-century cemeteries, writers such as Ebenezar Howard, while advocating new "garden cities" on the periphery of major cities, suggested plans that minimized the role of streets. Such "new towns" were to be characterized by superblocks, with school, shopping, and recreation facilities in the middle (surrounded by grass or parking). During the 1920s and 1930s, suburban neighborhoods with curvilinear streets designed to minimize through traffic began to appear. By the 1970s, the antistreet mentality was in full swing.

The ideal city changed from one organized around a grid of streets to one characterized by superblocks, cul-de-sacs, and curving lanes. Through traffic was to be relegated to the freeways. Commercial activity, instead of lining the strip, was to be concentrated in planned shopping centers of a variety of sizes. The organization of at least the newer portions of North American cities changed from grids to pods. The dominant image of the city was beginning to focus less on "paths" (Broadway, Wilshire Boulevard) and more on "nodes" (major shopping centers). Strips and streets were bad, while internally focused shopping complexes were good.

By the late 1980s, there were signs of some disillusionment with the city of pods. For one thing, major streets in "podded" cities were often sterile and boring. Four- and six-lane streets lined with residences (often walled off from the street for privacy and noise abatement) provided little visual stimulation or sense of connection to the intraurban traveler. Some people began to miss the excitement, stimulation, and information of the cluttered strip. Major streets seemed best suited to commerce. Additionally, as the pods or planned centers grew, they became clogged with cars (everyone had to drive to get to them), and vast parking lots dominated the pedestrian environments. While the traditional grids had tended to tie diverse parts of the city together, the pods tended to emphasize segregation because there was little connection between them.

The controversy is far from over. The future look of the American commercial strip will depend not only on changing building types, design ideologies, and needed urban functions but also on changes in very basic attitudes concerning the spatial organization of streets and neighborhoods. Both negative attitudes towards a messy, cluttered urban landscape and positive images of colorful "cruising" and neighborhood corner stores will no doubt have an impact on the kinds of commercial settings that will evolve in the future.

7 Architectural Innovations at Home and Abroad

Some Speculations on Future Trends

Over the past 150 years, two very prominent trends have affected the built environment and urban morphology of North American cities. The first is the invention and proliferation of new types of special-purpose buildings, and the second is the segregation or sorting out in space of those building types based on ability to pay land rent and/or planning ideologies. This book has explicitly conveyed those two trends. In the previous chapters, I have attempted to show how the relatively undifferentiated, architecturally uniform city of 1800—a city of "houses" including warehouses, banking houses, schoolhouses, storehouses, etc.—was gradually transformed into the late-twentieth-century city made up of a variety of very specialized buildings in very specialized types of locations. The twentieth-century city is far from undifferentiated. Each district has its own architecture and place imagery, be it skyscraper office towers downtown, drive-in restaurants along the strip, or rustic single-family houses in the suburbs. To a very real degree, the study of land use patterns in the North American city is the study of the location of building types.

For those speculating on future relationships between building types and urban land use patterns, there are two questions that must be addressed. First, are there completely new building types yet to be invented? And second, are there new ways to arrange in space the building types we already have? At least in the short run, the answers to these two questions seem to be no and yes.

Although both the external and internal character of houses, apartments, stores, and offices will change in the future, it is difficult to imagine the need for any really new types of structures. The quantum leap in style, scale, and spatial arrangement that occurred as the city of houses was transformed into the city of skyscrapers, department stores, and drive-in movies seems unlikely to be repeated in the foreseeable future. While some interesting ideas have been put forward over the past decades, such as Paolo Soleri's designs for Arcosanti (a megastructure with huge, open platforms for city building), the enthusiasm for such projects has substantially diminished in recent years. Today, visionary architects from Phillip Johnson to Andres Duany are more likely to focus upon reintegrating good ideas from the past into current projects.

On the other hand, we are rapidly changing our ideas of how existing building types should be sorted out in space. It seems clear that the postwar era of maximum segregation by building type has ended and that mixed-use developments are on the rise. While the architectural packaging may be quite different, the cities of the future may well come full circle to recreate at least some of the vibrant diversity of those from earlier centuries. They probably will not be so easily compartmentalized into homogeneous rings and sectors of land use, building type, and socioeconomic status as are the cities of today. The urban geographers of the future may have to take a closer look at the city in order to understand the locational decisions that are operating to produce a variety of spatial outcomes.

Still, the true mixed-use city is a long way off, and the various forces leading toward it are widely scattered. For example, some of the new enthusiasm for mixed-use projects has resulted from boredom with the sterile uniformity of the design of single-use developments, while in other cases, mixed use is primarily a way to reap more profit from the development of increasingly expensive urban land. In still other cases, transportation is a motivating factor, since the necessity of driving several miles to the nearest shop is creating gridlock in many areas. It is perhaps appropriate to speculate about some of the trends that are under way both within North America and abroad that may determine relationships between buildings and city structure in the future. There are at least three major themes worth developing here: the future design of buildings within existing North American cities; the use of American building types in new combinations in suburban and satellite megadevelopments; and the diffusion, acceptance, and modification of these building types in major metropolitan areas abroad.

Building Design: Back to the Future

Recently, it seems, we have been spending a great deal of time learning from the past. Many of the design features that were common 100 years ago are once more coming into vogue in North American cities. This topic has been dealt with in each of the preceding chapters, so I will try not to belabor it, yet it seems worth repeating that we have spent an inordinate amount of time reinventing the wheel. Not so long ago, we had office towers with decorative, ornate tops and a variety of retail shops at street level. After decades of trying to adjust to glass boxes, sterile lobbies, and empty plazas, the trend today is toward office towers with decorative tops and retailing at street level. We also once had glass-covered shopping arcades, two-story houses on relatively small lots, loft living above shops, luxury apartment buildings, densely built-up commercial strips, and streets organized on a grid pattern. All of these things are returning with the demise of space-extensive aesthetics and a diminishing supply of cheap, developable land. A combination of new environmental and design ideologies and new economic realities is pushing us to reevaluate the benefits of more traditional city design. As I said earlier, however, most of this has already been discussed in previous chapters, so let us move on to the next two themes.

Recombining the Pieces in New Mega-Nodes: Another Look at American Landscape Tastes

North Americans have long held an antiurban bias. When given the chance, we are quick to point out that we do not like high-density areas, congestion, tall buildings, apartment living, noise, mixed land use, and so on. We are also eager to emphasize that we do like an ideal landscape of vast open spaces, privacy, rustic surroundings, green grass, and trees. To us, these two types of settings are polar opposites. I am not so sure, however, that things are as simple as this dichotomy might suggest. If the design is appealing, for example, we love high density and congestion. On the other hand, it is becoming obvious that too much open space in a city can be boring and even dangerous. We need a better understanding and articulation of our likes and dislikes.

It may be that North Americans, like most people, have simply been upset by the process of change. Compared to their counterparts in most cities elsewhere in the world, the central areas of North American cities have been characterized by massive and rapid physical and social change throughout the twentieth century. As new buildings have gone up, old ones have fallen into disrepair, to be inhabited by marginalized people and activities. This sudden juxtaposition of new and old, rich and poor, big and small, healthy and sick, can be disturbing. We like temporal homogeneity. One reason we seem to like new places so much (new towns, suburban centers) is that they are all new—there has been no change. Ironically, we also like uniformly old (historic) places, for the same reason. In periods of rapid social and cultural change, perhaps we seek stability in our

New spatial arrangements of existing building types: an "edge city" in San Diego

landscapes (thus the appeal of images of unchanging forests and countryside). If new developments are to work better than the old ones,
architectural stability must be built into them.

While massive new developments have been constructed in relatively remote outer belt locations over the past two decades, they have
primarily utilized building types which evolved in the central city but
with new building arrangements and designs. From Costa Mesa,
California, to Stamford, Connecticut, shopping malls, high-rise office buildings, parking garages, and condominium projects have
sprung up to create booming new "edge cities" where mere villages
once stood.[1] Present only since the 1960s, such cities epitomize the
effects of strict land use planning requirements, and they have generally been quite successful economically. In many metropolitan areas,
they have been the direct cause of a declining downtown.

While traditional cities were originally quite mixed architecturally,
functionally, and socially, these new developments generally have
been dominated by large areas of homogeneity. Wide streets and
lawns separate vast office parks from huge shopping malls and immense condominium "villages." The densities are high as is the congestion, but there is none of the messy mixing of building types and
social classes that characterizes older cities. Everything is "clean"
and controlled, from signage, building color, and style to landscaping
and land use. Nothing can change without permission, everything
must be kept up to code, and no deterioration or disamenities will be

allowed to threaten the atmosphere of serenity. Everything has already been built at the regulated scale and in the proper style.

Given the apparent vitality of such developments, what can we say about the aesthetic tastes and ideologies of North Americans? Since most of the building types in these new developments, from office towers to apartment buildings, are much like those of the central city, it is really only spatial arrangement and temporal and social homogeneity that make them different. True, the office towers are often set apart by grassy lawns, and parking is more plentiful than it is downtown, but these are minor modifications. It is the newness, the uniformity, and the stability that seem to be most appealing.

Perhaps some of the design confusion in North America over the years has to do with the fact that we have unconsciously thwarted our basic aesthetic and social preferences in pursuit of "individual liberties." We have wanted to satisfy two very different and possibly mutually exclusive basic urban ideologies—economic individualism and Renaissance aesthetics. We have wanted to do whatever we wanted to do, but we have wanted the result to look aesthetically "orderly" in the tradition of European cities. North Americans, especially those in the United States, have often taken an individualistic stance and argued for frontier-like freedom from control and restraint. David Lowenthal has suggested that American landscape tastes exhibit a strong preference for the chaotic, featuristic, ragged, and big, as epitomized by the New York skyline or the Las Vegas strip.[2] "They're not going to tell *me* what to do" became a required American response to planning efforts during the 1950s and 1960s. Americans criticized neighborhoods where "all the houses look the same," and entrepreneurs sought individualistic symbols and signage. Ironically, no sooner were these individualistic landscapes created than Americans began to avoid them. Was there a mismatch between our rhetoric and our tastes?

Of course, it could be that everything in America simply goes in cycles. The extreme design individualism that characterized the period from the late nineteenth century to the mid-twentieth may have been largely a reaction to the rowhouse uniformity and egalitarian ideologies of the preceding century. Similarly, we may now be reacting (or overreacting) to the results of that unbridled individualism. Once we have urban areas filled with planned mega-nodes, we may well yearn once more for chaos and diversity.

Individualism is rare in the new mega-nodes, for corporatism reigns supreme. Acres of blue-glass office buildings sit in manicured green lawns, and endless shopping malls exhibit tasteful and uniform signage—logos which are immediately recognizable as belonging to national or multinational companies. Square miles of postmodern mauve condominium and apartment complexes are nearby, each with strict rules and regulations governing nearly all behavior from the allowable colors of curtains to the use of the pool. We can relax knowing that nothing will change. High density is fine if we know what the density is and will be. We object only when higher densities creep in and change the neighborhood (along with new types of high-density people). Most of the other clichéd complaints about city life (involving congestion, noise, pollution, etc.) are heard less often in the new nodes even though there may be no significant differences in these negative qualities between such areas and more traditional neighborhoods. Homogeneously clean and new congestion is okay.

Americans have generally been quite conservative in designing the new mega-nodes. Rarely has anything been done that would seem all that shocking to Ebenezer Howard and other New Town advocates of circa 1900. Everything is in its place. Total reliance upon the automobile is the rule (except in a few cities like Washington, D.C., where mega-nodes are being constructed at Metro stations), and pedestrians, while officially encouraged, are hard to find. The new nodes are urban in the sense that people can live at high density close to a variety of shopping, recreational, and work locations, but it is a new kind of "urban," one that is carefully controlled and economically exclusive. At the census-tract and neighborhood level, it is very mixed, but up close, there is unprecedented uniformity of architectural style and era and homogeneity of socioeconomic status.

In future years, aging mega-nodes may suffer from inflexibility unless new procedures and design guidelines can be developed. It will be very interesting to see how a political and economic system that has traditionally allowed and encouraged spontaneous individual decisions (to rebuild, abandon, upgrade, etc.) adjusts to a setting where thousands of buildings over several square miles all become obsolete at once. As society changes, the functional modifications associated with traditional neighborhoods (such as granny flats and accessory apartments) and with older commercial strips cannot take place in the new nodes (legally). Nothing can change until the pressure builds. What will happen then?

In some projects, there have been many attempts at greater mixing of uses, at least compared to the past few decades. Apartments have been built over stores, and retail shops have been built into the lower levels of office buildings. Developers have been justifiably cautious, however. After all, Americans have only just finished running from the "mixed" central city, and the "New Towns in Town" movement of the 1970s was a very limited success at best. The main trend is simply to arrange homogeneous districts in convenient, accessible ways.

Still, there are some signs that significant change is on the way. In southern California, the combination of a glut of office space and the large number of grassy, space-extensive office parks has led to plans to "fill in the lawns" with shops and houses. In San Diego's Mission Valley, the largest mega-node in the metropolitan area, the new district plan has zoned about half of the land simply as mixed-use, and city officials are waiting to see what develops.

Architecture Abroad: A New Scale Emerges in Europe

While North Americans have generally been content to simply arrange building types in increasingly orderly ways, innovations in both scale and design have occurred elsewhere. Much of this innovation has to do with the redesigning of building types, such as skyscrapers and shopping centers, which evolved primarily in North America. The diffusion and subsequent modification of architectural forms in new settings is nothing new, of course. Skyscrapers were accepted in Buenos Aires during the 1920s, and Stalin wholeheartedly embraced the 1920s-style tower as a way of embellishing postwar Moscow. In recent decades, however, the process has sped up. Many of the biggest and most interesting projects in the world are now in Europe and Asia. Europe leads the way when it comes to the sheer size and monumentality of projects. Even New York is beginning to pale in comparison. American cities no longer have a monopoly on bigness.

Much has been made of the fact that North American cities are multicentered, but this has been true in many European cities for centuries. In London, for example, the City, West End, and Westminster have long competed as important nodes. In Paris, several competing centers of activity have existed for centuries, from Notre Dame in the east to the Champs Elysées in the west. Over the past three decades, innovations in urban design have been more remarkable in the new nodes of European cities than in the relatively mundane multiple centers of North American cities. Much of this has to do with the acceptance and/or redefinition of "American" architectural forms, from the skyscraper to the fast-food restaurant. The La Défense development in Paris is a prime example.

Located just to the west of the city boundary on the site of the last set of walls (thus the name), La Défense consists of a huge, raised platform, or podium, built over a variety of transportation facilities and parking. One can arrive by train, subway, bus, or car. On the surface of the podium is a massive, mixed-use assemblage of office and residential towers, fountains, gardens, sculpture, and open plazas. Shops and restaurants are located both on and below the podium

Innovative architecture: La Défense, Paris

surface. Begun in the late 1950s, La Défense has always been controversial. While it relieved redevelopment pressure from the sacred
center of the city, many Parisians objected to the emerging, dominating skyline (à la Américain),which now includes towers of over 50
stories. Indeed, in the mid-1960s some French films (such as *Playtime*)
poked fun at the sterility of the project.

Over the years, however, La Défense has become a place. It has
become a confident center for truly innovative architecture, such as
La Grande Arche, a 30-story office building constructed in the shape
of a giant, rectangular doughnut. The Arche connects visually with
the other arch (the Arc de Triomphe) along the axis of the Champs
Elysées. La Défense has become a tourist and shopping attraction in
its own right, and it is far from complete.

Paris has generally led the way with innovations involving the creation of massive retail and office employment centers well-connected
to a transportation infrastructure. The Maine-Montparnasse project,
built between 1961 and 1973, is a mixed-use development built directly over the immense, five-level Gare Montparnasse (train station) near
the southern boundary of the city. It consists of eight levels (six underground) of shopping and parking, including several department
stores, a 52-story office tower (until recently the tallest in Europe),
and two 18-story wings each over 275 yards long containing offices,
museums, and a thousand apartments.

Developments like La Défense and Maine-Montparnasse are leading to a new spatial structure in Paris. The center of the city has become a largely preserved, sacred landscape of museums, churches, cafes, and expensive housing, while the working city is concentrated in a collar of mega-nodes just beyond but convenient to the sacred center. As we shall see, this pattern is also becoming apparent in other world cities, as along the Yamanote Line in Tokyo and the Docklands of London, and stands in contrast to the North American pattern of hyperdevelopment in the city center (Manhattan or Toronto) coupled with large numbers of relatively remote suburban shopping centers and office parks. It will be interesting to see if there is international convergence or divergence in the future as innovations in mega-node design diffuse.

No discussion of architectural innovations in Paris would be complete without some mention of the Georges Pompidou Centre. Since it is primarily a museum, it does not fit easily into the topics covered in this book, but still, it is difficult to ignore. In order to free the interior space for the activities of people, the infrastructure of the building was put on the outside. The building was constructed to be literally inside out. At first glance, it appears to be a tangle of steel tubing, stairways and escalators, ventilation pipes, and wiring. This is also true at second glance. It may be the last gasp of modernism or yet another variation on the postmodern theme, but it is *formidable*. Many of the critical terms used to describe it have not been heard since the Eiffel Tower went up 100 years ago ("the more things change . . ."). It may be the closest we can come in our search for a truly new building type.

By far the biggest urban redevelopment project in the world is now under way in London. If all the current plans for the London Docklands are brought to fruition, they will have an impact comparable to Haussmann's transformation of Paris in the nineteenth century. As in Paris, redevelopment on such a scale has been extremely controversial.

As the port of London gradually moved 20 miles downstream to new facilities closer to the North Sea, the old dock lands were largely abandoned. When the last docks closed in the early 1980s, there were still 40,000 people living in the area (mostly low-income people, with 90 percent living in council housing), as well as a vast stock of derelict warehouses. Plans were drawn up to turn the area into a new city, complete with financial towers, residential neighborhoods, renovated warehouses, art galleries and museums, a new airport, small industrial firms, restaurants, and pubs. The planning area consists of over 8 square miles, with 55 miles of waterfront along the Thames. Since the district begins only a few hundred yards from the Tower of London, with a main focal point at the Isle of Dogs only two miles further on, redevelopment could make the East End another version of the posh West End, thus surrounding the old center city with mega-nodes of activity. By the late 1980s, after huge government expenditures to clear the land and advertise its potential to private developers, things were under way. In 1990, the 800-foot-tall Canary Wharf Tower was completed, making London the home of one of Europe's tallest buildings. An above-ground, light railway system has been constructed to link Canary Wharf with the city center. It is too soon to tell just what architectural innovations will emerge in the Docklands, but its scale and central location alone make it a place to watch. The financial crunch of the 1990s has slowed development, but when the "Chunnel"—the railway tunnel under the English Channel connecting England with Continental Europe—is completed, the Docklands will be among the most accessible places in a newly enlarged Europe.

Architecture in East Asia: Innovative Hybrids

The rise of East Asia as an economic powerhouse has been accompanied by unprecedented building projects that seem to be bringing more and more "North American" architecture to the exotic East. The tallest buildings outside of North America are now in Singapore and Hong Kong, but Japan, Malaysia, and Korea are not far behind. In designing and creating places to shop, East Asia may already be the world leader. While department stores are generally getting smaller in North America as medium, mall-sized centers become the norm, Japan has continued to construct huge projects ringing the city center, often in conjunction with commuter railroad lines. These stores sometimes also include amusement rides and driving ranges on the roof. Huge and unusual department stores and shopping arcades are common from Seoul to Singapore.

Some of the largest and most interesting multipurpose structures in the world are now in Southeast Asian cities such as Bangkok, Hong Kong, Jakarta, and Singapore. It is common to have buildings several stories high and covering a large city block that include not only the usual range of department store activities but also traditional food markets and other types of street stalls. Often, small industrial spaces are included as well so that newly manufactured items can simply be moved downstairs for sale. Occasionally, all of these activities are included in the lower floors of massive housing projects so that the economic isolation so pervasive in American and European projects is absent. Sometimes an entire floor given over to activities to occupy young children while parents shop. There are rooms full of giant balls, castles, and dragons as well as large, automated animals being walked and ridden on throughout the store.

Innovative architecture in Tokyo

While such hybrid complexes do not really constitute architectural innovations in the strict sense of the term, they do represent a novel rearranging of internal spaces in ways which can change significantly our image of what shopping environments should be like. As we have seen in the case of the evolution of the shopping arcade and department store in Europe and North America, changing images and ideologies can be as important as more technical architectural breakthroughs. Rates of diffusion for future innovations, however, may be largely determined by types of legal systems. Most of the "fun zones" in Asian department stores, for example, would not be built in North America because businesses would fear possible injury and lawsuits. This is a significant and increasing constraint for urban designers in America.

East Asia is now the setting for some spectacular and unusual projects, many of which would seem outrageous and discordant to the rest of the world. Skyscrapers can be nearly any shape or color and often are. Decorations from dissimilar historical eras and national contexts can be applied to the same building in a random manner which would make the most enthusiastic postmodernist shudder. Still, many of the architectural innovations in East Asia, particularly those in Japan, are more subtle. Much of it has to do with the ability to compartmentalize.

In the West, we are used to being concerned with how everything fits together: we have a Renaissance perspective that emphasizes uni-

New extremes: apartments in Hong Kong

formity and coherence. In the United States, for example, historic districts must be uniformly historic; a new fast-food restaurant sticks out, aesthetically and ideologically, in a neighborhood of Victorian houses. This often makes design innovations involving combinations of old and new elements difficult to achieve. It also explains why Americans often view cities as discordant and stressful compared to the uniform atmosphere of, say, a park or homogeneous suburb.

The Japanese are less picky. In Japan, the design tradition is more likely to emphasize small, individual spaces which are experienced individually or sequentially rather than as part of an aesthetic whole. A Buddhist temple and a burger stand can exist serenely side by side, and it is common to see Coke machines next to a Shinto shrine.[3] New suburban houses often combine modern rooms (containing over-stuffed furniture and the like) and traditional rooms (containing tatami mats). The entire house need not have one theme. Along commercial streets, Tudor half-timbering and neon mix freely. It may seem chaotic to us but it does make for design flexibility, since anything can be built anywhere. As American commercial strips trend toward tasteful homogeneity and minimalist signage and away from vibrant diversity, Asian cities may need to compete only with Las Vegas for the undisputed lead in Neo-Boomerang Modern.

Flexibility in Asia goes far beyond aesthetic and temporal mixing, however. Most Asian cities have no zoning, at least in the Western sense, and so a variety of support activities can locate in a neighborhood which is chiefly dedicated to other functions. For example, homes are often used as factories, early morning food markets can appear on streets in the financial district, and small entrepreneurs often have stalls in the alleys between major corporate centers. We might do well to examine such settings for ideas about mixed-use design.

The combination of both aesthetic ideologies and zoning regulations which encourage building type mixing has an important impact upon city structure. In cities where the old and the new, the big and the small, the sacred and the profane, the historic and the avant-garde, the rich and the poor, and the messy and the clean, harmoniously occupy space together, the basic motivations and impulses behind North American–style segregation disappear. There is no reason to have official historic districts separate from modern developments or shopping areas set apart from residences.

An important dimension of design in many Asian cities is the continuing acceptance of multiple uses (often at different times of day) for any one space. North American cities are not just areally segregated but are also usually temporally (diurnally) divided, with certain places active only at certain times. We have nightclubs which are vacant all day and daycare centers which are unused at night. Even entire downtown financial districts can be ghost towns at night. Such temporal segregation may not be either economically plausible or culturally desirable in the future.

Architecture, Urban Design, and Whimsy: Building Types and the Vibrant City

In our quest for efficiency, we have developed building types that are (at least theoretically) ideally suited for the activities that go on within them. We have designed houses around notions of the needs of families, factories and offices on the basis of time and motion studies, shopping centers and department stores on the advice of specialists in consumer psychology, and even parks on the recommendation of scientists concerned with environmental conservation. All of this is well and good, but I can't help feeling that somewhere along the way we started taking it all a bit too seriously. Or perhaps, like other trends, we simply abandoned other goals and put all our eggs in one basket. We have too many "perfectly" designed buildings in too many "optimum" locations. All very nice, but it can be boring. We don't have enough fun anymore.

The two design objectives—efficiency and fun—are by no means mutually exclusive. Indeed, a major trend in the reorganization of city spaces lies in the recombination of building types so as to integrate fun zones with other activities. Las Vegas provides the most famous examples, with hotel-casinos that include circus acts and medieval jousting tournaments. The Edmonton (Canada) Mall, the largest in the world with 800 stores covering the equivalent of 108 football fields, is also a case in point. It includes not only shopping, eating, and the usual entertainment facilities, but also a huge indoor waterpark with machine-made waves and a lake complete with Spanish galleons, submarines, and a shark tank. The shopper can round out the day with a game of miniature golf on the way to the petting zoo.

There are many other examples. In Brisbane, Australia, the Meyer Center, a new downtown shopping complex, includes examples of all that is best in conventional urban design. It is located in the heart of the city over a commuter rail line and bus center as well as a parking structure. The center itself occupies part of the block, while smaller-scale, traditional street facades have been preserved or recreated to perpetuate the sense of a pedestrian-oriented atmosphere ong the major shopping street.

These attributes are nice but not unusual. Inside the center, however, the fun begins. The entryway is topped by a Ferris wheel, and mixed right into a huge atrium filled with shopping space is a mini-roller coaster. You can hop on at men's accessories and zoom through lingerie and slippers in a bright red dragon car. When buildings are constructed in the cities of the future, I hope that they will be characterized by efficiency and taste, but I wouldn't mind a few red dragon cars here and there either.

Notes

Thinking about Cities

1. See, for example, Thurber 1945.

Merging the Traditions of Space and Place

1. See, for example, Cromley 1990; Foley 1980; Girouard 1985; Goldberger 1981; King 1980; Kostof 1987; and Olsen 1986.

2. Garreau 1991; Hayden 1985; Wright 1981.
3. Boyer 1980; Plunz 1989.
4. Bourne 1982.
5. Goss 1988.

Chapter One: Downtown Buildings

1. For good descriptions of the built environments of late medieval cities, see Vance 1971 and Girouard 1985. For information on the evolution of the skyscraper, see Goldberger 1981 and Mujica 1977.
2. Based on Vance 1971.
3. See, for example, Girouard 1985.
4. See Carter 1983 and Gray 1982.
5. Gibbs 1984; Severini 1983.
6. Bunce 1954, 26.
7. Shultz and Simmons 1959; Gibbs 1984, and Gad and Holdsworth 1987a provide data on and pictures of early office buildings.
8. Kingston and Clark 1930, 51.
9. Gad and Holdsworth 1987b.
10. Colby 1933.
11. See, for example, Murphy and Vance 1954 and 1955.

12. Kingston and Clark 1930, 80.
13. Shultz and Simmons 1959, 113.
14. Starrett 1928, 88.
15. Most of the data on the financial and occupancy histories of major buildings can be found only in building records and in local library files of newspaper reports. City directories are also invaluable.
16. The story of Rockefeller Center is well told in Karp 1982.
17. Fisher 1967 provides a good review of the postwar office boom.
18. Gad and Holdsworth 1987a, 225.
19. Liston 1965, 65. Liston provides a good review of urban renewal procedures in the 1960s.
20. Shultz and Simmons 1959, 249.
21. Carruth 1969, 114.
22. Pygman and Kately 1985 provide

data on size and year of construction for major buildings.

23. Ibid.
24. Ford 1984c.
25. Costonis 1974.
26. San Francisco 1981.
27. Lake 1987.

Chapter Two: The Downtown Frame

1. Bogue 1963.
2. Skolnik 1976.
3. Groth 1983, 32. Groth provides an excellent review of the problems and prospects of residential hotels in America.
4. Ibid., 55.
5. Anderson 1970.
6. Sacramento Historical Structures Advisory Committee 1976.
7. Skolnik 1976; Kreisman 1985.
8. Chapman 1976, 13.
9. Lewis 1980.
10. Jacobs 1961; Gans 1962; Lynch 1972; Press 1979; Wright 1980; Hayden 1984; Newman 1973; Sennett 1978.
11. Gans 1962.
12. The Urban Land Institute 1983 provides a review of projects.
13. Kersten and Reid 1968.
14. Clay 1973.
15. Lynch 1972, 234.

Chapter Three: Places to Shop

1. See, for example, Girouard 1985, Rudofsky 1969, and Vance 1971.
2. Girouard 1985, 203. Girouard provides an excellent overview of Renaissance developments, especially in London and Paris.
3. Geist 1983 provides the best information on the arcade as a building type.
4. See, for example, Lockwood 1976 and Boyer 1980.
5. Girouard 1985, 245.
6. See, for example, Adburgham 1979, Michael Miller 1981, and Ferry 1960
for data on early department store development.
7. Geist 1983, 79.
8. Domosh 1988.
9. Charles Moore as quoted in Freeman 1986.
10. Ibid.
11. See Diamonstein 1986 for an overview of rehabilitation projects.
12. Gordon 1985 reviews the evolution of the Horton Plaza concept.
13. Ibid., 147.
14. Riley 1980.
15. Goss 1993.

Chapter Four: The American Single-Family House

1. See, for example, Adams 1987, Bourne 1981, and Goetze 1983.
2. See, for example, Wright 1981, Clark 1986, Foley 1980, Handlin 1979, Hayden 1985, and Kostof 1987.
3. Vance 1990.
4. Gray 1982 provides a concise look at the development of London over the centuries.
5. Vance 1990. See also Burnett 1978 and Muthesius 1982.
6. Engels as cited in Vance 1990, 304; Park, Burgess, and McKenzie 1925.
7. See, for example, Jakle, Bastian, and Meyer 1989.
8. Both Clark 1986 and Wright 1981 are excellent sources of information on the relationship between house form and the development of a

middle-class culture. Many of the figures presented here are from those books.

9. See, for example, King 1984 and Winter 1980.
10. Clark 1986, 162.
11. Wright 1981, 158, provides an excellent review of the social history of housing.
12. Clark 1986, 191.
13. See, for example, Stevenson and Ward 1986.
14. Wright 1981, 208.
15. Ibid. See also Fusch and Ford 1983.
16. See Adams 1982, 1987 for information on housing construction and financing.
17. Park, Burgess and McKenzie 1925.
18. For a review of urban models and changes therein, see Hoyt 1971.
19. Clark 1986, 233.
20. For a variety of perspectives on the historic preservation movement and its impact on cities, see Cybriwsky 1978, Ford and Fusch 1978, Laska and Spain 1980, Smith and Williams 1986, and Weinberg 1978.
21. Ford 1988.
22. Fusch and Ford 1983.

Chapter Five: Multiunit Housing and City Structure

1. Groth 1983.
2. An excellent review of the evolution of high-density housing types in New York is found in Plunz 1989. Much of the data on early tenements presented here is from that source.
3. Borchert 1980 looks at alley housing as an alternative to the tenement.
4. There is now a great deal of literature on the evolution of the luxury apartment. See, for example, Alpern 1975; Cromley 1990; Girouard 1985; Goode 1988; Hancock 1980; Olsen 1986; and Wright 1981.
5. Riis 1890.
6. Goode 1988.
7. Compare, for example, the development history of New York (Plunz 1989) with that of Baltimore (Olson 1976).
8. See, for example, Hayden 1985 and Wright 1981.
9. Plunz 1989 includes valuable information on various regulations impacting high-density housing in New York.
10. Plunz 1989 and Cromley 1990 provide clear depictions of interior plans for various projects.
11. Hoyt 1939.
12. Wright 1981.
13. Goode 1988 is an excellent source for photographs of and data on huge garden apartments.
14. See, for example, Chase 1981 and Curtis and Ford 1988.
15. Plunz 1989.
16. Newman 1973.
17. Ford 1986a.

Chapter Six: Drive-in Dreams

1. Some of the best sources are Jakle (1979, 1980, 1982, and 1985), Liebs (1985), and Venturi, Brown, and Izenour (1988).
2. As quoted in O'Connor 1988, 112.
3. Venturi, Brown, and Izenour 1988, 13.
4. Clay 1973, 87.
5. See, for example, Rifkind 1977.
6. Jakle 1985, 121.
7. Jakle 1979; Sculle 1981.
8. See, for example, Rubin 1979.
9. Jakle 1985, 136.
10. Wolfe 1965, 82.

11. Hess 1986, 43.

12. Quoted in Hess 1986, 61.

13. Blake 1979, 24.

14. Lowenthal 1968.

15. Relph 1976.

16. Liebs 1985, 65.

17. All data for San Diego commercial strips are from O'Connor 1988.

18. MacDonald 1985, 19.

19. See, for example, Boal and Johnson 1971.

20. See, for example, Berry 1963.

21. Pred 1963.

22. Franklin 1983.

23. Riccio 1988.

Chapter Seven: Architectural Innovations at Home and Abroad

1. Garreau 1991.

2. Lowenthal 1968.

3. See, for example, Greenbie 1988.

References

Abbott, Edith. 1970. *The Tenements of Chicago: 1908–1935*. Chicago: University of Chicago Press.

Adams, John S., ed. 1976. *Contemporary Metropolitan America*. Vol. 1. Cambridge, Mass.: Ballinger.

———. 1982. "Residential Structure of Midwestern Cities." In Bourne 1982.

———. 1984. "The Meaning of Housing in America." *Annals of the Association of American Geographers* 74:515–52.

———. 1987. *Housing in America in the 1980s*. New York: Russell Sage Foundation.

Adburgham, Alison. 1979. *Shopping in Style: London from the Restoration to Edwardian Elegance*. London: Thames & Hudson.

Alpern, Andrew. 1975. *New York's Fabulous Luxury Apartments*. New York: Dover.

Anderson, Jack. 1970. "Urban Renewal Hits Sacramento's Poor." *Sacramento Bee*, August 18.

Andrew, Caroline, and Beth Milroy. 1988. *Life Spaces: Gender, Household, and Employment*. Vancouver: University of British Columbia Press.

Andrews, Wayne. 1964. *Architecture, Ambition, and Americans*. New York: Free Press.

Andrus, Phillip, et al. 1976. *Seattle*. Cambridge, Mass.: Ballinger.

Armstrong, Regina B. 1972. *The Office Industry: Patterns of Growth and Location*. New York: Regional Planning Association.

Arreger, Hans, and Otto Glaus. 1967. *Highrise Building and Urban Design*. New York: Praeger.

Arreola, Donald. 1981. "Fences as Landscape Taste: Tucson's Barrios." *Journal of Cultural Geography*, 2:96–105.

Attoe, Wayne. 1981. *Skylines: Understanding and Molding Urban Silhouettes*. Chichester, U.K.: John Wiley & Sons.

Badcock, Blair. 1984. *Unfairly Structured Cities*. Oxford: Basil Blackwell.

Baeder, John. 1982. *Gas, Food, and Lodging*. New York: Abbeville Press.

Baerwald, Thomas. 1978. "The Emergence of a New Downtown." *Geographical Review* 68:293–307.

Ball, Michael, Michael Harloe, and Maartje Martens. 1988. *Housing and Social Change in Europe and the USA*. London: Routledge.

Banham, Reyner. 1971. *Los Angeles: The Architecture of Four Ecologies.* New York: Harper & Row.

————. 1976. *Megastructures: Urban Futures and the Recent Past.* New York: Harper & Row.

Barley, Maurice. 1986. *Houses and History.* London: Faber & Faber.

Barnett, Jonathan. 1974. *Urban Design as Public Policy.* New York: McGraw-Hill.

————. 1982. *An Introduction to Urban Design.* New York: Harper & Row.

————. 1986. *The Elusive City: Five Centuries of Design, Ambition, and Miscalculation.* New York: Harper & Row.

Barnett, Roger. 1978. "The Libertarian Suburb: Deliberate Disorder." *Landscape* 22:44–48.

Barth, Gunther. 1980. *City People: The Rise of Modern City Culture in Nineteenth-Century America.* New York: Oxford University Press.

Bassett, Keith, and John Short. 1980. *Housing and Residential Structure.* London: Routledge & Kegan Paul.

Bastian, Robert. 1975. "Architecture and Class Segregation in Late-Nineteenth-Century Terre Haute, Indiana." *Geographical Review* 65:166–79.

Beamish, Jane, and Jane Ferguson. 1985. *A History of Singapore Architecture.* Singapore: Graham Brash.

Belasco, Warren James. 1979. *Americans on the Road: From Autocamp to Motel, 1910–1945.* Cambridge: MIT Press.

Berry, Brian. 1963. *Commercial Structure and Commercial Blight.* Chicago: University of Chicago, Department of Geography Research Paper 85 and 86.

————. 1967. *Geography of Market Centers and Retail Distribution.* Englewood Cliffs: Prentice-Hall.

Binford, Henry. 1985. *The First Suburbs: Residential Communities on the Boston Periphery, 1815–1860.* Chicago: University of Chicago Press.

Black, Thomas J. 1978. *The Changing Economic Role of Central Cities.* Washington, D.C.: Urban Land Institute.

Blackmar, Elizabeth. 1989. *Manhattan for Rent, 1785–1850.* Ithaca: Cornell University Press.

Blake, Peter. 1979. *God's Own Junkyard: The Planned Deterioration of America's Landscape.* New York: Holt, Rinehart & Winston.

Boal, F. W., and D. B. Johnson. 1971. "The Functions of Retail Service Establishments on Commercial Ribbons." In Bourne 1971.

Bogue, Donald. 1963. *Skid Row in American Cities.* Chicago: Community and Family Study Center, University of Chicago.

Borchert, James. 1980. *Alley Life in Washington: Family, Community, Religion, and Folklife in the City, 1850–1970.* Urbana: University of Illinois Press.

Boston Redevelopment Authority. 1976. *Recycled Boston.* Boston.

Bottles, Scott. 1987. *Los Angeles and the Automobile: The Making of a Modern City.* Berkeley and Los Angeles: University of California Press.

Bourne, Larry S., ed. 1971. *Internal Structure of the City: Readings on Space and Environment.* New York: Oxford University Press.

————. 1981. *The Geography of Housing.* New York: John Wiley & Sons.

————, ed. 1982. *Internal Structure of the City: Readings on Urban Form, Growth, and Policy.* Oxford: Oxford University Press.

Boyer, Christine. 1980. *Manhattan Manners.* New York: Rizzoli International Publications.

Bowden, Martyn. 1971. "Downtown through Time: Delimitation, Expansion, and Internal Growth." *Economic Geography* 47:121–35.

Bruegmann, Robert. 1982. "Two Post-Modernist Visions of Urban Design." *Landscape* 26:31–37.

Bunce, O. B. 1954. "A Prophecy of Skyscrapers." *Landscape* 3:26.

Burchard, John, and Albert Bush-Brown. 1961. *The Architecture of America: A Social and Cultural History.* Boston: Little, Brown.

Burgess, Ernest W. 1929. "Urban Areas." In *Chicago: An Experiment in Social Science Research*, ed. T. V. Smith and L. D. White, 114–23. Chicago: University of Chicago Press.

Burnett, John. 1978. *A Social History of Housing, 1815–1970.* Cambridge: Cambridge University Press.

Burns, Elizabeth. 1980. "The Enduring Affluent Suburb." *Landscape* 24:33–41.

Burton, Lydia, and David Morley. 1979. "Neighborhood Survival in Toronto." *Landscape* 23:33–40.

Buttenwieser, Ann L. 1987. *Manhattan Water Bound.* New York: New York University Press.

Cadwallader, Martin. 1988. "Urban Geography and Social Theory." *Urban Geography* 9:227–51.

Cannadine, David, and David Reeder, eds. 1982. *Exploring the Urban Past.* Cambridge: Cambridge University Press.

Carruth, Eleanor. 1969. "Manhattan's Office Building Binge." *Fortune*, October, p. 114.

Carter, Harold. 1975. *The Study of Urban Geography.* London: Edward Arnold.

———. 1983. *An Introduction to Urban Historical Geography.* London: Edward Arnold.

Chapman, Bruce. 1976. "The Growing Public Stake in Urban Conservation." In Latham 1976, 9–13.

Chase, Laura. 1981. "Eden in the Orange Groves: Bungalows and Courtyard Houses of Los Angeles." *Landscape* 25:29–36.

Choko, Marc, and Richard Harris. 1990. "The Local Culture of Property: A Comparative History of Housing Tenure in Montreal and Toronto." *Annals of the Association of American Geographers* 80:73–95.

Christensen, Terry. 1982. "A Sort of Victory: Covent Garden Renewed." *Landscape* 26:21–28.

Christian, Charles, and Robert Harper. 1982. *Modern Metropolitan Systems.* Columbus: Charles E. Merrill.

Clark, Clifford. 1986. *The American Family Home, 1800–1960.* Chapel Hill: University of North Carolina Press.

Clark, W. C., and J. L. Kingston. 1930. *The Skyscraper: A Study in the Economic Height of Modern Office Buildings.* New York: American Institute of Steel.

Clay, Grady. 1973. *Close-Up: How to Read the American City.* Chicago: University of Chicago Press.

Clout, Hugh, and Peter Wood, eds. 1986. *London: Problems of Change.* Harlow, Essex: Longman Group.

Cohn, John. 1979. *The Palace or the Poorhouse.* East Lansing: Michigan State University Press.

Colby, Charles. 1933. "Centrifugal and Centripetal Forces in Urban Geography." *Annals of the Association of American Geography* 23:1–20.

Coleman, Alice. 1985. *Utopia on Trial: Vision and Reality in Planned Housing.* London: Hilary Shipmant.

Condit, Carl. 1960. *American Building Art.* Chicago: University of Chicago Press.

———. 1964. *The Chicago School of Architecture: A History of Commercial and Public Buildings in the Chicago Area, 1875–1912.* Chicago: University of Chicago Press.

Condon, George. 1967. *Cleveland: The Best-Kept Secret.* Garden City, N.Y.: Doubleday.

Conzen, Michael P. 1978. "Analytical Approaches to the Urban Landscape." In *Dimensions in Human Geography: Essays on Some Familiar and Neglected Themes* ed. Karl W. Butzer, 128–65. University of Chicago, Department of Geography Research Paper 186. Chicago: University of Chicago.

Costonis, John. 1974. *Space Adrift: Landmark Preservation and the Marketplace.* Urbana: University of Illinois Press.

Cromley, Elizabeth. 1990. *Alone Together: A History of New York's Early Apartments.* Ithaca: Cornell University Press.

Cruikshank, Dan, and Neil Burton. 1990. *Life in the Georgian City.* New York: Viking Penguin.

Cudahy, Brian. 1988. *Under the Sidewalks of New York.* Lexington, Mass: Stephen Greene Press.

Curtis, James. 1981a. "The Boutiquing of Cannery Row." *Landscape* 25:44–48.

———. 1981b. "Miami's Little Havana: Yard Shrines, Cult Religion, and Landscape." *Journal of Cultural Geography* 1:1–15.

———. 1982. "Art Deco Architecture in Miami Beach." *Journal of Cultural Geography* 3:51–63.

Curtis, James, and Larry Ford. 1988. "Bungalow Courts in San Diego." *Journal of San Diego History* 34:78–92.

Cybriwsky, Roman. 1978. "Social Aspects of Neighborhood Change." *Annals of the Association of American Geographers* 68:17–33.

Datel, Robin, and Dennis Dingemans. 1980. "Historic Preservation and Urban Change." *Urban Geography* 1:229–53.

Dawson, John. 1980. *Retail Geography.* London: Croom Helm.

Diamonstein, Barbaralee. 1986. *Remaking America: New Uses, Old Places.* New York: Crown.

Dingemans, Dennis. 1975. "The Urbanization of Suburbia: The Renaissance of the Row House." *Landscape* 20:20–31.

———. 1979. "Redlining and Mortgage Lending Rates in Sacramento." *Annals of the Association of American Geographers* 69:225–39.

Domosh, Mona. 1988. "The Symbolism of the Skyscraper: Case Studies of New York's First Tall Buildings." *Journal of Urban History* 14:320–45.

———. 1989. "A Method for Interpreting Landscape: A Case Study of the New York World Building." *Area* 21:347–55.

———. 1990. "Shaping the Commercial City: Retail Districts in Nineteenth-Century New York and Boston." *Annals of the Association of American Geographers* 80:268–84.

Doucet, Michael, and John Weaver. 1985. "Material Culture and the North American House: The Era of the Common Man, 1870–1920." *Journal of American History* 72:560–87.

Doughty, Martin, ed. 1986. *Building the Industrial City.* Leicester: Leicester University Press.

Downs, Anthony. 1976. *Urban Problems and Prospects.* Chicago: Rand McNally.

Duncan, James. 1973. "Landscape Taste as a Symbol of Group Identity." *Geographical Review* 63:334–55.

———, ed. 1982. *Housing and Identity: Cross-Cultural Perspectives.* New York: Holmes & Meier.

Eckert, Kevin J. 1980. *The Unseen Elderly.* San Diego: Campanile Press.

Entrikin, Nicholas. 1980. "Robert Park's Human Ecology and Human Geography." *Annals of the Association of American Geographers* 70:43–58.

———. 1991. *The Betweenness of Place: Towards a Geography of Modernity.* Baltimore: Johns Hopkins University Press.

Epstein, Amy Kallman. 1980. "Multifamily Dwellings and the Search for Respectability." *Urbanism Past and Present* 5 (Summer): 29–39.

Evansen, Norma. 1979. *Paris: A Century of Change.* New Haven: Yale University Press.

Ferry, John W. 1960. *A History of the Department Store.* New York: Macmillan.

Firey, Walter. 1947. *Land Use in Central Boston.* Cambridge: Harvard University Press.

Fisher, Robert. 1959. *Twenty Years of Public Housing.* New York: Harper.

———. 1967. *The Boom in Office Buildings.* Washington, D.C.: Board of Governors of the Federal Reserve System.

Fitch, James. 1948. *American Building: The Forces That Shape It.* Boston: Houghton-Mifflin.

Foley, Mary Mix. 1980. *The American House.* New York: Harper & Row.

Ford, Larry. 1984a. "Architecture and Geography: Toward a Mutual Concern for Space and Place." *Yearbook of the Association of Pacific Coast Geographers* 46:7–33.

———. 1984b. "The Burden of the Past: Rethinking Historic Preservation." *Landscape* 28:41–48.

———. 1984c. "Preserving Diversity: The Importance of Street-Level Doors." *California Geographer* 24:1–20.

———. 1986a. "Multiunit Housing in the American City." *Geographical Review* 76 (October): 390–407.

———. 1986b. "The Enduring Romantic Cottage: Rethinking Historic Preservation." *Landscape* 29:17–23.

———. 1988. "Housing and Inner-City Population Change in Columbus and San Diego." *Yearbook of the Association of Pacific Coast Geographers* 50:105–15.

———. 1991. "A Metatheory of Urban Structure." In *Our Changing Cities*, ed. John Fraser Hart. Baltimore: Johns Hopkins University Press.

Ford, Larry, and Richard Fusch. 1978. "Neighbors View German Village." *Historic Preservation* July, 37–41.

Ford, Larry, and Ernst Griffin. 1979. "The Ghettoization of Paradise." *Geographical Review* 69:140–58.

———. 1981. "Chicano Park: Personalizing an Institutional Landscape." *Landscape* 25:42–46.

Foster, R. H. 1980. "Wartime Trailer Housing in the San Francisco Bay Area." *Geographical Review* 70:276–90.

Francaviglia, Richard. 1977. "Main Street USA: The Creation of a Popular Image." *Landscape* 21:18–23.

Franklin, Robert. 1983. "Ethnicity and an Emerging Indochinese Commercial District in Orange County." *Yearbook of the Association of American Geographers* 45:85–99.

Freeman, Allen. 1986. "'Fine Tuning': A Landmark of Adaptive Use." *Architecture*, November.

French, Jere S. 1978. *Urban Space: A Brief History of the Urban Square.* Dubuque: Kendall Hunt Publishing Co.

Frieden, Bernard, and Lynnes Sagalyn. 1990. *Downtown, Inc.: How America Rebuilds Cities.* Cambridge: MIT Press.

Fusch, Richard, and Larry Ford. 1983. "Architecture and the Geography of the American City." *Geographical Review* 73:324–40.

Gad, Gunter, and Deryck Holdsworth. 1987a. "Corporate Capitalism and the Emergence of the High-Rise Office Building." *Urban Geography* 8:212–30.

———. 1987b. "Looking Inside the Skyscraper: The Measurement of Building Size and Occupancy in Toronto Office Buildings, 1880–1950." *Urban History Review* 16:176–89.

Gallion, Arthur, and Simon Eisner. 1963. *The Urban Pattern.* New York: D. Van Nostrand.

Gans, Herbert. 1962. *The Urban Villagers.* New York: Free Press.

———. 1967. *The Levittowners.* New York: Pantheon.

Gardiner, Stephen. 1976. *Evolution of the House.* St. Albans: Granada Publishing.

Garreau, Joel. 1991. *Edge City.* New York: Doubleday.

Gebhard, David. 1958. "Fifty Years of the American House." *Landscape* 8:5–9.

Geist, Johann F. 1983. *Arcades: A History of a Building Type.* Cambridge: MIT Press.

Gellon, Martin. 1985. *Accessory Apartments in Single-Family Housing.* New Brunswick: Center for Urban Policy Research.

Gibbs, Kenneth. 1984. *Business Architectural Imagery in America, 1870–1930.* Ann Arbor: UMI Research Press.

Girouard, Mark. 1985. *Cities and People.* New Haven: Yale University Press.

Goetze, Rolf. 1983. *Rescuing the American Dream.* New York: Holmes & Meier.

Goldberg, Michael, and John Mercer. 1986. *The Myth of the North American City.* Vancouver: University of British Columbia Press.

Goldberger, Paul. 1979. *The City Observed: New York.* New York: Vantage Books.

———. 1981. *The Skyscraper.* New York: Alfred A. Knopf.

Goode, James. 1988. *Best Addresses: A Century of Washington's Most Distinguished Apartment Houses.* Washington: Smithsonian Institution Press.

Gordon, Jacques. 1985. *Horton Plaza: A Case Study of Private Development.* Cambridge: MIT Center for Real Estate Development.

Goss, Jon. 1988. "The Built Environment and Social Theory: Towards an Architectural Geography." *Professional Geographer* 40:392–403.

———. 1993. "The 'Magic of the Mall': An Analysis of Form, Function, and Meaning in the Contemporary Retail Built Economy," *Annals of the Association of American Geographers* 83:18–47.

Gottfried, Herbert. 1985. *American Vernacular Design, 1870–1940*. New York: Van Nostrand Reinhold.

Gottman, Jean. 1966. "Why the Skyscraper?" *Geographical Review* 56:190–212.

Gowans, Alan. 1964. *Images of American Living: Four Centuries of Architecture and Furniture as Cultural Expression*. Philadelphia: J. B. Lippincott.

———. 1966. *Building Canada: An Architectural History of Canadian Life*. Toronto: Oxford University Press.

———. 1987. *The Comfortable House: North American Suburban Architecture, 1890–1930*. Cambridge: MIT Press.

Gray, Robert. 1982. *A History of London*. London: Hutchinson.

Greenbie, Barrie. 1988. *Space and Spirit in Modern Japan*. New Haven: Yale University Press.

Groth, Paul. 1983. *Forbidden Housing: The Evolution and Exclusion of Hotels, Boarding Houses, Rooming Houses, and . . .* Ann Arbor: University Microfilms International.

———. 1990. "Lot, Yard, and Garden: American Distinctions." *Landscape* 30:29–35.

Gruen, Victor. 1964. *The Heart of Our Cities*. New York: Simon & Schuster.

Hall, Peter. 1978. *Europe 2000*. New York: Columbia University Press.

Halpern, Kenneth. 1978. *Downtown USA: Urban Design in Nine American Cities*. New York: Whitney Library of Design.

Hamlin, Talbot. 1926. *The American Spirit in Architecture*. New Haven: Yale University Press.

Hancock, John. 1980 "The Apartment House in Urban America" In King 1980.

Handlin, David. 1979. *The American House: Architecture and Society, 1815–1915*. Boston: Little, Brown.

Harries, Keith. 1971. "Ethnic Variations in Los Angeles Business Patterns." *Annals of the Association of American Geographers* 61:736–43.

Hart, John Fraser. 1982. "The Bypass Strip as an Ideal Landscape." *Geographical Review* 72:218–23.

Hartshorn, Truman. 1980. *Interpreting the City: An Urban Geography*. New York: John Wiley & Sons.

Harvey, Thomas. 1981. "Mail-Order Architecture in the Twenties." *Landscape* 25:1–9.

Hayden, Dolores. 1984. *Redesigning the American Dream*. New York: Norton.

———. 1985. *The Grand Domestic Revolution*. Cambridge: MIT Press.

Hecht, M. E. 1975. "The Decline of the Grass Lawn Tradition in Tucson." *Landscape* 19:3–10.

Heimann, Jim, and George Rip. 1980. *California Crazy: Roadside Vernacular Architecture*. San Francisco: Chronicle Books.

Hess, Alan. 1986. *Googie: Fifties Coffee Shop Architecture*. San Francisco: Chronicle Books.

Hine, Thomas. 1987. *Populuxe*. New York: Alfred A. Knopf.

Historic Seattle Preservation and Development Authority. 1975. *An Urban Resource Inventory for Seattle*. Seattle: City of Seattle.

Hoffman, Mark S., ed. 1988. *The World Almanac and Book of Facts*. New York: Pharos Books.

Holcomb, Briavel, and Robert Beauregard. 1981. *Revitalizing Cities.* Washington, D.C.: Association of American Geographers.

Holdsworth, Deryck, ed. 1985. *Reviving Main Street.* Toronto: University of Toronto Press.

Hoover, Edgar, and Raymond Vernon. 1959. *The Anatomy of a Metropolis.* Garden City, N.Y.: Doubleday.

Horowitz, Carl F. 1983. *The New Garden Apartment.* New Brunswick: Rutgers University Press.

Hosmer, Charles. 1965. *Presence of the Past.* New York: G. P. Putnam's Sons.

Howe, Barbara, et al. 1987. *Houses and Homes.* Nashville: American Association of State and Local History.

Hoyt, Homer. 1933. *One Hundred Years of Land Values in Chicago.* Chicago: University of Chicago Press.

——. 1939. *The Structure and Growth of Residential Neighborhoods in American Cities.* Washington, D.C.: Federal Housing Administration.

——. 1971. "Recent Distortions of the Classical Models of Urban Structure." In Bourne, 1971, 84–96.

Hugil, Peter. 1980. "Houses in Cazenovia: The Effects of Time and Class." *Landscape* 24:10–15.

——. 1984. "Good Roads and the Automobile in the United States, 1880–1929." *Geographical Review* 74:327–49.

Huxtable, Ada Louise. 1984. *The Tall Building Artistically Reconsidered: The Search for a Skyscraper Style.* New York: Pantheon Books.

Jackson, J. B. 1984. *Discovering the Vernacular Landscape.* New Haven: Yale University Press.

Jackson, Kenneth. 1985. *The Crabgrass Frontier: The Suburbanization of America.* New York: Oxford University Press.

Jacobs, Allan. 1985. *Looking at Cities.* Cambridge: Harvard University Press.

Jacobs, Jane. 1961. *The Death and Life of Great American Cities.* New York: Vintage Books.

Jakle, John. 1979. "The American Gasoline Station, 1920–1970." *Journal of American Culture* 2:520–42.

——. 1980. "Motel by the Roadside: America's Room for the Night." *Journal of Cultural Geography* 1:34–49.

——. 1982. "Roadside Restaurants and Place-Product Packaging." *Journal of Cultural Geography* 3:76–93.

——. 1983. "Twentieth-Century Revival Architecture and the Gentry." *Journal of Cultural Geography* 4:28–45.

——. 1985. *The Tourist: Travel in Twentieth-Century North America.* Lincoln: University of Nebraska Press.

——. 1987. *The Visual Elements of Landscape.* Amherst: University of Massachusetts Press.

Jakle, John, Robert Bastian, and Douglas Meyer. 1989. *Common Houses in America's Small Towns.* Athens: University of Georgia Press.

Jackle, John, and David Wilson. 1992. *Derelict Landscapes: The Wasting of America's Built Environment.* Savage, Md.: Rowman and Littlefield.

Jencks, Charles. 1971. *Architecture 2000: Predictions and Methods.* New York: Praeger.

——. 1991. *The Language of Post-Modern Architecture.* New York: Rizzoli.

Jennings, Jan, ed. 1990. *Roadside America: The Automobile in Design and Culture*. Ames: Iowa State University Press.

Johnston, R. J. 1969. "Towards an Analytical Study of the Townscape: The Residential Building Fabric." *Geografiska Annaler* 51:20–32.

Kain, Roger. 1981. *Planning for Conservation*. London: Mansell.

Karp, Walter. 1982. *The Center: A History and Guide to Rockefeller Center*. New York: American Heritage Publishing Co.

Kaufman, Edgar, Jr., ed. 1970. *The Rise of an American Architecture*. New York: Praeger.

Kersten, Earl, and Ross Reid. 1968. "Clayton: A New Metropolitan Focus in the St. Louis Area." *Annals of the Association of American Geographers* 58:637–49.

King, Anthony. 1980. *Buildings and Society: Essays on the Social Development of the Built Environment*. Boston: Routledge & Kegan Paul.

———. 1984. *The Bungalow: The Production of a Global Culture*. London: Routledge & Kegan Paul.

Kingston, J. L., and W. C. Clark. 1930. *The Skyscraper: A Study in the Economic Height of Modern Office Buildings*. New York: American Institute of Steel Construction.

Kniffen, Fred. 1965. "Folk Housing: Key to Diffusion." *Annals of the Association of American Geographers* 55:549–77.

Kniffen, Fred, and Henry Glassie. 1966. "Building in Wood in the Eastern United States: A Time-Place Perspective." *Geographical Review* 56:40–66.

Knox, Paul L. 1987. "The Social Production of the Built Environment: Architects, Architecture, and the Post-Modern City." *Progress in Human Geography* 11:354–77.

Kostof, Spiro. 1987. *America by Design*. Oxford: Oxford University Press.

Kowinski, W. S. 1985. *The Malling of America: An Inside Look at the Great Consumer Paradise*. New York: William Morrow.

Kreisman, Lawrence. 1985. *Historic Preservation in Seattle*. Seattle: Historic Seattle Preservation and Development Authority.

Krim, Arthur. 1970. "The Three Decker as Urban Architecture in New England." *Monadnock* 44:45–55.

Lake, Robert. 1981. *The New Suburbanites: Race and Housing in the Suburbs*. New Brunswick: Rutgers Center for Urban Policy Research.

Lancaster, Clay. 1985. *The American Bungalow, 1880s–1920s*. New York: Abbeville Press.

———. 1987. "Employment and Housing Transformations in New York City." Paper presented at the Second Conference on Geography Sponsored by the American Council of Learned Societies and the Soviet Academy of Sciences, Milwaukee.

Langdon, Philip. 1986. *Orange Roofs and Golden Arches: The Architecture of American Chain Restaurants*. New York: Alfred A. Knopf.

Laska, Shirley, and Daphne Spain. 1980. *Back to the City: Issues in Neighborhood Renovation*. New York: Pergamon.

Latham, J. E., ed. 1976. *The Economic Benefits of Preserving Old Buildings*. Washington, D.C.: Preservation Press.

Lewis, Peirce. 1975a. "Common Houses, Cultural Spoor." *Landscape* 19:1–22.

————. 1975b. "To Revive Urban Downtowns, Show Respect for the Spirit of the Place." *Smithsonian*, September, 33–41.

————. 1976. *New Orleans: The Making of an Urban Landscape*. Cambridge, Mass.: Ballinger.

————. 1980. "Preservation, Ecology, and Money." Address to conference on historic preservation, Charleston, S.C.

Ley, David. 1980. "Liberal Ideology and the Postindustrial City." *Annals of the Association of American Geographers* 70:238–58.

————. 1987. "Styles of the Times: Liberal and Neo-Conservative Landscapes in Inner Vancouver." *Journal of Historical Geography* 13:40–56.

Liebs, Chester. 1985. *Main Street to Miracle Mile: American Roadside Architecture*. Boston: Little, Brown.

Lipton, S. 1977. "Evidence of Central City Revival." *Journal of the American Institute of Planners* 43:136–47.

Liston, Robert. 1965. *Downtown: Our Challenging Urban Problems*. New York: Delacorte.

Lockwood, Charles. 1976. *Manhattan Moves Uptown*. New York: Houghton Mifflin.

Longstreth, Richard. 1987. *The Buildings on Main Street: A Guide to American Commercial Architecture*. Washington, D.C.: Preservation Press.

Lottman, H. 1976. *How Cities Are Saved*. New York: Universe Books.

Low, Setha, and Erve Chambers, eds. 1989. *Housing, Culture, and Design*. Philadelphia: University of Pennsylvania Press.

Lowe, David. 1975. *Lost Chicago*. Boston: Houghton Mifflin.

Lowenstein, Louis. 1971. *Urban Studies*. New York: Free Press.

Lowenthal, David. 1968. "The American Scene." *Geographical Review* 58:61–88.

Lowenthal, David, and Hugh Prince. 1965. "English Landscape Tastes." *Geographical Review* 55:188–222.

Luxenberg, Stan. 1985. *Roadside Empires: How the Chains Franchised America*. New York: Viking Penguin.

Lynch, Kevin. 1960. *The Image of the City*. Cambridge: MIT Press.

————. 1972. *What Time Is This Place?* Cambridge: MIT Press.

————. 1981. *A Theory of Good City Form*. Cambridge: MIT Press.

Lynes, Russell. 1949. *The Tastemakers*. New York: Grosset & Dunlap.

McAlester, Virginia, and Lee McAlester. 1984. *A Field Guide to American Houses*. New York: Alfred A. Knopf.

McAusland, Randolph. 1980. *Supermarkets: Fifty Years of Progress*. Washington, D.C.: Food Marketing Institute.

MacDonald, Kent. 1985. "The Commercial Strip: From Main Street to Television Road." *Landscape* 29:12–19.

Mackay, David. 1977. *Multiple Family Housing*. New York: Architectural Books.

Mackay, Donald. 1987. *The Building of Manhattan*. New York: Harper & Row.

Mackey, Sean, ed. 1963. *Symposium on the Design of High Buildings*. Hong Kong: Hong Kong University Press.

McSheehy, William. 1979. *Skid Row*. Boston: Schenkman.

Manners, Ian. 1974. "The Office in Metropolis: An Opportunity for Shaping Metropolitan America." *Economic Geography* 50:93–109.

Marchand, Bernard. 1986. *The Emergence of Los Angeles: Population and Housing in the City of Dreams, 1940–1970*. London: Pion.

Martin, Judith, and David Lanegran. 1983. *Where We Live: The Residential Districts of Minneapolis and Saint Paul*. Minneapolis: University of Minnesota Press.

Mattson, Richard. 1981. "The Bungalow Spirit." *Journal of Cultural Geography* 1:75–92.

———. 1983. "Changing Face of Main Street: Store Front Remodeling from 1930 to the Present." *Journal of Cultural Geography* 4.

Mayer, Harold, and Clyde Kohn. 1959. *Readings in Urban Geography*. Chicago: University of Chicago Press.

Mayer, Harold, and Richard Wade. 1969. *Chicago: Growth of a Metropolis*. Chicago: University of Chicago Press.

Mazey, Mary E., and Theresa Seiler. 1982. "Women in Suburbia." *Journal of Cultural Geography* 3:122.

Meinig, D. W., ed. 1979. *The Interpretation of Ordinary Landscapes*. Oxford: Oxford University Press.

———. 1989. "The Historical Geography Imperative." *Annals of the Association of American Geographers* 79:79–87.

Messler, Norbert. 1981. *The Art Deco Skyscraper in New York*. New York: Peter Lang.

Meyer, David. 1973. "Intraurban Differences in Black Housing Quality." *Annals of the Association of American Geographers* 63:347–52.

Miller, Michael. 1981. *The Bon Marché: Bourgeois Culture and the Department Store, 1869–1920*. Princeton: Princeton University Press.

Miller, Roger. 1982. "Household Activity Patterns in Nineteenth-Century Suburbs: A Time-Geographic Exploration." *Annals of the Association of American Geographers* 72:355–71.

Miller, Ronald. 1982. *The Demolition of Skid Row*. Lexington, Mass.: Lexington Books.

Morgan, William. 1980. "Strongboxes on Main Street: Prairie-Style Banks." *Landscape* 24:35–40.

Mujica, Francisco. 1977. *History of the Skyscraper*. New York: De Capo Press.

Muller, Peter. 1981. *Contemporary Suburban America*. Englewood Cliffs: Prentice-Hall.

Mumford, Lewis. 1961. *The City in History*. New York: Harcourt, Brace & World.

———. 1971. *The Brown Decades: A Study of the Arts in America, 1865–1895*. New York: Dover.

Murphy, Raymond. 1972. *The Central Business District*. Chicago: Aldine-Atherton.

Murphy, Raymond, and James Vance. 1954. "Delimiting the Central Business District." *Economic Geography* 30:189–222.

———. 1955. "Internal Structure of the CBD." *Economic Geography* 31:21–46.

Murtaugh, William. 1957. "The Philadelphia Row House." *Journal of the Society of Architectural Historians* 16: 8–13.

Muthesius, Stefan. 1982. *The English Terraced House*. New Haven: Yale University Press.

National Trust for Historic Preservation. 1976. *A Guide to Delineating Edges of*

Historic Districts. Washington, D.C.: National Trust for Historic Preservation.

Naumberg, Elsa. 1933. *Skyscraper.* New York: John Day.

Nelson, Howard. 1963. "Townscapes of Mexico: An Example of the Regional Variation of Townscapes." *Economic Geography* 39:74–83.

Neutze, Max. 1968. *The Suburban Apartment Boom.* Baltimore: Johns Hopkins University Press.

Newman, Oscar. 1973. *Defensible Space.* New York: Macmillan.

New York City Department of City Planning. 1981. *Midtown Development.* New York: Department of City Planning.

Noble, Allen. 1984. *Wood, Brick, and Stone: The North American Settlement Landscape.* Vol. 1, *Houses.* Amherst: University of Massachusetts Press.

Norton, Thomas, and Jerry Patterson. 1984. *Living It Up: A Guide to the Named Apartment Houses in New York.* New York: Atheneum.

O'Connor, Anne. 1988. "Gas or Class: Towards an Interpretation of the Commercial Strip." Master's thesis, San Diego State University.

Olsen, Donald. 1986. *The City as a Work of Art.* New Haven: Yale University Press.

Olson, Sherry. 1976. *Baltimore.* Cambridge, Mass.: Ballinger.

Owens, Bill. 1972. *Suburbia.* San Francisco: Straight Arrow Books.

Palm, Risa. 1976. "Real Estate Agents and Geographic Information." *Geographical Review* 66:266–80.

Park, Robert, Ernest Burgess, and R. D. McKenzie. 1925. *The City.* Chicago: University of Chicago Press.

Pevsner, Nikolaus. 1976. *A History of Building Types.* Princeton: Princeton University Press.

Pillsbury, Richard. 1970. "The Urban Street Pattern as a Cultural Indicator: Pennsylvania, 1682–1815." *Annals of the Association of American Geographers* 60:428–46.

———. 1990. *From Boarding House to Bistro: The American Restaurant Then and Now.* Boston: Unwin Hyman.

Plunz, Richard. 1989. *A History of Housing in New York City.* New York: Columbia University Press.

Pred, Allan. 1963. "Business Thoroughfares as Expressions of Urban Negro Culture." *Economic Geography* 39:217–39.

Press, Irwin. 1979. *The City as Context.* Urbana: University of Illinois Press.

Price, Edward. 1964. "Viterbo: Landscape of an Italian City." *Annals of the Association of American Geographers* 54:242–75.

———. 1968. "The Central Courthouse Square in the American County Seat." *Geographical Review* 58:29–60.

Pygman, James, and Richard Kately. 1985. *Tall Office Buildings in the United States.* Washington, D.C.: Urban Land Institute.

Raitz, Karl, and John Paul Jones. 1988. "The City Hotel as Landscape Artifact and Community Symbol." *Journal of Cultural Geography* 9:17–36.

Rannells, John. 1956. *The Core of the City: A Pilot of Changing Land Uses in Central Business Districts.* New York: Columbia University Press.

Rapoport, Amos. 1969. *House Form and Culture.* Englewood Cliffs: Prentice-Hall.

Rasmussen, S. E. 1951. *Towns and Buildings.* Cambridge: Harvard University Press.

Rathbun, Robert. 1986. *Shopping Centers and Malls (2)*. New York: Retail Reporting Corporation.

Redstone, Louis. 1976. *The New Downtowns: Rebuilding Business Districts*. New York: McGraw-Hill.

Relph, Edward. 1976. *Place and Placelessness*. New York: Pion.

———. 1987. *The Modern Urban Landscape*. Baltimore: Johns Hopkins University Press.

Reps, John. 1965. *The Making of Urban America: A History of City Planning in the United States*. Princeton, N.J.: Princeton University Press.

Rhoads, William. 1976. "The Colonial Revival and American Nationalism." *Journal of the Society of Architectural Historians* 35:239–54.

Riccio, Rita. 1988. "The Landscape of Visible Prostitution." Master's thesis, San Diego State University.

Ricciott, Dominic. 1981. "Symbols and Monuments: Images of the Skyscraper in American Art." *Landscape* 25:22–29.

Rickert, John. 1967. "House Facades of the Northeastern United States: A Tool of Geographic Analysis." *Annals of the Association of American Geographers* 57:211–38.

Rifkind, Carole. 1977. *Main Street: The Face of Urban America*. New York: Harper & Row.

Riis, Jacob. 1890. *How the Other Half Lives: Studies of the Tenements of New York*. New York: Charles Scribner's Sons.

Riley, Robert. 1980. "Speculations on the New American Landscapes." *Landscape* 24:1–9.

———. 1987. "Vernacular Landscapes." In *Advances in Environmental Behavior and Design*, ed. Ervin Zube and Gary Moore. 1:129–58. New York: Plenum Press.

Rosen, Barbara, and Wolfgang Zuckermann. 1982. *The Mews of London*. Exeter: Webb & Bower.

Rosenberry, Sara, and Chester Hartman, eds. 1989. *Housing Issues of the 1990s*. New York: Praeger.

Roth, Leland. 1977. *A Concise History of American Architecture*. New York: Harper & Row.

Rowntree, Lester, and Margaret Conkey. 1980. "Symbolism and the Cultural Landscape." *Annals of the Association of American Geographers* 70:459–74.

Rubin, Barbara. 1977. "A Chronology of Architecture in Los Angeles." *Annals of the Association of American Geographers* 67:531–37.

———. 1979. "Aesthetic Ideology and Urban Design." *Annals of the Association of American Geographers* 69:339–61.

Ruchelman, Leonard. 1977. *The World Trade Center: Politics and Policies of Skyscraper Development*. Syracuse: Syracuse University Press.

Rudofsky, Bernard. 1969. *Streets for People: A Primer for Americans*. Garden City, N.Y.: Doubleday.

Sacramento Historical Structures Advisory Committee. 1974 (rev. 1976). *Sacramento Old City: A Preservation Program*. Sacramento Preservation and Development Authority.

San Francisco, Department of City Planning. 1981. *Guiding Downtown Development*. San Francisco: Department of City Planning.

Schafer, Robert. 1974. *The Suburbanization of Multifamily Housing*. Lexington, Mass.: D. C. Heath.

Schnore, Leo F., ed. 1975. *The New Urban History.* Princeton: Princeton University Press.

Schuyler, David. 1986. *The New Urban Landscape: The Redefinition of City Form in Nineteenth-Century America.* Baltimore: Johns Hopkins University Press.

Schwirian, Kent. 1974. *Comparative Urban Structure.* Lexington, Mass.: D. C. Heath.

Sculle, Keith. 1981. "The Vernacular Gas Station: Examples from Illinois and Wisconsin." *Journal of Cultural Geography* 1:56–74.

Scully, Vincent. 1969. *American Architecture and Urbanism.* New York: Praeger.

Sennett, Richard. 1978. *The Fall of Public Man.* New York: Random House.

Severini, Lois. 1983. *The Architecture of Finance.* Ann Arbor: UMI Research Press.

Shapiro, Ann-Louise. 1985. *Housing the Poor of Paris, 1850–1902.* Madison: University of Wisconsin Press.

Sharpe, William, and Leonard Wallock. 1987. *Visions of the Modern City.* Baltimore: Johns Hopkins University Press.

Shoenfeld, Oscar, and Helene MacLean, eds. 1969. *City Life.* New York: Grossman.

Shultz, Earle, and Walter Simmons. 1959. *Offices in the Sky.* Indianapolis: Bobbs-Merrill.

Simpson, Charles. 1981. *Soho: The Artist in the City.* Chicago: University of Chicago Press.

Sjoberg, Gideon. 1960. *The Preindustrial City.* New York: Free Press.

Skolnik, A. 1976. "A History of Pioneer Square." In *Economic Benefits of Preserving Old Buildings,* ed. J. Latham. Washington, D.C.: Preservation Press.

Smith, Kathryn Schneider, ed. 1988. *Washington at Home.* Northridge, Calif.: Windsor Publications.

Smith, Neal, and Peter Williams. 1986. *Gentrification of the City.* Boston: Allen & Unwin.

Solomon, R. J. 1966. "Procedures in Townscape Analysis." *Annals of the Association of American Geographers* 56:254–68.

Sorkin, Michael, ed. 1992. *Variations on a Theme Park: The New American City and the End of Public Space.* New York: Noonday Press.

Spann, Edward. 1981. *The New Metropolis: New York City, 1840–1857.* New York: Columbia University Press.

Starrett, Paul. 1939. *Changing the Skyline.* New York: McGraw-Hill.

Starrett, William. 1928. *Skyscrapers and the Men Who Build Them.* New York: Scribners and Sons.

Stern, Robert. 1986. *Pride of Place.* Boston: Houghton-Mifflin.

Stevenson, Katherine, and Jandl Ward. 1986. *Houses by Mail: A Guide to Houses from Sears, Roebuck and Company.* Washington, D.C.: Preservation Press.

Stilgoe, John. 1983. *Metropolitan Corridor: Railroads and the American Scene.* New Haven: Yale University Press.

———. 1988. *Borderland: Origins of the American Suburb, 1820–1939.* New Haven: Yale University Press.

Strasser, Susan. 1982. *Never Done: A History of American Housework.* New York: Pantheon.

Sutcliffe, Anthony. 1974. *Multi-storey Living: The British Working-Class Experience*. London: Croom Helm.

Thurber, James. 1945. *The Thurber Carnival*. New York: Harper & Row.

Trindell, Roger. 1968. "Building in Brick in Early America." *Geographical Review* 58:484–87.

Tuan, Yi-Fu. 1974. *Topophilia*. Englewood Cliffs: Prentice-Hall.

———. 1983. "Moral Ambiguity in Architecture." *Landscape* 27:11–17.

———. 1989. "Surface Phenomena and Aesthetic Experience." *Annals of the Association of American Geographers* 79:233–41.

Tunnard, Christopher. 1968. *The Modern American City*. Princeton: D. Van Nostrand.

Tunnard, Christopher, and Henry Reed. 1956. *The American Skyline*. New York: New American Library.

Upton, Dell, and John Michael Vlach. 1986. *Common Places: Readings in American Vernacular Architecture*. Athens: University of Georgia Press.

Urban Land Institute. 1983. *Urban Waterfront Development*. Washington, D.C.

Vance, James. 1971. "Focus on Downtown." In Bourne 1971, 112–20.

———. 1990. *The Continuing City: Urban Morphology in Western Civilization*. Baltimore: Johns Hopkins University Press.

Van Leeuwen, Thomas. 1986. *The Skyward Trend of Thought*. Cambridge: MIT Press.

Venturi, Robert, Denise Scott Brown, and Robert Izenour. 1988. *Learning from Las Vegas*. Cambridge: MIT Press.

Vlach, John. 1976. "The Shotgun House: An African Architectural Legacy." *Pioneer America* 8:47–70.

Ward, David. 1966. "The Industrial Revolution and the Emergence of Boston's Central Business District." *Economic Geography* 42:152–71.

———. 1968. "The Emergence of Central Immigrant Ghettoes in American Cities." *Annals of the Association of American Geographers* 58:343–59.

———. 1971. *Cities and Immigrants: A Geography of Change in Nineteenth-Century America*. New York: Oxford University Press.

———. 1976. "The Victorian Slum: An Enduring Myth?" *Annals of the Association of American Geographers* 66:323.

Ward, J. 1975. "Skid Row as a Geographic Entity." *Professional Geographer* 27:286–96.

Warner, Sam Bass. 1962. *Streetcar Suburbs*. Cambridge: MIT Press.

———. 1968. *The Private City: Philadelphia in Three Periods of Its Growth*. Philadelphia: University of Pennsylvania Press.

———. 1972. *The Urban Wilderness: A History of the American City*. New York: Harper & Row.

Webb, Michael. 1990. *The City Square*. New York: Whitney Library of Design.

Weinberg, Nathan. 1978. *Preservation in American Towns and Cities*. Boulder: Westview Press.

West, Pamela. 1976. "The Rise and Fall of the American Porch." *Landscape* 20:42–47.

Westfall, Caroll William. 1987. "From Home to Towers: A Century of Chicago's Best Hotels and Tall Apartment Buildings." In *Chicago Architecture, 1872–1922: Birth of a Metropolis*, ed. John Zukowsky. Chicago: Art Institute of Chicago.

White, Norval. 1987. *New York: A Physical History.* New York: Atheneum.

White, Paul. 1984. *The West European City.* London: Longman Group.

White, William. 1988. *City: Rediscovering the Center.* New York: Doubleday.

Whitehand, J. W. R., ed. 1981. *The Urban Landscape: Historical Development and Management. Papers by M. R. G. Conzen.* London: Academic Press.

Wilson, Margaret Gibbons. 1979. *The American Woman in Transition: The Urban Influence, 1870–1920.* Westport, Conn.: Greenwood Press.

Winter, Robert. 1980. *The California Bungalow.* Los Angeles: Hennessey & Ingalls.

Winters, Christopher. 1979. "The Social Identity of Evolving Neighborhoods." *Landscape* 23:8–14.

Wolfe, Gerard. 1988. *New York: A Guide to the Metropolis.* New York: McGraw-Hill.

Wolfe, Tom. 1965. *Kandy-Kolored Tangerine-Flake Streamline Baby.* New York: Farrar, Straus and Giroux.

———. 1982. *From Bauhaus to Our House.* New York: Pocket Books.

———. 1987. *Bonfire of the Vanities.* New York: Farrar, Straus and Giroux.

Wong, Luke, ed. 1978. *Housing in Hong Kong: A Multi-Disciplinary Study.* Hong Kong: Heinemann Educational Books.

Wright, Gwendolyn. 1980. *Moralism and the Model Home: Social Conflict in Chicago, 1873–1913.* Chicago: University of Chicago Press.

———. 1981. *Building the Dream: A History of American Housing.* New York: Pantheon.

Zelinsky, Wilbur. 1973. *The Cultural Geography of the United States.* Englewood Cliffs: Prentice-Hall.

Zukin, Sharon. 1982. *Loft Living: Culture and Capital in Urban Change.* Baltimore: Johns Hopkins University Press.

———. 1991. *Landscapes of Power.* Berkeley and Los Angeles: University of California Press.

Index

About the Author

Larry Ford teaches in the Geography Department at Diego State University and specializes in urban design and comparative urbanization. He has published primarily in the areas of urban preservation and comparative city structure. For the past twenty-five years, he has kept busy examining the relationship between architectural traditions and urban morphology in a variety of cultural contexts.

Books in the Series

LIBRARY OF CONGRESS CATALOGING-IN-PUBLICATION DATA

Ford, Larry.
    Cities and buildings : skyscrapers, skid rows, and suburbs / Larry R. Ford.
            p.   cm. — (Creating the North American landscape)
    Includes bibliographical references and index.
        ISBN 0-8018-4646-3 (hc : acid-free paper). — ISBN 0-8018-4647-1
    (pbk. :   acid-free paper)
        1. Architecture—United States.   2. City planning—United States.
    I. Title. II. Series.
    NA705.F67   1994
    720'.973—dc20   93-5752